A Seventh Child
and the Law

I dedicate this book to

Arthur Walton M.A. (Cantab)

to whom I owe my Oxford education and,
more particularly, my privilege to qualify for the Bar

A Seventh Child
and the Law

Patrick Yu Shuk-siu

香港大學出版社
HONG KONG UNIVERSITY PRESS

Hong Kong University Press
14/F Hing Wai Centre
7 Tin Wan Praya Road
Aberdeen, Hong Kong

© Hong Kong University Press 1998
Reprinted 1998

ISBN 962 209 457 0

Printed in Hong Kong by ColorPrint Production Co.

Contents

Foreword by D.A.L. Wright   vii

Acknowledgements   xi

PART ONE   *1*

Introduction   3

 1 Scholarship to England   5

 2 A Seventh Child   7

 3 Wah Yan College and the Irish Jesuits   11

 4 The Fairy Tale of My Matriculation   15

 5 An Apology and Explanation   21

 6 Mystery Unravelled   23

 7 A Vintage Year   25

 8 The University of Hong Kong   29

 9 The Fall of Hong Kong: Before and After   35

10 The War Years (Part One)   43

11 The War Years (Part Two)   53

12 The War Years (Part Three): Drama in Huizhou   61

13 A Very Merry Christmas   69

14 Merton College Oxford   71

15 Unique 1947 Friendship Ties   79

16 Changes in the Wind   83

17 A Crucial Decision   87

18 Wrangling with Officialdom   93

19 End of Oxford Sojourn   97

20 Reading Law at Last   101

21 Discipline Rewarded   105

22 Leisurely Year of Pupillage   109

23 Malayan Undertaking Contemplated   113

24 Year of Mixed Fortune in Malaya   117

25 First Chinese Crown Counsel   123

26 No. 9 Ice House Street Also Known as Holland House   129

27 My Family and the Bar   135

28 The Institution of Silk   139

29 Looking Ahead   145

PART TWO   149

Introduction   151

 1 The Case of the Suicide Pact   153

 2 The Case of the Midnight Court   163

 3 The Case of the Murder Trial without the *Corpus Delicti*   175

 4 The Case in Which the Crown Failed to Prove That
    Gold Was Gold   183

 5 The Case of the Traffic Policeman and the Pak-pai Taxi
    Driver   191

 6 The Case of the Ruptured Kidney   203

 7 The Case of the American Who Was in *Two* Places at
    the Same Time   219

 8 The Case of the Hunter Who Became the Hunted   235

Index   245

Foreword

It is a unique occasion when one of Hong Kong's most eminent and esteemed Counsel publishes his autobiography.

Patrick Yu unfolds the story of a long life which, though not without its vicissitudes and setbacks, is full of interest, endeavour and achievement, and spans a momentous period of Hong Kong's history.

Of great interest is his account of school and university life in Hong Kong before the Pacific War, the early days of the Japanese Occupation of Hong Kong, and the hardships endured by himself and his family during wartime on the mainland of China. There is, additionally, an intriguing description of the author's service in China during the war with British Naval Intelligence and later with the Chinese Nationalist Army.

In his day Patrick Yu was a high profile criminal lawyer. His personality and temperament well fitted the role of a criminal law advocate. Impressively tall, histrionic, and persuasive, it is not surprising that he captivated juries. One of his occasional forays into the realm of civil law was a case tried by a jury — a rare event in Hong Kong. The case attracted extensive public and media attention. The author's final address, delivered, as was his custom, without notes, made such an impact on the jury that against all the odds he succeeded in obtaining a favourable verdict. It does not detract from his performance that the verdict was later overturned on appeal but he did have the satisfaction of taking part in an important case which, incidentally, established a new legal principle that soon received recognition in leading legal textbooks published in the United Kingdom and elsewhere.

One of the Patrick Yu's accomplishments of which he is justly proud is the part he played in the establishment of a Department of Law in the University of Hong Kong which has since been elevated to be a Faculty of Law. The faculty has happily flourished and now enjoys international prestige.

He adopted a firm stand against unfair discrimination in government service regarding the terms of pay and privileges enjoyed by expatriate officers compared with the terms of employment of their local counterparts. The dawdling reluctance of the administration to put an end to this inequitable treatment led the author to resign when serving as Hong Kong's first Chinese Crown Counsel and later to reject offers of appointment as a Judge of the High Court.

Patrick Yu uncompromisingly censures the hallowed institution of Queen's Counsel (now Senior Counsel) and, conceding that his view is a minority view, his trenchant criticism, if it does not make some hackles rise, will certainly induce some reproachful tut-tutting amongst the members of that select circle.

A judicious selection of cases of exceptional interest, aptly and wittily captioned, is separately incorporated in this volume. The diversity of events shown in these cases demonstrates the author's virtuosity, resourcefulness and talents as well as his penetrating insight into the psyche of his fellow countrymen.

A recurrent theme running like a golden thread throughout this autobiography is the author's devotion to traditional Chinese family values. Today he is the paterfamilias of a large and devoted family and his infectious exuberance and zest for life remain undiminished.

This book will be read with delight by lawyers and laymen alike, and overseas by all who have an affection for and affinity with Hong Kong. A contemporaneous Chinese translation will make it available to a widespread readership.

D.A.L. Wright
August 1997

Postscript

On 22 February 1998, Leslie Wright passed away peacefully at the Hong Kong Sanatorium after a short illness. At the time he wrote this Foreword he must have been aware of the fatal illness with which he was afflicted. It was typical of Leslie not to let even his close friends know the condition he was in until he was finally hospitalized.

Since his arrival in Hong Kong in 1947, Leslie Wright had been a great asset to the local Bar and the legal profession, neither of which will be the same again without him. Leslie loved Hong Kong, and had looked upon it as his permanent home these past fifty years. His countless friends in the territory will always remember and sadly miss him. One of the last things Leslie did was to finance and set up an education fund to promote a better mutual understanding of the respective laws and legal systems of the mainland and Hong Kong. This fund has been aptly named the 'Leslie Wright China-Hong Kong Legal Education Fund' to perpetuate the memory of one of the most esteemed members ever of the local Bar.

The civil law-suit referred to in the Foreword by Mr Wright was best known as the Case of the One-Armed Swordsman, which was a legal battle between two giants in the local film industry. With his customary modesty, Mr Wright altogether omitted to mention his part as leading Defence Counsel in the case or the assistance he rendered thereby to Mr Justice Huggins in arriving at the latter's landmark decision on the law of passing-off and intellectual property rights.

Patrick Yu Shuk-siu
2 March 1998

Acknowledgements

Anita Wong was my secretary from the latter part of 1993 until August 1996. During this period I wrote the eight court cases which made up Part II of this book as well as the first ten chapters of my autobiography. May Ip took over from Anita after August 1996 and has been my secretary up-to-date. She helped me compile the remaining nineteen chapters of my autobiography during this latter period. Over the past twelve months Yvonne Tin and Josephine Lee had also on occasions rendered assistance when May went on leave. Without the tireless efforts and solid secretarial assistance of these young ladies, the publication of this work would probably have taken a much longer time.

Susan Kwan was not only responsible for talking me into writing this book but also spent more time than anybody else reading my manuscript and checking up on my behalf on dates, names, places and events. Similarly, Mok Yeuk Chi and my son Denis, although perhaps not nearly to the same extent as Susan. Victoria Woo has been conscientiously and industriously translating each and every chapter of my manuscript upon receipt, and has thus found it necessary to amend her translation every time I amend my manuscript, which unfortunately happens far too often regrettably although inevitably.

My good friend L. Cyril Kotewall has also been a great help and a source of endless positive encouragement from the moment he discovered I was writing my autobiography and memoirs.

To Professor Raymond Wacks of the Faculty of Law of the University of Hong Kong I owe the title of this book which originally I had intended to name as 'The Law and I'. But 'A Seventh Child and the

Law' does sound so much more apt, intriguing, romantic and attractive, thanks to Professor Wacks.

I would like to thank also my daughter-in-law Marianne; my brother Brian in Toronto; his son Peter; my sister Winnie in Michigan, USA; my son-in-law Dr Richard Cauldwell of Birmingham University in England; and my two daughters Estella and Dominica, for the various forms of assistance rendered.

Part One

Introduction

I stopped going to court in the early 1980s although I did not officially retire until some years later. I spent the next ten odd years idling and having very little, if anything, to do with law, but fully occupied with pleasurable pursuits of my own choice such as travelling, reading, racing, playing mah-jong, and more particularly, tinkling on my piano, no doubt to the utter chagrin of the fellow occupants of Bowen Mansions where I live.

In the latter part of 1993, shortly before I departed for London to attend the wedding of my younger son Dominic, three members of my Chambers at New Henry House, namely, Susan Kwan, Mok Yeuk Chi and my son Denis, talked me into writing up some of my old cases. As a result, I found myself doing nothing else for the next two years. This was even harder work than going to court, mainly because the experience was altogether novel and I felt at times as if I was writing my first essays in college all over again. Besides, I had not kept any of my old files, and the Records Office surprisingly could render me very little assistance. In actual fact the only court file I could secure was in the case of the Ruptured Kidney, although I did manage to lay hands on a copy of Judge Hopkinson's judgment in the case of Augustine Chung. The respective accounts of the remaining cases had to be written entirely from memory.

While I was thus engaged, my brother Ping Tsung fell seriously ill and was hospitalized for long periods. Before he passed away in February 1996, I spent many hours with him daily, sometimes at his home and sometimes in hospital. Naturally, we regularly recalled events in our childhood, our school and university days as well as the war years. As a result many a fond memory of the ancient past was rekindled. In the end I decided to commit all of it, together with the main part of my life story, to writing as well.

1 Scholarship to England

In the early part of 1946, the Hong Kong government commemorated the capitulation of Japan by awarding five Victory Scholarships, advertised as such, to local students, with no strings attached, to further their studies at various universities in the United Kingdom. There were many applicants for the award, from whom seven were eventually chosen to share the five scholarships. I was one of the lucky seven. So was my younger brother Brian. In those days, air travel was far less common than now. Even travel by sea was severely restricted because of the large number of ships sunk during the war. It was not until late in August that year that the SS Menelaus, a cargo boat ploughing the South China seas, was available to take us to Singapore, where, after a further considerable delay and much red tape, we finally set sail for England on board the troopship SS Britannic arriving in Liverpool only in the middle of October.

Of the seven scholarship students from Hong Kong, three were admitted into London University, one was admitted into Leeds University, and one into Manchester University. I was accepted by Merton College, Oxford to read Politics, Philosophy and Economics, while my younger brother Brian gained admission into Pembroke College, Cambridge to read Economics. The Michaelmas term had already commenced when Brian and I finally arrived at and settled into our respective colleges. Brian had taken a course in Economics as an undergraduate at Lingnan University in China during the war. It was only natural that he should want to carry on with the study of Economics at Pembroke. I chose PPE for totally different reasons.

In point of fact, on the eve of my departure from Hong Kong, my father had urged me to read law and qualify as a barrister. However, I had other ideas. The law and the legal profession, especially the Bar, were in those days altogether unknown and alien to me, and, indeed, to most of the Chinese population in Hong Kong. Until then neither I nor any other member of my family was aware that anyone we knew had made a success of practising at the local Bar. Besides, I had spent several years in China during the war, had witnessed the pitiful ignorance and poverty in most parts of the mainland, and had pledged that I would return to do what little I could to better the lot of my people after receiving my education abroad. In the circumstances I felt almost justified in turning a deaf ear to my father's advice.

If anyone were to have told me then that I would eventually end up reading law at Lincoln's Inn in London and return to practise law in the courts of Hong Kong, I would probably have laughed it off as sheer fantasy on their part. I could hardly be expected to know that ere long subsequent events in China would force upon me a different outlook for the future, that I would indeed as a result switch to studying and practising law, and be the first one in the family to fulfil his parent's dear wish.

However, more of this later.

2 _A Seventh Child_

I was born on 22 August 1922. Not that I know anything about it, other than that my birth certificate says so. My parents had four sons and seven daughters. I was their third son and seventh child. My father was himself the seventh child of his parents. The Chinese believe that the seventh child of a seventh child is specially blessed. Over the years, I have certainly had a greater measure of good fortune than most of the people I know.

My first clear recollections as a child came with Nos. 15–17 Upper Shelley Street (上些利街). Until the end of the last war, these consisted of two adjoining two-storey twin houses into which my family had moved when I was less than six years old. Shelley Street is divided into two sections. Lower Shelley Street (下些利街) adjoins Hollywood Road at one end and Caine Road at the other. Upper Shelley Street is a steep sloping walkway which is less than twenty feet wide, and about two hundred yards long, bounded at the top by Mosque Street, and at the bottom by Caine Road, with residential houses lining both sides of the street almost all the way with the exception of a large vegetable garden fenced by walls facing houses Nos. 15–17 directly across the walkway. Immediately past the vegetable garden is the entrance to a Muslim mosque with surrounding walls which take up the rest of that side of the walkway right up to Mosque Street. Walking up Shelley Street from Caine Road, one would, after some fifty yards, come to an opening on the right which leads into Prince's Terrace. Lying another fifty yards further up and beyond this opening on the right would be Nos. 15–17 Upper Shelley Street.

The majority of the houses in this area are extremely close to or otherwise actually adjoining one another. In those days Nos. 15–17 Upper Shelley Street had the unique distinction in the whole of that area of being able to boast of a long strip of verandah some three to four feet wide overhanging the walkway from the first floor and extending continuously over the entire frontage of the two houses. This overlooked not only the whole length of Shelley Street, but also a vast area in the vicinity. Standing on this verandah one could even sight a part of the harbour and something of Kowloon for a long way beyond. When lined with pots of multi-coloured flowers, this unusual structural addition to the property made a very attractive sight. Very regrettably this historic residence of my family was sold in the 1950s, and has since been replaced by a mundane building of multiple storeys with no verandah or view whatever.

It was at this address that I grew up together with my brothers Ping Tsung and Brian. Shortly after the family moved into Shelley Street, my eldest brother Pak Chuen left for England and was soon joined by my eldest sister Sheung Woon. My two other elder sisters Josephine and Margaret were then already attending school. My two younger sisters Winnie and Rosalind came respectively into this world at Shelley Street in 1929 and 1931. Yet another two sisters, one older and one younger than I, had died in their infancy. My father was a Senior Inspector of Schools employed by the Hong Kong government. At dinner he frequently told us fascinating stories about our literary giants and historic heroes which were unforgettable lessons in themselves. On Sundays, we would more often than not be taken to watch either a cinema film or a soccer match, to be followed by a meal in town in one of our favourite restaurants. Those were overwhelmingly happy years.

My brother Ping Tsung, who passed away in February, 1996, was one and a half years older than I. Together we learnt our ABCs as well as our first Chinese characters at Nos. 15–17 Shelley Street. A Eurasian woman surnamed Shum was engaged to teach us English and arithmetic, while a Chinese male tutor surnamed Li taught us Chinese. Being much cleverer than I, Ping Tsung was naturally the teachers' favourite. It did not explain, though, why Miss Shum should constantly find fault with me, frequently for no reason whatever. Whenever she picked on me unfairly, Ping Tsung would rally to my side, and do his utmost to console and comfort me. Although this did not always suffice to pacify my injured ego and outraged sense of justice, an intimate comradeship grew up between us as a result which continued right through our school and university days as well as during and after the war.

My brother Brian is two years younger than myself. He too received his initial education at Nos. 15–17 Upper Shelley Street, save that he was given separate lessons from Ping Tsung and myself. The three of us regularly played together when we were not at work. We often pretended to divide the family residence into three separate kingdoms, and each of us would occupy one of them. We would then play hide-and-seek fighting against one another as kings defending our respective realms. No. 15 and No. 17 Shelley Street in those days each had a winding staircase leading from the ground floor to a common dining room straddling the first floor of both houses. A third smaller winding staircase led from the kitchen, the servants' quarters, and an open yard at the rear of the ground floor of both houses to a narrow corridor serving only the first floor of No. 15, ending likewise in the common dining room. This intriguing layout offered ideal opportunities for our game. Although Ping Tsung won most of our imaginary combats, Brian and I enjoyed nonetheless the sheer excitement of dashing up and down the several staircases trying to outmanoeuvre, outwit and outguess one another as if we were seasoned strategists.

At the beginning of 1932, my father decided that the time had come for his three younger sons to go to school. Accordingly, he took us to see the headmaster of Wah Yan College, then situated at No. 2 Robinson Road. Robinson Road adjoins the east end of Mosque Street and is no more than a stone's throw from Shelley Street. The school was then divided into eight grades. The highest grade was class 1 which was the matriculation class. The lowest was class 8. Ping Tsung and I were put into class 7 while Brian was put into class 8. Thus began my education at Wah Yan College. I was then nine years old.

3 *Wah Yan College and the Irish Jesuits*

Walking every morning to Wah Yan and back again in the afternoon was not only good exercise. As I carried my books daily up Shelley Street across and beyond Mosque Street into Robinson Road, I felt sheer pride in being able to fend for myself at last, and no longer needing to be constantly watched over by my parents. Sharing a classroom with some forty other students was also a new and pleasurable experience. Hitherto attending classes at home with Ping Tsung alone had invariably given me an inferiority complex. The discovery that not a few of the other students were not much cleverer than I, if at all, was in itself both comforting and reassuring. Besides, being the youngest member of my class, and more than articulate in expressing myself, I enjoyed more immediate attention from the teachers at Wah Yan than Miss Shum and Mr Li had ever shown me at home. This gave me no small measure of a newly acquired confidence.

Wah Yan College was founded by a Mr Peter Tsui in 1919 in Hollywood Road with no more than a handful of pupils at its inception. However the number of its students and classes grew steadily over the years. In 1921, it moved into No. 2 Robinson Road. In 1922, it became a grant-in-aid secondary school with more than one hundred students, after which its complement of students and classes increased further from year to year. In 1931, it was sold to the Society of Jesus from Dublin, Ireland, and was in due course taken over by the representatives of that religious order. Under the expert supervision and management of the Irish Jesuits, Wah Yan College continued to expand and flourish in the years which followed, and has long since won recognition as one of the best-run and most successful local secondary schools.

In 1932, when admission into Wah Yan was sought by my father for Ping Tsung, Brian, and myself, it was Fr Gallagher who received, interviewed, and admitted us. Fr Gallagher was the first Irish Jesuit headmaster of Wah Yan. He was a perpetually cheerful and affable man, whose somewhat stern looks belied his gentle and selfless inner nature. At first we could not help feeling a little afraid of him, but his overflowing friendliness quickly put us at our ease. It did not take us long to discover that since becoming headmaster, he had readily won over the love and respect of all the teachers, staff, and students alike of the school.

I owe a special debt of gratitude to Rev Fr D. Donnelly SJ who taught me mathematics in 1936, 1937, and 1938 in Wah Yan College. With Miss Shum as my former teacher, I had had no end of problems with my arithmetic. This continued initially in Wah Yan throughout 1932, 1933, 1934 and 1935. I experienced a similar difficulty, although to a lesser degree, with algebra, geometry and trigonometry, when I was first taught those subjects in 1934 and 1935. Strange as it may seem, after Fr Donnelly took over teaching me in 1936, I saw daylight immediately, and became completely at home in all four mathematics subjects. Whereas I used previously to loathe my mathematics lessons, from 1936 onwards I found myself looking forward daily to them with Fr Donnelly as teacher. One exciting facet of Fr Donnelly's teaching was that he habitually cited intriguing mathematical problems which were not available in our textbooks, and challenged us to solve them. The high marks which I scored in mathematics from 1936 onwards not only pulled me up several places in class. I was awarded a distinction in both my school leaving examinations in 1937, and my matriculation examinations in 1938. In 1938 in particular, this played a major part in winning a government scholarship for me at a time when my father's financial ability to send both Ping Tsung and me to the university was very much in doubt. To this day, I still wonder how Fr Donnelly managed to effect that transformation in me so promptly and completely.

My best friends and favourite teachers at Wah Yan were undoubtedly a Mr F. Cronin, and a Mr T. Sheridan. These were two young Irish scholastics who had been sent out to Hong Kong to acquire some experience. Mr Cronin taught me history for several years at Wah Yan, and invariably gave me more marks than I deserved. I can hardly forget the emphasis he constantly laid on cause and effect to explain historical events. Mr Sheridan on the other hand played a big part in getting the students at Wah Yan interested in ex-curricular activities such as public speaking, debates, and drama. In the course of time he wrote a number of extremely clever and amusing Chinese operas in English which never failed to bring the roof down whenever they were produced. I participated in several of those productions, and was usually given the part of a general because of my imposing size and height, even though I could not sing.

Mr Sheridan also very successfully directed and produced a number of Shakespearean plays in Wah Yan in the middle and late 1930s. I took part in all of them. Perhaps the best remembered of his productions was *The Merchant of Venice* in which I played the part of Portia. I can still recall how I extolled the quality of mercy in the dramatic court scene in which Ping Tsung played the Doge, and Brian his page. However it was Joseph Lim who stole the show as Shylock. I cannot help wondering whether I was not already destined then to make my living as a lawyer and advocate twenty years hence. Joseph Lim is a born actor of many talents. He was a contemporary of mine at Wah Yan and also subsequently at the University of Hong Kong. His father, Mr Lim Hoy Lan (林海瀾), was a well-known and distinguished headmaster of Wah Yan in the 1920s, and a very good friend of my father. Although neither of us knew it at the time, Joseph Lim and I were later to team up to act together in many more successful dramatic productions in the Arts Faculty of the University of Hong Kong.

Mr Cronin and Mr Sheridan were not much older than my classmates and I. While in their spare time they taught us how to speak and write English properly, we taught them Chinese. They each occupied a room in the living quarters of the school, where I used to spend not a little of my time almost daily after school and during weekends and holidays. Although they were my teachers, I was made to feel more like their friend than student. In the course of time, they were both duly ordained as priests, and became close friends of mine and my family.

For a number of years, Fr Cronin was the warden of Ricci Hall, the Catholic hostel for undergraduates, and a lecturer in logic at the University of Hong Kong. In due course he became Father Superior of the Irish Jesuits in Hong Kong. In 1952 it was Fr Cronin who solemnized my marriage. After the 1967 riots in Hong Kong, I decided to send my children abroad for their schooling, and Fr Cronin was mainly instrumental in securing my elder son Denis' admission into Stonyhurst College in England. This was a renowned boarding school run by the English Jesuits in Lancashire. Denis' entrance in 1968 into Stonyhurst to continue his studies paved the way for the sons of quite a number of my friends in Hong Kong to follow suit. My younger son Dominic did likewise in 1981.

Fr Cronin died in Hong Kong in 1987 some years after celebrating his fiftieth anniversary as a Jesuit. Fr Sheridan on the other hand tragically died at an early age in Manila in the 1950s in somewhat mysterious circumstances, although no foul play was suspected.

The influence of the Irish Jesuits on me as a teenager was not limited to the priceless lessons they taught me in the classroom. As I grew older and more mature with every year spent at Wah Yan, I could see for myself how very learned and knowledgeable and yet how very humble and unassuming these Jesuits all were, how charitable and kind they were towards everyone who came into contact with them, and what a simple life they lived and had chosen to live. Apart from the time when we were taught our religious knowledge lessons in the classroom, I seldom heard any of my Jesuit teachers talk religion outside the classroom or try to convert anyone to their particular professed faith. Yet their example from day to day made me ask myself time and again what these wonderful people were seeking in life, while denying themselves so many of the cherished earthly pleasures and commonly desired rewards of this world.

4 The Fairy Tale of My Matriculation

By June 1938, Ping Tsung and I had completed six and a half years of tuition from our Irish Jesuit mentors. Already the University of Hong Kong was beckoning to us as we prepared for our matriculation. The impending examinations did not pose much of a hurdle for either of us, and we had rather taken our eventual entry into the university for granted. One evening my father sent for Ping Tsung and myself. This was something he had never done before. In his private sitting room on the first floor of No. 17 Shelley Street, he disclosed that the education of my eldest brother Pak Chuen and my eldest sister Sheung Woon in England and that of my two other elder sisters Josephine and Margaret at the University of Hong Kong had taxed his financial resources to the utmost. As a result, he regretted that he could send only one but not both of us immediately to the university to continue our studies. As Ping Tsung was the elder brother, my father explained that he must be given the option to go to the university ahead of me. Thus, unless I won a scholarship for myself, I would have to wait until Josephine and Margaret had taken their degrees before I could have my post-secondary education. This was a real bombshell for me. I knew only too well that although I had surpassed myself in my School Leaving Examinations in the previous year, it was extremely doubtful whether I could match strides with the best of Hong Kong's matriculation candidates in the normal course of events and win a scholarship in order to gain admission into the university. Obviously my father thought likewise. Consequently he invited me to defer my matriculation, repeat one year at Wah Yan, and aim instead at winning a scholarship in the following year.

I do not know what gave me the audacity at the time. I flatly refused even to consider deferring my matriculation. My reaction is not difficult to understand. I had shared the same tuition and classes with Ping Tsung from the day we were taught our ABCs, and had experienced some very difficult times keeping pace with him. Now that I had caught up with him, I was naturally unwilling to be left behind through no fault of my own. Life is frequently not without its irony. It is not unknown that once in a while ill-considered decisions are made, which, at the time of making, may not be the most logical or the best, but which turn out sometimes to be the wisest later on and in the long run. I can only say that the decision I made for myself in the summer of 1938 fell directly into that category. Without doubt, it was only my pride at the time which made me refuse to defer my matriculation. My father could do nothing to change my mind. Nor could my form-master Rev Fr T. Ryan SJ, who strongly supported my father's suggestion that I repeat my final year at Wah Yan. I was in no mood whatever to listen to any suggestion from anybody to do otherwise than take my place in the matriculation examination hall in 1938. What I did not tell anyone was that I immediately went to the chapel at Wah Yan, where I made a promise to the good Lord that if I should win a scholarship for myself that year, I would carry out a number of undertakings in later life to repay Him for the special favour granted me.

It was in those circumstances that I proceeded to sit for my matriculation examinations. The remaining part of my story was comparable to a fairy tale, which I found myself reliving every so often in later life. To begin with, I ran a high fever for no less than a week just before the examinations. On the very first day I misread my Chinese examination paper, and wrote a critique on a famous battle in Chinese history which was not the one set out in the examination paper. My mistake was only discovered after I had gone home to compare notes with Ping Tsung who was most sympathetic although as shocked as I was. As I was visibly upset, he comforted me saying I must put this unfortunate mistake behind me and not allow it to detract from my performance in the remainder of the examinations. This was of course excellent advice, but more easily said than done. Try as I might, I was unable to sleep that evening, but lay awake instead tormenting myself with the thought of the likely consequences of my stupid error.

On the following morning, I went into the examination hall for my algebra paper literally in a state of physical exhaustion and mental stupor. I could think of nothing else other than the misfortune which had befallen me, and was totally incapable of concentrating on the subtle algebraic calculations I was required to do. In the end I came away without being able to recall what exactly I had done that morning, save that whatever it was, it was not algebra. Indeed one misfortune had led to another. Without doubt I was floundering, and all seemed lost.

Two examination papers had been set down for that day with a luncheon break of two hours between the first and the second paper. At lunch Ping Tsung could see that I was mentally and emotionally shattered, and must have sensed what had happened. This time, instead of sympathizing, which most certainly would not have helped, he went out of his way to give me a stiff warning, bless him, which more than just made me sit up. Unless I pulled myself together, he said, no one, not even God Almighty, could help me. Unlike me, he was known to be a total non-believer, and his altogether unexpected reference to the Creator suddenly and very effectively reminded me of the plea I had made at the Wah Yan chapel. This caused me immediately to feel more ashamed of than sorry for myself. As I made my way back to the examination hall after lunch, I was calmer, more relaxed and resigned, and ready to try my best all over again. In the afternoon, by sheer coincidence, there was an unexpected turn of events which changed the whole scene.

In those days matriculation candidates in Wah Yan were daily given a totally free private study period of one hour each. In 1938, there was a Chinese teacher in Wah Yan who was a returned student from Paris, and more than proficient in French. With the special permission of the Prefect of Studies of the school, Ping Tsung and I and two other matriculation candidates had elected to take French lessons from this gentleman during our daily private study period, and had been doing so since the commencement of the current school year. In the course of time, encouraged by our teacher, we had offered French as an optional third language in our matriculation examination, indeed only out of fun, and not really caring whether we passed or failed. I had hardly expected that this bold venture on our part would come to my rescue on the second day of my matriculation.

On that afternoon, our French examination was fatefully due. It turned out to be pleasantly easier than expected and completely to my liking. This paper consisted of two parts. The first half was all French grammar. The second half contained two pieces of translation which I was required to do, one from French into English, and the other vice-versa. My French teacher had somehow amazingly anticipated almost the whole contents of the first half so that I had no difficulty applying my limited knowledge to its fullest use. Although the translations were a little more difficult, nonetheless at the end of the day, I felt almost as if I was a specialist in this foreign language. I knew then that whatever happened to my Chinese, it could no longer hurt me as much.

My French paper not only restored my overall equanimity but also conveniently reminded me of another known factor which could well work in my favour. One of the rules of matriculation in those days was that every candidate need offer only three of the four mathematics subjects if he so desired. In other words, so long as I did well in arithmetic, geometry, and trigonometry, the day might yet be saved. This gave me further fresh hope. Consequently, as from the third day I was able to perform like my normal self again. No more setbacks occurred, and I sailed through my remaining subjects.

Waiting for the matriculation results was both long and anxious. Eventually they were announced on 22 August which coincided with my sixteenth birthday. I remember that it was on a Monday. Perusing the names of the successful candidates published in the local newspapers initially caused me fresh consternation. There were in 1938 two matriculation classes in Wah Yan so that some eighty students had taken the examinations from Wah Yan alone, and the list of those who had passed was necessarily fairly long and in alphabetical order. As our surname started with a 'Y', Ping Tsung had no difficulty finding his name immediately at the very bottom of the alphabetical list. My name, which should have immediately followed his if I had passed, was not there. A single glance was sufficient to tell me so, which, I thought, could only mean that I had failed after all. As I moved quietly away feeling totally downcast and lost, Ping Tsung suddenly shouted his congratulations to me at the top of his voice, because my name was the second one at the very top of the list and one of the only two from Wah Yan who had been awarded honours, which meant that I had attained a minimum standard of excellence in all my subjects. Ping Tsung was of course overjoyed for my sake, but could not help querying immediately afterwards whether I could have in fact written a wrong Chinese essay on the first day, and subsequently mucked up my algebra paper on the second day, as I said I had done. I was so happily taken aback by the published results that I could do no more than shake my head in total disbelief, especially because I had scored a distinction in mathematics as well.

There was natural rejoicing in the family that evening. It was also one of the most jubilant birthdays I have ever celebrated. One week after the publication of the results, a letter of congratulations arrived from the Education Department offering me a government scholarship to do a bachelor's degree in education at the University of Hong Kong, but only on condition that I would teach for a period of not less than three years in one of the government schools after my graduation. I was of course more than delighted to accept the offer, which spared me from having to choose what to read. Needless to say, I lost no time before hastening to the Wah Yan chapel to do my thanksgiving, and reaffirm my promised undertakings to the good Lord. My father was probably the most pleased, because my scholarship had saved him from the embarrassment of being unable to send his two sons concurrently to the university. The mystery surrounding my Chinese essay and algebra papers, and how I could have qualified as an honours student despite fumbling those two papers was not unravelled until late in September, after I had started my first year at the university. In the meantime, I was left to enjoy the rest of my summer vacation in peace and without a worrying thought of any kind other than what might be lying in wait for me at this new landmark in my life called the University of Hong Kong.

5 An Apology and Explanation

It was not without good reason that I went to such great length to describe my matriculation. Nor was the reason merely that it might make interesting reading. I was underlining the importance of two particular incidents each of which made a huge impact on my later life. The first was of course my unexpected scholarship, which had the immediate effect of altogether removing the financial obstacle to my joining the university. The second incident, consisting of my foolhardy refusal to defer my matriculation, had just as important a bearing on my life as the first, although its effect was not immediately obvious. This refusal on my part could have boomeranged if my matriculation results had proven to be otherwise. As things turned out, it was essential in enabling me to enrol as an undergraduate in 1938. Otherwise there would be no way I could have joined the university earlier than September 1939 with or without a scholarship.

The all important difference between enrolling at the University of Hong Kong in 1938 and enrolling instead in 1939 lay in the fact that when the Japanese attacked and occupied Hong Kong in December 1941, I was already in my fourth and final year in the Arts Faculty thanks to my having matriculated in 1938. When the university authorities, as a result of the Japanese occupation of Hong Kong, decided to award without further ado a war-time degree to all final year arts students of whom I was one, I became immediately entitled to the benefit of that decision. If I had enrolled in 1939, I would not have been in my final year in 1941 and would not have been so entitled.

At the time the award of the war-time degree was announced, I doubt if its full significance was appreciated, save that the lucky recipients must have felt grateful to be spared the agony of having to return and complete their course after the war. In the years which followed, however, this war-time degree proved to be much more important to me than I could possibly have visualized. The fact was that with the award I was at least a finished product, namely, a university graduate with a bachelor's degree. Without it, I would have been a mere undergraduate still studying at the university, which could have meant anything, and would have had nothing to recommend me for work. In due course this degree enabled me to secure two war-time jobs one after another on the Chinese mainland where I went shortly after the Japanese occupation of Hong Kong. I doubt if I would have landed either of them without my degree. Furthermore the war service I rendered as a result of those two jobs played no small part in eventually winning for me my Victory Scholarship in 1946, without which I would certainly not have had the necessary means to further my education in England.

Today as I recall those happenings of some sixty years ago, it certainly looks as if every single material incident, whether big or small, which took place in 1938 and the years which followed, was part of a predestined plan to chart the charmed life of the seventh child of a seventh child which I am only too happy to be.

6   *Mystery Unravelled*

I had the most loving parents, who were, however, over protective to an incredible degree. They would readily not let any of their young children out of their sight, if that were possible, just to ensure from day to day that they did not come to any harm. While we were still at Wah Yan, my brothers and I had finally succeeded, after many futile attempts, in persuading our parents to let us play soccer with some of our classmates and friends on a large piece of open ground in Robinson Road during weekends and public holidays. Unbelievably, our parents only agreed to sanction those games on condition that we promised not to perspire, lest we caught cold as a result, and that Ping Tsung's former nanny watched over us throughout the game, lest we got hurt.

In the fall of 1938, Ping Tsung and I thought we had secured a psychological victory over our parents when they agreed to let us live as boarders in Ricci Hall, the Catholic hostel for undergraduates. Like Wah Yan, Ricci Hall was run by the Irish Jesuits, quite a number of whom had by this time become my father's personal friends. But this permission to live at Ricci was accompanied by a most unusual condition, namely, that we lunched and dined at home every day, and returned to Shelley Street to live during weekends and public holidays. To facilitate our constant travelling between the university and home, my father even purchased each of us a monthly bus ticket.

Accordingly in the autumn of 1938, Ping Tsung and I found ourselves lunching and dining at Shelley Street every day, and catching the last No. 3A bus in Caine Road at 10.30 p.m. every evening in order to be back at our hostel before 11 p.m., after which hour, leave of absence would have to be obtained from the warden. For a while we were the laughing stock of Ricci, when our daily domestic routine became known to our contemporaries. However the joke only lasted a short while. This routine was followed for no more than the first couple of months. Our sheer impatience to get back to the university every day and Ricci Hall every evening became so painfully obvious that our parents soon felt obliged to relax the rule; and from the end of that year we were permitted to come and go as we desired.

However, first things first, before I proceed further with my account of life at Pokfulam. Within days of my enrolment at the university, I was sent for first by Professor Ma Kam of the Chinese school, and subsequently by a Mrs Faid who was the pure mathematics lecturer, and the examiner for the matriculation algebra paper. Professor Ma revealed that when he first read my essay on the wrong battle, his immediate reaction was to have me disqualified because no candidate deserved to be forgiven for such blatant ignorance of Chinese history. Eventually, however, he decided to wait first for the result of my Chinese history paper. After he learned that I had received a good mark in the latter paper, he concluded that no more than a genuine mistake must have been made, brought on not by ignorance but by illness or some other reasonable excuse. So, miraculously as far as I was concerned, he had marked my essay on its own merit as if there had been no mistake made about the subject matter.

The interview on my algebra paper started with Mrs Faid inquiring if I took drugs! I was of course stunned. When I asked what she meant, she simply took out my algebra paper and showed it to me. I had written across the face of the otherwise blank sheet nothing other than the words 'I have failed my Chinese essay paper' no less than six times. Naturally I told her my side of the story. She said she had guessed as much. She revealed that after due consideration she felt convinced that what had happened reflected sheer dejection on my part as a result of an unfortunate accident, and not incompetence as far as algebra was concerned. Accordingly, she had recommended to the board of examiners that my case be treated as if I had neither handed in an algebra paper at all nor even offered algebra as one of my matriculation subjects, and that each of my other mathematics papers, namely, arithmetic, geometry, and trigonometry, be allowed respectively to stand on its own merit.

It is difficult to imagine how anyone could be so fortunate as to have all at once two such considerate examiners. But I certainly did. In the absence of either one of them, I would not have been awarded my scholarship to enter the university in September 1938.

7 — *A Vintage Year*

I met many outstanding people at the University of Hong Kong in 1938. In the Arts Faculty alone, there was already an imposing array of young talents from each of whom I soon discovered that I had much to learn. 1938 certainly seemed to be a vintage year for the students of Hong Kong.

Oswald Cheung, now Sir Oswald Cheung, QC, better known to all his friends simply as Ossie, was a King Edward scholar of my year when he was only sixteen years of age. Immediately after the last war he became the headmaster of Diocesan Boys' School for a while before he was awarded a government scholarship to read law at University College, Oxford. Since the early 1950s, he has been a prominent member of the local Bar. In 1987 he was knighted in recognition of services rendered by him as legislative and executive councillor respectively in the 1960s and 70s. He was voted a life member of the Hong Kong Bar Association in 1996.

Rayson Huang was another talented young government scholar of my year. He was one of the most conscientious hard workers, both in and out of the classroom, that I have ever known. We attended the same mathematics classes in 1938 and 1939. The meticulous notes he invariably took at every lecture were a great help to me whenever I missed any lesson as a result of illness or some other reason. After the war he took a doctorate degree in chemistry at Magdalen College, Oxford and, in due course became the Vice-Chancellor first of Nanyang University in Singapore, and a little later of the University of Hong Kong.

Lau Din Cheuk, another outstanding sixteen-year-old government scholar of 1938, was small in stature but a giant in intellectual prowess.

He carried away almost every available prize in the Arts Faculty during the three odd years he spent at the University of Hong Kong. I remember being almost jealous of his successes because he never seemed to have to do much work for his achievements. After the war, he went to Glasgow for his master's degree. I was then reading law in London. Whenever he visited me in my digs at Earls Court, he would hold me spellbound while initiating me into the beauty of the Chinese language, the Chinese classics, and Chinese philosophy. It was no surprise that after Glasgow, he was promptly made a member of the teaching staff of the School of Oriental and African Studies in London, where his expert knowledge was put to full use for some years before he returned to Hong Kong to teach at the Chinese University. He was duly appointed Professor in 1970 at the latter institution. Although he has long since retired from active teaching, he has been retained permanently by the Chinese University as an honorary professor. He has for many years been and still is a recognized authority on the Chinese language and the Chinese classics.

Kam Ying Hei was another King Edward scholar of my year and, likewise, a brilliant exponent of Chinese literature and the Chinese classics. He was always seen going around wearing a cheong-sam, that is to say a long Chinese gown which was hardly the fashion in those days especially among undergraduates. He was soft spoken and polite to an incredible degree. When not attending lectures, he appeared to spend all his time reading or working in the university library. A Chinese chess fiend, he had a fantastic memory, and could memorize any poem whether Chinese or English after reading through the text no more than once. We used to call him the walking encyclopaedia, because he could reproduce almost any literary quotation when requested in either language off the cuff. I do not know what happened to him during the war years. After the war I believe he became at one time a top government official of the Guangdong Provincial Government. I am truly sorry I never saw Kam Ying Hei again after 1941, because we were such good friends at the university. Like a lot of good people, he died young in the early 1990s!

Clifford Matthews is a dear friend of mine who was yet another HKU government scholar of my year, likewise at the age of sixteen. To him I owe my acquired interest in many good things and, in particular, in the wonderful world of opera. I cannot help remembering the many delightful hours we spent together as undergraduates in his room at St John's Hall, the hostel where he lived, just listening to his gramophone recordings of *La Bohème* and other works of Puccini. Nor can I forget the occasion when he made a number of casual comments about Sir

Walter Scott's epic novels, which impressed me tremendously. Several weeks later, I unashamedly reproduced those comments of his when doing a test paper for Professor Simpson on Sir Walter Scott, and was given top marks in the class. I never told anybody about the incident with Clifford, because that was the only time I ever won top marks. Clifford is currently Professor of organic chemistry at the University of Illinois in Chicago, USA. After all these years, he still calls me by no other name than 'Steamship' because of my Chinese initials S.S.

I must not forget to mention an amazing young lady in my class by the name of Lam Yung Tai. Yet another government scholar in 1938, she scored full marks in all her mathematics papers not only in her matriculation but also throughout the three odd years when she was at the University of Hong Kong. A demure and petite teenage girl of no more than five feet, she was the personification of modesty despite her mathematical genius. Professor Brown, somewhat reminiscent of Fr Donnelly at Wah Yan, used every now and again to pose difficult mathematical questions to our class in the course of his lectures. Whenever this happened, it was always Miss Lam who put up her hand to answer those questions, and most of the time correctly too. At the end of which, Professor Brown would tease me by saying 'I do not expect Y(o)u would know that, would you?'. After the war Miss Lam was appointed headmistress of one of the best schools in Hong Kong.

I wonder how many of these exceptional individuals I would have had the good fortune of knowing if I had not enrolled at the university in 1938.

8   *The University of Hong Kong*

For me, life at the Arts Faculty of the University of Hong Kong began with a somewhat unnerving experience. When I turned up for the first of my lectures, I was overwhelmed by the sight of nearly twenty pretty young ladies already seated in the lecture room, chatting, joking, laughing, and creating almost a minor disturbance. There were of course many male occupants in the room too, but in the company of the flamboyant members of the fair sex, their presence became barely noticeable. Hitherto my sisters and a couple of my cousins had made up the sole female company I ever had. Learning how to conduct myself in the company of the opposite sex soon became a revelation and an education in itself.

One shortcoming of a Wah Yan education was that I was never taught any English verse. As a result I frequently found myself at sea when attending poetry classes at the university. The lecturers without exception seemed to assume that every one in the class had had some basic knowledge of the subject. Unfortunately I had known nothing hitherto about scansion or the different verse forms. The good ladies of my class, on the other hand, were all on familiar ground. When they heard of my predicament, they were instantly sympathetic, although somewhat sceptical at first. As a result, sometimes in the university library and sometimes over a cup of tea in the students' union, they would take turns to explain to me like teachers to their pupils at school what I ought to but did not know about the subject.

One of the many attractions of undergraduate life, especially for a newcomer like myself, lay in the numerous functions organized in the evenings from time to time by the students themselves to enable their friends and associates of the different years, faculties, and hostels, to come together and get to know one another better. Those gatherings took various forms including debates, speech competitions, musical performances, and intellectual discussions. The biggest and most popular social function was undoubtedly the annual ball sponsored by the students' union. This event was always staged at the Lok Yew Hall of the university main building, for which the best orchestral band in town and the most noteworthy food and beverage caterers would be hired. Admission tickets were costly, and dress for the occasion was invariably black tie. As Ping Tsung and I did not even have a tuxedo, but dearly wished to attend, we felt obliged to take the matter to our parents to seek their assistance. We were pleasantly surprised when they raised no difficulty, readily gave us the money for the tickets, and forthwith sent for the tailor to have our tuxedos made. Before we could even begin to rejoice, however, they made the bombshell announcement that we would of course be taking sisters Josephine and Margaret to the ball. Judgment had been pronounced, and no room was left whatever for argument or discussion. The couple of beautiful faces whom we had originally in mind of inviting to the ball quickly vanished into oblivion. That was how sisters Josephine and Margaret became the dancing partners of Ping Tsung and myself at our first ball at the university. We never found out which of the four of us enjoyed the evening least.

Another event staged at the Lok Yew Hall was the annual dramatic production by the Arts Faculty. This was always undertaken by one of the junior lecturers as a showpiece not only for the faculty, but also for the university at large. Joseph Lim and I found ourselves being given leading parts in each of the productions respectively in the years 1938, 1939, and 1940, namely, George Bernard Shaw's *You Never Can Tell*, and *Androcles and the Lion*, and S.I. Hsiung's *The Professor from Peking*. 'Androcles and the Lion' deserves special mention. It was in the course of this production that the acting genius of Joseph Lim, who played the part of the Roman emperor, became manifest. On opening night, at the juncture when the lion pursued him across the stage, he completely forgot his lines. To stall for time, he raced several times instead of just once round the stage, while the poor lion struggled on all fours to follow him. Meanwhile, his false imperial paunch came loose and had to be held up with both his hands. As he ran, he uttered extemporaneous exclamations which would undoubtedly have amused even Bernard Shaw. Not surprisingly, on stage and in the audience, pandemonium erupted and continued for several minutes before the production returned to its normal course. As the curtain finally rang down after the producer and all the cast had taken their bow, the audience started calling again for Joseph Lim, who had to reappear to take yet another bow while still holding his false paunch. It was rumoured that not a few members of the audience who had not read *Androcles and the Lion* genuinely thought that Joseph Lim's spontaneous improvisations that evening were all part and parcel of Bernard Shaw's play superbly translated into action by the genius of the actor.

Because of the way my matriculation went, I felt I owed a measure of loyalty to the French language, and accordingly registered early for the French class conducted at the university by a very sweet lady by the name of Madame Martie. For the next two weeks, however, I was totally unable to tell when she was speaking English, and when French. In the end, I saw no point in further attending her classes. However, Madame and I remained good friends, nonetheless. When a little later she requested me to participate in her French play, I felt obliged to do so, because she had very few male students from whom to choose her players. Ping Tsung thought I must have lost my head to agree to take part in a French play, because he knew better than anybody else how little French I spoke. My response was that he must come to the play and witness how much I had improved in my spoken French. I did not tell him then that my part only required me to say 'Oui' three times, 'Non' twice, and 'Monsieur' once in the course of the whole play. Obviously Madame Martie knew and chose her players well.

The only ball game I could play reasonably well was soccer, thanks no doubt to my parents encouraging their sons to practise their skills at Robinson Road without perspiring. In my first year, history was made when the Arts Faculty won the inter-faculty football championship for the first time ever. As members of the team representing the Arts Faculty, Joseph Lim, Ping Tsung, and I stood ten feet tall in the eyes of our lady friends who turned up in full force to cheer us to victory. In the following year, all three of us represented Ricci Hall in the inter-hostel football championship. A lucky draw in the six-hostel tournament soon sent us challenging Eliot Hall for the title. Nine members of the latter team played regularly for the university in the open league in Hong Kong, so that few gave us any chance of winning. But soccer is so very unpredictable. In the final match, we were besieged and bombarded for the whole of the ninety-minute game. Somehow we held out to the end, thanks to the magnificent feats of George Choa at goal. In the dying minutes of the second half, after a scramble in midfield, a loose ball was seen flying through the air towards the Eliot goal. Ratna Kutrakal, a Thai national and another former student from Wah Yan, sprinted after the ball while the Eliot goalkeeper raced out to intercept him. The two players collided heavily and fell. As they both lay on the ground, the ball rolled into the Eliot goal to give underdog Ricci Hall the match. As was customary, the winning team celebrated the victory by holding a dance. This time Ping Tsung and I made sure we could partner our favourite young ladies to the occasion by the early inclusion of sisters Josephine and Margaret and their respective boyfriends as invitees. Later in life, Ratna Kutrakal took Holy Orders after returning to his home country, was first ostracized and later disinherited by his family for forsaking the Buddhist faith, but stuck to his religious conviction, and eventually became a cardinal in Bangkok. The hero of the match, George Choa, was a medical student at the University of Hong Kong in those days. After the war he became an outstanding golfer and tennis star as well as the leading ear, nose and throat specialist in the territory.

One of the biggest events in my life took place at Ricci Hall on the first day of January 1939. I was baptized and received into the Catholic Church. This had been on my mind for some time. It was one of the several undertakings I promised to the good Lord in the Wah Yan chapel, and the first one of its kind to be fulfilled. The others, I am afraid, will take a whole life-time to fulfil. In those days, to be baptized was not an easy decision for me to make. My parents were then essentially pagans. They knew little or nothing about Christianity, and believed only in what had long been translated into English as ancestor worship. I have often wondered whether there might not be a better translation for this particular filial rite. There was a special room at the back of Nos. 15–17 Shelley Street where the Yu family ancestor tablets were meticulously and respectfully set up. On all festive occasions, and whenever celebration of any kind occurred in the family, our parents would kow-tow before the tablets, that is to say, kneel and bend one's head until it touched the ground, and offer thanksgiving to the ancestors. The rest of the family would then follow suit in accordance with their respective age and seniority.

I never discussed with my parents the essential principles involved in this form of ancestor worship. But I have never had any doubts in my own mind that according to traditional Chinese belief, while ancestor worship cannot be entirely separated from spiritualism and the supernatural, it is only paying homage and respect to and a long way from deifying one's ancestors. For a very long time, children in Chinese families used regularly to kow-tow and pay similar homage to their living parents. I certainly did so throughout my parents' lifetime. Surely there can be no question of deifying one's living parents by this filial rite.

Unfortunately the Vatican held a different view of things, and for a long time kneeling before one's ancestor tablets was prohibited as worshipping false gods. On the other hand my parents had always taken it for granted that their children would honour and perpetuate the traditional practice of ancestor worship. That was why I had not even dared to ask them for permission to become a Catholic. This stalemate was not in fact resolved until some years later when the Vatican eventually, albeit belatedly, lifted the prohibition against ancestor worship.

When towards the end of 1938 my parents no longer required me to return home to dinner every evening, I felt I could not keep the good Lord waiting for me to become a Catholic any longer. Fr Gallagher, who had admitted me into Wah Yan, was specially invited to perform the necessary rites. In the months and years which followed, I had to absent myself from home whenever there was any ancestor worship to be performed. On those occasions when I could not help being present at Shelley Street, I would make every possible excuse to appear before the ancestor tablets only after my parents had left the room. After a while my parents must have suspected the truth, although being such loving parents they elected to say nothing, and pretended not to notice anything. In the course of time, when brother Brian and sisters Josephine and Margaret saw that I managed to get by without having to kneel in front of our ancestor tablets, they too became Catholics. During the war my two younger sisters Winnie and Rosalind also joined us in embracing the Catholic faith. This led eventually to my parents becoming Catholics as well, although only at a much later date.

9   *The Fall of Hong Kong: Before and After*

Time sped by almost unnoticed. By December 1941 Ping Tsung and I had expended three full academic years at the university, and had entered upon our fourth and final year. Those were very profitable years during which I could easily have acquired an excellent education. Instead, I merely had a wonderful time. In September 1940, younger brother Brian had joined us at Ricci Hall. He had in fact matriculated in 1939 at the precocious age of fourteen winning a scholarship in the process, but was denied admission into the University until the following year because he was too young. Meanwhile ugly clouds of war had been gathering on the not too distant horizon. In 1937, Japan had openly invaded China in the north. In 1938, Canton had fallen to its Imperial army in the south. During this period, the Western countries had enough problems of their own trying to contain the aggression of Nazi Germany in eastern Europe. After war had been declared against Germany in 1939, rumours were rife that Japan would soon link up with the Axis powers to further its own military and territorial aggrandizement. These rumours grew louder by the day as Hitler's armies quickly overran Europe in 1940 and 1941. Nonetheless many people in Hong Kong still found it difficult to believe that Japan would all at once challenge the hitherto invincible might of the British Navy as well as incur the total wrath of the North American continent. Thus, when on 8 December 1941 the Japanese launched their simultaneous attack on Pearl Harbour and Hong Kong, my parents, among others, were caught entirely by surprise.

On the morning of that historic day, I was awakened in Ricci Hall by the air-raid sirens announcing the first bomb attacks on Kai Tak airfield. From the incessant radio broadcasts which followed, Hong Kong learnt with a shock that after all the unsubstantiated rumours hitherto, war had in truth visited the island at last. In the summer of 1941, I had enlisted as a volunteer worker with what was known as the War Auxiliary Services, and was duly assigned to the War-time Rice Control Department which had an office in the western section of town. I was instructed to report to that office for duty in the event of war. After the Japanese had dropped their first bombs on Hong Kong, however, there was an emergency announcement repeated again and again over the radio advising all volunteer workers of that department not to attend at its western office until further notice. It transpired that a huge fire had mysteriously broken out engulfing not only the whole of that office building, but also several adjoining godowns where much of the government rice was stored.

On that first day of the war, Ping Tsung, Brian, and I had to walk home from Ricci Hall, because all bus services had been suspended. At home in Shelley Street, a picture of utter gloom and despair sadly met our eyes. At one stage my father asked me to cash a cheque for him in town, and send a telegram on behalf of the family to my eldest brother Pak Chuen on the Chinese mainland where he had gone after coming home from England in the mid 1930s. I can still remember the look of total disbelief on his face, when I enquired where and how his two requests could be carried out. I wonder which of the two of us was more stunned on that occasion. I was then nineteen years old, and a final year student at the university. Yet I had never once been inside a bank, a post office, or a telegraph office. The outbreak of war had all of a sudden mercilessly awakened me to the realisation that I had lived hitherto in an altogether unrealistic world of books and make-believe. Things like literature and mathematics, and doing well in examinations were all of no immediate help to me and the family in the face of the numerous inexorable problems instantly created by war.

My father as head of the family was probably the one hardest hit by the outbreak of hostilities. The war with Japan was obviously going to last a long time from which there would be no immediate foreseeable relief. Everywhere constant reverses were reported to be suffered by the Allies. My father had a large family to support, and very little savings. Innumerable uncertainties lay ahead; his eldest son was fighting the Japanese on the Chinese mainland, while the rest of his family was trapped in Hong Kong. The immediate problem of providing for the inmates of the household was already by no means an easy one.

My mother's younger brother Lam Pak Chung and his sizeable family were also residing at Shelley Street after their residence in Caine Road had been damaged by a shell. There were thus more than thirty mouths to feed including the servants. My mother turned out to be a pillar of strength in a crisis. To the relief of everyone, especially my father, she produced surprise savings in cash, and sent several of her children into different parts of town to acquire forthwith a substantial stock of tinned food, rice, and other essentials for the household in anticipation of the siege to come. Everything in Shelley Street was thereafter ordered to be rationed until further notice.

Right from the start of the hostilities, the Japanese air force had complete command of the skies. They bombed Kai Tak airfield and whatever shipping there was in the harbour at will. The rest of Hong Kong seemed to be deliberately spared, no doubt because the Japanese army was confident of taking over the island completely ere long. At first, only sporadic gun-fire in the distance could be heard. Soon this became more clearly audible, after the Japanese had stormed and landed in the eastern end of the island. Ugly stories of Japanese atrocities began to filter through. Prisoners of war were murdered, and women raped. Hong Kong was valiantly defended by two British battalions, two Indian battalions, two Canadian battalions, as well as a brave contingent of local volunteers. They were however no match for the seasoned Imperial Japanese army who had had years of disciplined training and hard fighting in China. Capitulation was only a question of time, and it duly came on Christmas day 1941. The battle of Hong Kong had lasted just seventeen days.

On the day Hong Kong surrendered, a family council was immediately formed. Numerous conferences were held from time to time at Nos. 15–17 Shelley Street to decide what should be done. An early announcement by the Japanese Occupation Army surprisingly advised local inhabitants to leave Hong Kong if they so desired, despite the fact that there was nowhere they could go other than to the Chinese mainland. Obviously there was no way the Japanese could feed the one and a half million inhabitants on the island. This was the first bit of welcome news for the incarcerated Hong Kong population. Almost immediately those who could depart forthwith did so. Others made the necessary preparations before following suit. Soon hundreds and thousands left by the day, and in the course of time many more followed. From day to day we heard only of relatives and friends having departed, just about to leave, or planning to go. This mass exodus continued for a very long time, until, at the end of the war, there were less than half a million people remaining in Hong Kong.

At one of our early family conferences, it was unanimously decided that we too must leave Hong Kong, and as soon as possible, even though we had no idea what would be lying in wait for us at the end of our journey. We realized that if we stayed, we would either starve or have eventually to seek work under the Japanese. We were not prepared to accept either alternative. Besides, dire consequences might follow if the Japanese became aware that my eldest brother was fighting against them in China. Once the decision to leave was reached, we settled down to raising as much money as we could for the intended journey and our forthcoming stay on the Chinese mainland. Again my mother's resourcefulness came to the fore. She produced a number of items of jewellery which had been given her by my father or purchased with her savings from the housekeeping money. They all fetched good money. Even the three brothers managed a limited contribution as we each sold a water-proof wrist watch recently given to us. Water-proof wrist watches had just become fashionable in Hong Kong in those days and enjoyed substantial prices in the black market because the Japanese loved watches. A good collection of Chinese stamps which I had hitherto kept was likewise sold at an exceptionally handsome price. The total amount of money raised did not amount to a fortune by any standard, but probably would suffice to sustain the family until we could find work in China.

There were two available routes which people leaving Hong Kong could take. One was by land and on foot via Shenzhen (深圳). The other by sea via Macau to Guangzhou Wan (廣州灣). Macau was a Portuguese colony, and Guangzhou Wan, a French colony, which until then the Japanese had left alone. Surprisingly a number of small passenger boats had resumed regularly ploughing between Hong Kong, Macau, and Guangzhou Wan. As the land route was reported to be infested with bandits, the family further decided to proceed by sea to Guangzhou Wan, and from there cross into Guangxi Province (廣西省) of free China. We divided ourselves into three groups. Ping Tsung and Brian requested to be the vanguards and were the first to leave. The second group comprised my parents, sisters Margaret, Winnie, and Rosalind, and my eldest brother's wife Norma and their young son Anthony. They would follow suit as soon as word reached home from Ping Tsung that all was well. Sister Josephine decided to go to Shanghai instead, where her fiancé was waiting to marry her. It fell on my shoulders to see her safely off before I brought up the family rear. I was also instructed to try selling off some more of the family belongings remaining at Shelley Street prior to my departure.

One evening at the beginning of January 1942, somewhat alarmingly, a Japanese officer in full military uniform suddenly appeared and rang our door bell at Nos. 15–17 Shelley Street, asking to see Yu Wan, which

was my father's name. Not knowing what to expect, we initially feared
the worst, but, thank heavens, those fears proved to be ill-founded. He
turned out to be a Mr Sagamoto, the former headmaster of a Japanese
school in Wanchai. At one time or another before the war, the Education
Department had raised various problems concerning his school, which
time and again my father had helped him to surmount.

Sagamoto was a devout Christian, a Chinese scholar himself, although
he could speak only a little Cantonese, and apparently a great admirer
of my father. He had never been to Nos. 15–17 Upper Shelley Street
before, but almost as soon as he had arrived back in Hong Kong with
the Japanese army, he had found his own way there. He even ordered
a consignment of rice to be delivered to our house. My father was at first
worried and embarrassed by this thoughtful gift. But Sagamoto
immediately declared it was no more than a token appreciation, with no
strings attached, of my father's goodwill shown hitherto towards his
school. He further inquired whether my father cared to work for the
Japanese government. If so, he could easily arrange it. He added, however,
that he was not unaware that my eldest brother was in the Chinese
army, so that if my father preferred to be left alone, it was alright with
him.

Sagamoto spoke half the time in English and half in Cantonese, and
was hardly fluent in either language. His bona fides, however, was more
than evident despite his hesitant speech, and his friendly disposition was
completely convincing. In response to his kind gesture, my father told
him just as candidly that all our family would shortly be leaving for
Guangzhou Wan in order later on to cross into free China. Sagamoto
was speechless for a few moments. He then volunteered, when the time
came, to guide my parents and the family personally through the Japanese
customs officers in order to spare them any undue inspection of their
luggage or other difficulty which might arise. And he was true to his
word.

The only request Sagamoto made was a touching one. He asked my
father to compose a few lines of Chinese poetry for him to perpetuate
the memory of their friendship. My father immediately took out his
brush and ink and complied with his request. As Sagamoto kept the
piece of paper on which my father's poem was written, I very much
regret I can only recall the opening line, which, translated into English,
should read something like this: 'There is no love more profound than
the pledging of brotherhood in No-Man's-Land.' (戰地桃園情至真)

On the day my parents and the second group of my family were due
to leave Hong Kong, Sagamoto turned up as promised in order to escort

everybody and all their baggage safely through to the boat scheduled to take them to Macau. On the way to the pier, he asked me how old I was. When I told him, he said that he too had a son in Japan of about my age. He seriously doubted whether he would survive the war and ever see his son again, because he would soon be despatched further and further away from home. That was the last time I or any member of my family saw Sagamoto. After the war, we made every effort to trace and locate him, but in vain. To this day, I still wonder whether he ever told his superior officers about my eldest brother. I only wish we had had a better chance to show him how very much we appreciated the kindness he had bestowed on our family.

After sister Josephine had embarked for Shanghai, I packed my own few belongings, and proceeded to rejoin my family in Guangzhou Wan. Before I left Hong Kong, I surprised even myself by successfully concluding a deal whereby a sizeable stock of coal subsisting at Nos. 15–17 Shelley Street was sold for a substantial amount of cash. The price of coal had appreciated unbelievably after the Japanese occupation. When I handed over the money to my father in Guangzhou Wan, he patted me on my shoulders saying that I was learning fast, as not so long ago I had not even known how to cash a cheque. My response was that there was nothing unusual about it because selling coal was one of my subjects at the university whereas cashing cheques was not.

Eventually the family gathered together again in Guilin (桂林), the capital of Guangxi Province, but not for long. My eldest brother Pak Chuen, who had met my parents in Guangzhou Wan, departed shortly thereafter with his wife and son to Qujiang (曲江), the headquarters of the Seventh War Zone in Guangdong, and my other brother Ping Tsung went with him. Sister Margaret had a teaching job at Mei Lu (梅綠) just inside the Guangxi border from Guangzhou Wan, which turned out to be in fact a Chinese military intelligence post. After a brief stay, younger brother Brian left initially to enrol as an undergraduate at Zhongshan (中山) University in Pingshi (平石) just inside Guangdong. He later transferred to Lingnan University at Qujiang. As I waved him *au revoir* at the Guilin railway station, it dawned upon me that had it not been for my war-time degree, I too, like Brian, would be scurrying to find a Chinese university to grant me a place, and, under a totally different academic system, might have difficulty in completing my bachelor's degree whether in the space of months or at all. My father went ahead by himself to Qujiang to take up an appointment as an assistant to the British Consul there. I was entrusted with the job of looking after my mother and sisters Winnie and Rosalind in Guilin until such time when a better and perhaps safer place could be found for them in Qujiang or elsewhere.

In Guilin, my mother, my two sisters and I lived far away from town in a stone hut which was cold and damp and without running water or electricity. During this period, though, I witnessed the first real air battles in my life. Those were breathtaking dog fights over the Guilin skies between the American Flying Tigers and the Japanese air force. However, they took place very infrequently. Most of the time I had practically nothing to do. There were neither any books to read nor other undertakings to keep myself usefully occupied. My two younger sisters Winnie and Rosalind were then respectively twelve and ten years old. For a while, we tried our hand at raising chickens. It gave us no end of satisfaction for the first couple of weeks just watching our chickens grow. Then suddenly disaster struck. It broke our hearts to see them all dying of malaria one by one in rapid succession. There was nothing we could do to save them. The only comforting thought was that their death at least spared us the pain of otherwise having in due course either to kill them for food, or part with them to total strangers for money.

We were in fact fortunate not to have died of malaria ourselves. The abundance of infected mosquitoes in Guilin, and, indeed, everywhere in China, and the alarming shortage of the appropriate medicines and medical attention in those days rendered malaria a real curse which we quickly learnt to dread throughout our stay on the Chinese mainland. Long before the war was over, we all caught malaria at one time or another. I myself only ceased to have recurrent malarial attacks after I arrived in England in 1946.

One gratifying aspect of this otherwise uneventful Guilin episode stood out in my mind right through the years. During this period, my mother, Winnie, Rosalind, and I lived a long way from civilization in an exclusive environment. From day to day, we had neither visitors nor friends, but just the four of us for company, and all the time in the world on our hands. As a result, we learnt much more about one another than we could ever have known. My mother had always been fond of me, but it was during this period of time that we were made to feel especially close to each other. Similarly a rare attachment grew up between my two younger sisters and myself which has continued to this day.

In the course of time, I was more than happy to receive instructions from my father to escort my mother and two sisters to rejoin him at the British Consulate in Qujiang. With the permission of the British consul, a Mr Sedgwick, who had known my father back in Hong Kong, we erected a somewhat primitive bungalow at the back of the consulate grounds where we all lived. Even though overall living conditions remained trying, it was nonetheless altogether a welcome change. We had left Japanese occupied Hong Kong behind; my mother could resume her housekeeping role and look after her husband again; Winnie and Rosalind soon gained admission into one of the local schools to catch up on their interrupted studies; while I started looking for a job for the first time in my life. Although I did not realize it at the time, another noteworthy phase in my life had begun.

10   *The War Years (Part One)*

While I was in Guilin, circumstances were totally unsuitable for employment of any kind to be undertaken. To begin with, I had my mother and two little sisters to look after. Besides, where we lived made it altogether difficult to go regularly to work. There was no road as such, but only a narrow winding footpath through the hills leading to our far-away humble residence. Whenever it rained, the sole means of access was nothing but mud and marshes, which rendered walking along it slippery and even dangerous, especially after dark. There were no street lamps of any kind. In good weather, covering the distance to town would take at least an hour and a half. In rain and mud, twice as long.

After the family had settled into the sanctuary of the consulate grounds in Qujiang, I felt it was long overdue for me to look for work. My brother Ping Tsung had by this time flown off to the war-time capital Chungking to act as English secretary and interpreter to Lt. General Wong Chun Kau who was then the head of the Chinese Air Defence. My eldest brother Pak Chuen, on the other hand, was waiting for official confirmation of his appointment as regiment commander entrusted with the defence of Qujiang. Their progress made me even more impatient to seek employment. I was soon to discover that for a young man and a stranger in China like myself, this was by no means an easy task.

On arrival in Qujiang, I had spotted an advertisement in the local newspapers inviting applications for a fair number of vacancies for trainees in the Chinese Customs and Excise Department. Applicants with a university degree would be preferred, it said. Immediate remuneration sounded reasonable, but ultimate prospects promised to be excellent. I hardly hesitated before sending in my application. To my disappointment, I did not even receive an acknowledgment of receipt of my application.

Not long thereafter, the Bank of Communications similarly advertised vacancies for six trainees to be employed in Qujiang. After the disappointment of my Chinese Customs and Excise application, I was naturally of two minds whether I should answer this second advertisement. It was difficult to imagine that I could do worse than in the earlier instance. While trying to make up my mind, I came across quite by chance the manager of the advertising bank, a Mr Pang, who knew my father and used to play the odd game of bridge with him in the evening. He not only encouraged me to apply for one of the vacancies, but offered himself as my referee. This almost sounded too good to be true, and naturally made up my mind for me on the spot. So, on the following day, I duly sent in my application. In time, I was required to sit for an examination in both English and Chinese, which presented no difficulty whatever. Nothing more happened for a little over a fortnight, until one day, I went to the bank to pay in a cheque for my father. There, to my surprise and utter dismay, I saw several of my fellow candidates at the examination, each sitting behind a desk in the bank, and obviously already at work.

My father naturally asked Mr Pang what had gone wrong if anything. Initially, Mr Pang insinuated that I had performed poorly in my examination. In the end, he was honest enough to admit and apologize in strict confidence to my father that all six successful candidates had powerful backers whom he could not afford to ignore or offend. Accordingly there was nothing he could do to take me into his bank. I must confess to feeling at the time somewhat envious of the several young men who were thus assured of a banking career. Some ten years later, I came across one of those successful candidates again in Hong Kong. He remembered me well. Although by then he had become a sub-department head in the said bank, he was a totally disgruntled man, and it was his turn to envy my success at the local Bar. He said he wished he could change places with me. I realized then how fortunate I had been to be rejected by the bank in Qujiang, otherwise I would have ended up being disgruntled instead.

After my two unsuccessful attempts to find work, I was resigned to helping my father process some of his papers at the British consulate. Apart from the consul Mr Sedgwick, there were only two employees other than my father in that office, namely, a messenger, and a clerk. The main work of the establishment consisted of giving out immediate monetary relief in the form of interest-free loans to new refugee arrivals from Hong Kong. One day Mr Sedgwick saw me at my father's desk, and expressed surprise that I was not otherwise employed. He said he wished he could offer me employment in his office. But, as I could see for myself, I would only be wasting my time there. Several days later, however, he called me into his private office, and told me in confidence that British Naval Intelligence had just opened an office, and was looking for a bilingual assistant to accompany one of its officers on a secret mission to the Fujian (福建) and Guangdong coast. The pay offered was good, but the trip would be hazardous and the mission might even be dangerous. He said that the post would not be advertised, although he expected there would be other people vying for the job. He thought however that my Hong Kong University degree and the fact that my father was working at and well-known to the consulate would stand me in good stead. He also offered to give me his personal recommendation if I was interested. Needless to say, I immediately indicated my willingness to try for the job.

In due course, I was interviewed at great length by a Lieutenant Commander John Davies of the British Navy. Although he did not strike me as being as kind a man as Mr Sedgwick, our interview proceeded smoothly, and I told him everything he wanted to know about myself and my family. When asked I told him I knew nothing about ships generally, especially warships. He said that that was not important because he could teach me what I needed to know, provided that I had an adequate knowledge of the English language. He proceeded to ask me a considerable number of questions about my degree, and what I was taught at the university, and then rigorously tested my knowledge of English. He next asked me how familiar I was with (1) Cantonese, (2) Mandarin, and (3) written Chinese. I told him that Cantonese was my mother tongue, that I had picked up a fair amount of Mandarin at school, although I was never taught phonetically how to speak it, and finally that I could read and write Chinese without difficulty. He asked further whether written Chinese was the same in both Mandarin and Cantonese despite the difference in speech. I told him that this was essentially although not entirely correct and that, if necessary, a northern and a southern Chinese should have no real difficulty understanding each other once they reduced their spoken language into writing. Obviously he was concerned about my ability to interpret satisfactorily for him in the event of Mandarin being spoken. It was evident from the interview that he and I would be travelling beyond the Cantonese speaking province of Guangdong, where, at one stage or another, only Mandarin would be spoken. Apparently Lt. Comdr. Davies had spent a considerable number of years in the Harbour Office in Hong Kong, but surprisingly never learnt to speak or understand even Cantonese, not to mention Mandarin.

In time, I was notified that I had been chosen for the post. I was further told that the main objective of Lt. Comdr. Davies' mission, and indeed mine, was to set up a number of observation posts along the south China coast in order to report the movement of every single Japanese warship from day to day seen going in either direction, so that the deployment of the Japanese navy could be gauged, and aerial attacks or other plans could be carried out whenever feasible or expedient. During the fortnight which followed, I had to survive a crash course, whereby I was initially made to learn a new vocabulary relating to the different parts of naval vessels. Next, I was shown an album containing a set of photographs of all the Japanese warships known to be in service at the time, and was taught how to identify each and every ship in the different classes of vessels making up the Japanese navy, which included aircraft carriers, battleships, cruisers, destroyers, submarines, gunboats, as well as numerous other supporting vessels. I was particularly required to memorize the individual characteristics in the structure of each vessel which distinguished it from the other vessels in the same class, and thus learn to identify it from those known characteristics.

I was given exactly a fortnight to complete the exercise. I was also provided with a copy of a special English-Chinese dictionary of naval terminology and told to familiarize myself thoroughly with the equivalent in Chinese of what I had been taught in English. This course of training, although short, was at once exciting and challenging, and most instructive. During those two weeks, I learnt more about warships generally, and in particular, those making up the Japanese navy, than I could ever have believed possible. I was required to do so because one of the main duties of my job was to pass on that knowledge to others in due course. It is a pity that after all these years I can now scarcely tell the difference between any of those Japanese warships and the Star Ferry.

Fuzhou (福州), the capital of Fujian Province, was targeted as the first and primary destination of our travelling, because the British Consulate there would best be able to provide the personnel to be trained for one or more of the observation posts. Furthermore, it was in Fuzhou that the Headquarters of the Chinese Third War Zone were situate. The co-operation and assistance of the Chinese Nationalist Army stationed there was naturally also indispensable, because the latest information regarding the deployment of the Japanese army in that area was essential to ensure the safety not only of Lt. Comdr. Davies and myself, but also of the observations posts to be established. I should mention that Lt. Comdr. Davies had in his possession an extremely impressive document signed personally by Generalissmo Chiang Kai-shek authorizing the holder of the document to call on the Commander-in-Chief and all other officers of every war zone visited by him to provide all and every assistance necessary to set up the observation posts.

The planned journey from Qujiang to Fuzhou was to be by road via Jiangxi (江西) Province. Because of the war, travelling by postal truck was the only means then available. Before leaving Qujiang where the British Naval Intelligence Office was based, we called on General Yu Hon-mou (余漢謀), the Commander-in-Chief of the Seventh War Zone, to pay our respects. However, instead of General Yu, it was a Lieutenant General Lee Yen-wor (李彥和) who received us. Lt. Gen. Lee was the right hand man of General Yu, and the second most powerful man in the Seventh War Zone. He was educated in Paris, and had been mainly responsible for General Yu rallying to the support of Chiang Kai-shek and the Kuomintang regime when the Japanese invaded China in the north. The meeting with Lt. Gen. Lee was comparatively short. To my surprise, he seemed to be more interested in me than Lt. Comdr. Davies, which did not please the latter at all. General Lee was delighted to hear that I was the younger brother of Pak Chuen and Ping Tsung, because apparently he was mainly responsible for their respective appointments in Qujiang and Chungking. He inquired out of curiosity how much I was being paid by British Naval Intelligence for my job. When I told him, he observed that I was better paid even than he was, and regretted that much as he would love to have me work for him, the Chinese army simply could not afford my kind of salary. It was unfortunate although inevitable that this conversation had to be translated for the benefit of Lt. Comdr. Davies, because, as things turned out later on, it led to not a little unpleasantness between him and me when our relationship subsequently turned sour.

On the very next day after we had met Lt. Gen. Lee, we embarked on our journey first to Ganzhou (贛州) and later on from there to Shang Rao (上饒) both in Jiangxi Province. The postal truck service was not a daily one so that we had perforce to spend a couple of days at each place, and it was not until the sixth day that we turned southwards from Shang Rao into Fujian Province, ending up in Nan Ping (南平). I cannot now remember why we had to travel so far north before turning southwards. It could well be because certain of the roads were at the time not entirely safe from day to day. From the very first day of our journey, my relationship with Lt. Comdr. Davies took on an unpleasant note. In every postal truck, there was ample room next to the driver's seat to accommodate two passengers more than comfortably. But for some strange reason Lt. Comdr. Davies would not let me sit with him in front. There were of course no seats as such of any kind at the back of the truck other than sacks and sacks of postal parcels of different shapes and sizes which were piled up to varying heights. I had thus perforce to make the most of rearranging some of those sacks, and ride on top of them. On a bumpy road, this was not only uncomfortable; at times it was hurtful to the extreme. Even before we left Qujiang, we had already been warned against the appalling condition of the roads in war-ravaged China. The worst of such warning was fully confirmed soon after we embarked on our journey. This was most unfortunate for me. As a result, long before we returned to Qujiang, both pairs of flannel trousers which I had brought along with me were completely worn out and torn at places, and I even suffered cuts and bruises to certain obvious parts of my anatomy from being constantly tossed about on those sacks. However Lt. Comdr. Davies paid no attention whatever either to my protests or discomforts. Perhaps on the very first day I should have insisted on being allowed to sit with him in front, or quit there and then. But I was at the time too young and inexperienced, and thus allowed him to bully me into sitting at the back. The journey through Jiangxi Province was altogether uneventful save that like the rest of our journey it was most uncomfortable for me.

On the sixth day of our journey, the postal truck carrying Lt. Comdr. Davies and myself arrived at Nan Ping in the early afternoon. There we unexpectedly had our first row. After making inquiries in town, Lt. Comdr. Davies immediately made a beeline for a Protestant Missionary House standing at the top of a small hill known to be run by an elderly English couple. I never found out whether they were his friends. All that he said to me before leaving the modest inn into which we had checked was to wait for his return. I waited until 9 p.m. before going to a nearby restaurant to have a simple meal of noodles, after leaving a note for him in his room. I returned no more than half an hour later to find him waiting for me in my room in a fury, asking how I dared to absent myself for so long, and claiming to have been waiting for me for two full hours. So, I simply took him over to his room where I had left my note for him, in which I expressly put down the time of my departure which was just after 9 p.m. The time then was only 9:30 p.m. He had no answer of course. Very unfortunately, from that time, everything I did seemed to be wrong in his eyes. This trivial event was only the first of a large number of similar, unnecessary and unpleasant incidents which contributed eventually to my immediate resignation from my job as soon as we arrived back in Qujiang.

On the following day we drove down to Fuzhou, where Lt. Comdr. Davies stayed with the British consul and his wife at the consulate, while I was fortunate enough to be able to enjoy the hospitality of a Eurasian family employed by the consulate. Fuzhou was a beautiful city with wide clean streets, and plenty of open spaces even in town, and many awe-inspiring Buddhist temples in the outskirts. Like the Romans, people in Fuzhou bathed in public baths instead of at home. We spent a little over one month in this delightful town, during which, for the benefit of three young intelligent Chinese men specially selected by the consulate, I conducted special training classes on Japanese warships just like those I myself had undergone in Qujiang. Upon the conclusion of those classes, the three young trainees were duly dispatched beyond the city limits to the Fujian coast each with three months' advance pay and a pair of binoculars with which to watch the waterfront. There they were instructed to take turns to carry out the requisite lookout for all Japanese warships, and forthwith to report back to the consulate the result of what they had seen in order to have the information flashed to Qujiang in the shortest possible time. The details of finalizing the arrangements for the observation posts were left to a couple of senior officials of the consulate after Lt. Comdr. Davies and I had inspected and approved of the site.

The objective of our mission was to set up at least three such observation posts along the coastline, one outside Fuzhou, another outside Amoy (廈門), and a third outside Shantao (汕頭). At one stage, several more such posts had in fact been contemplated along the Fujian and Guangdong coastline. But those original plans were doomed to be drastically curtailed. While in Fuzhou, we were strongly advised by both the British consulate and the Chinese army to leave Amoy alone, because units of the Japanese army had been going in and out of that town at will, and there was no way to tell when, if ever, it would be safe for us to go near the place, or for any one of our agents to set up an observation post there. Besides, according to the latest information received, practically the whole of the Fujian and Guangdong coastline was infested with pirates with the connivance of the Japanese, so that we were further warned in no uncertain terms to steer clear not only of Amoy, but also of the remainder of the Fujian coast altogether, and to return to Nan Ping before turning westwards in order to cross into Guangdong to carry out the remaining part of our mission. For several more days, we waited in vain in Fuzhou hoping for an improvement in the situation. When it became obvious that this was not forthcoming, we reluctantly started our journey back to Nan Ping.

In Nan Ping we remained only long enough to enable us to find transport to take us to Lien Cheng (連城), which was about half way to the Guangdong border. At Lien Cheng, however, we were delayed for quite some time before we could resume our journey. Beyond this small town, there was no longer any regular postal service, and the only means of travel by road was on board private commercial trucks. Because of the acute fuel shortage, the postal trucks were driven by a mixture of petrol and alcohol, but even this makeshift mixture was not available for use by ordinary private commercial trucks. In consequence these latter vehicles were all charcoal burners, which were not only filthy but every so often broke down in the course of almost every journey. If the roads hitherto were bad, those leading westwards from Nan Ping were even worse, and became progressively more so as the Guangdong border approached. Only a limited number of these commercial trucks would travel all the way into Guangdong. As travellers without goods, it took us quite a while and much bargaining and persuasion before we found the owner-cum-chauffeur of a decent charcoal burner who was willing to take us into Guangdong. In the end, we were only too happy to be on our way again, although very regrettably, as far as I was concerned, my seating discomforts inevitably resumed and drastically worsened, as the condition of the road and, indeed, of my trousers continued to deteriorate. Shortly after we left Lien Cheng, the land began to rise, which necessarily rendered progress on our charcoal burner even slower and more trying. Needless to say, there were repeated breakdowns and consequent delays on the way. As we scaled the hills along the Guangdong border, we frequently had to alight from the truck in order to reduce its load as much as possible.

After crossing into Guangdong, we passed through Jiao Ling (蕉岭) before arriving and stopping first at Mei Xian (梅縣) and later at Xing Ning (興寧). In Xing Ning, we called on and paid our respects to General Hsiang Hon-ping (香翰屏) who was the second in command of the Seventh War Zone, and the highest ranking officer in the East River area. General Hsiang gave us a personal letter of introduction to his subordinate officer-in-charge stationed just outside Shantao (汕頭), which we duly visited next. There we spent several weeks setting up our second observation post with the invaluable assistance of the officers and men of the Seventh War Zone. I need hardly add that once again a similar course of training to identify warships was repeated, save that this time my task was rendered considerably easier because everybody spoke Cantonese. As there was no consulate in Shantao in those days, those manning the observation post were instructed to report every Japanese warship seen to the Chinese army HQ outside Shantao for transmission to Qujiang.

A pleasant surprise occurred during my stay in Shantao. There I came across a former Wah Yan classmate of mine who had returned home in the late 1930s after his matriculation. He and his family owned one of the biggest lacquer factories for which Shantao was famous. He not only treated me to the best meal I had had for a long time, but also made me a lovely gift of a rare lacquer tea-set as a souvenir. Unfortunately this friendly gesture provoked another of those distasteful confrontations between Lt. Comdr. Davies and myself. He queried my having the money with which to buy such an expensive set, and insinuated that I must have been misappropriating the cash he had provided me with from time to time to pay for our meals, accommodation, and our travelling expenses. Although he had nothing more to say after learning about my former classmate, I decided there and then that this was the last straw, and that I would resign my job as soon as I got back to Qujiang. It was one thing to be facetiously accused of incompetence, but altogether another, of misappropriation of official funds. Lt. Comdr. Davies loved habitually to remind me that I would never find another similarly well-paid job, and ask sarcastically whether I would care to work instead for Lt. Gen. Lee at a fraction of my British Naval Intelligence salary.

After Shantao (汕頭), our mission along the South China coast was more or less completed, although not to the full extent of what had originally been planned. Accordingly we returned to Xing Ning, and from there proceeded back to Qujiang by way of Long Chuan (龍川) and Lian Ping (連平). On the very next day after our arrival back in Qujiang, I duly handed in my formal resignation to the British Naval Intelligence Office. I can still remember with relish the look of total disbelief on the face of Lt. Comdr. Davies as he read my letter of resignation.

The journey from Qujiang to Fuzhou and back had taken just over four months.

11 The War Years (Part Two)

For almost one week after my return to Qujiang, I lay sprawling face downwards on my bed in order not to aggravate the numerous cuts sustained around the seat of my anatomy. Several of them had turned septic, and for a couple of days I ran a fever from blood poisoning. Lying in bed during those few days did me a world of good. First and foremost, I badly needed to rest after the exhausting journey and to recuperate from my ugly wounds. What I appreciated most was the opportunity to do a little quiet thinking and planning for the future. The fiasco of my respective applications to the Chinese Customs and Excise Department and the Bank of Communications convinced me that it would be futile trying to obtain employment by answering advertisements. My experience with British Naval Intelligence made me realize on the other hand that notwithstanding my lack of working experience, my knowledge of the English language and my ability to communicate readily in both Chinese and English were both useful assets.

I had not hitherto offered my services to the Chinese army only because it had not crossed my mind to do so. The Customs and Excise advertisement, Mr Pang's offer to be my referee for the Bank of Communications, and Mr Sedgwick's introduction to the British Naval Intelligence Office had taken place one after another in rapid succession after my arrival in Qujiang, and I had responded to each event as any young aspirant looking for employment would have done. Besides, I had not seen or been in touch with my two elder brothers since Guilin, so that even if I had wanted to follow in their footsteps and join the Chinese army, I would not have known how to begin. I had no idea how much they were paid by the Chinese army, and frankly was not concerned with the question of pay. As a single young man of twenty with hardly any responsibility on my shoulders, I was simply eager to find work of any kind in order to make myself useful. The adequacy or otherwise of the remuneration offered had never entered into my calculations.

Meeting with Lt.-Gen. Lee Yen-wor at the headquarters of the 7th War Zone had left a deep impression on my mind. He was such an imposing character and yet such a kind and simple man. The exceptional interest he showed towards me almost made me forget my own unimportance. His stunning disclosure that I was better paid than he was gave me food for thought. It explained in part why Chinese university graduates preferred to join the banks, the customs and excise department, and other better paying institutions. The promptitude with which my brother Ping Tsung had been snapped up by the Chinese Air Defence in Chungking only served to underline the acute shortage of bilingual personnel with an adequate knowledge of the English language ready and willing to work for the Chinese military authorities. Lt.-Gen. Lee had himself said he would love to have me work for him, save that the Chinese army could not afford my kind of pay. In the weeks and months which followed, I found myself chewing over everything he said to me on that occasion again and again.

Lt. Gen. Lee was reputed to be one of the few incorruptible high ranking officers of the 7th War Zone. He had a wife and four young children to support. The thought foremost in my mind was that if he and his family could survive on his army emoluments, there was no reason why I could not do likewise on the standard pay, however meagre, of the Chinese Nationalist Army. Lt.-Commander Davies' sarcastic suggestion that I work for Lt.-Gen. Lee at a fraction of my British Naval Intelligence pay helped me make up my mind to do just that. I reasoned that if other young men invariably opted for the more attractive emoluments offered by the British or the American establishments, then surely it must be the Chinese military authorities who most needed and would best appreciate my kind of services. I felt much happier once I arrived at this conclusion.

Lt.- Gen. Lee lived in the outskirts of Qujiang not too far away from the British Consulate. As soon as I recovered sufficiently from my wounds, I walked right up to his residence one late afternoon without an appointment, and asked to see him. To my surprise, Mrs Lee, who opened the door, enquired almost immediately whether I was the brother of Pak Chuen and Ping Tsung, because, she said, she could easily see the family resemblance. I could not help feeling gratified that she should mention my two elder brothers. Her husband must have discussed my family with her. As we were talking on the doorstep, Lt.-Gen. Lee arrived home riding his bicycle, as usual. He had no difficulty in recognizing me. Obviously he knew about the bungalow in the consulate grounds in which my parents lived, because he immediately asked with great concern whether anything had gone wrong in my home which required his assistance. I assured him nothing untoward had happened. With considerable audacity on my part, I proceeded to ask him instead whether he was serious when he said a few months ago that he would be glad to have me work for him. If so, I said, I was ready and willing to serve him. He was clearly surprised by the directness of my approach and instead of answering my question, invited me into his home where he formally introduced me to his wife and his four young children.

Lt.-Gen. Lee and his family lived in a small single storey stone house with a minimum amount of furniture and ornamentation. Over a cup of tea in the sitting room, he tactfully enquired what had happened since he last saw me. I spent the next hour telling him about my trip to Fuzhou ending with my resignation from the British Naval Intelligence Office, and what had since been going through my mind. Although he listened with great patience and attention, his reaction appeared at one stage to be a trifle hesitant and embarrassed, which had me wondering momentarily whether he had changed his mind about wanting to have me work for him. As we spoke further, it soon transpired that my anxiety was altogether uncessary. The Chinese Nationalist Army was apparently somewhat particular about degrees and qualifications. My brother Ping Tsung had been quickly accepted by the Chinese Air Defence mainly because of his HKU war-time degree. As I was almost two years his junior, Lt.-Gen. Lee had assumed that I did not hold a similar degree. Thus he was afraid that the Personnel Department of the 7th War Zone might raise difficulties about giving me a proper assignment. He was more than happy to hear that I, too, held a war-time degree just like that of Ping Tsung, although he could not help asking how that was possible. So I explained to him that the two of us had been classmates ever since we were kids.

Lt.-Gen. Lee declared that he had for some time longed for the luxury of having an English secretary himself. But regrettably no such post existed hitherto in the 7th War Zone. That was why he had despatched Ping Tsung to work for the Chinese Air Defence in Chungking instead. He explained that his was the so-called Political Department of the 7th War Zone with a sizeable section of headquarters and a substantial staff assigned to him. He said he would be delighted to take me forthwith into his department, and leave the details of my employment to be worked out later. He was almost apologetic when he touched on the question of remuneration. I hastened to assure him that I was completely happy to accept the standard pay of whatever post he could offer me. Before I departed, he thanked me warmly for my willingness to work for him on those terms. I only wished I could tell him in return exactly how much I appreciated his readiness to offer me an opportunity to make myself useful, especially after my repeated frustrating experiences since my arrival in Qujiang from Guilin.

Despite this happiest of understandings arrived at between Lt.-Gen. Lee and myself at his home, the Personnel Department of the 7th War Zone appeared to take its time processing the necessary documents relating to my appointment, and more than a month elapsed before I was able to don a military uniform as an officer of the Chinese Nationalist Army. While I cannot pretend not to have been impatient waiting for my official appointment to materialize, those few weeks turned out to be more rewarding and instructive for me than the whole of the two odd years I subsequently spent working in the political department of the 7th War Zone. During this period of waiting, most of my evenings were spent with Lt.-Gen. Lee at his home where he would never tire of telling me about his hopes and misgivings about the war, about corruption in China at large, about the many difficult problems he was confronted with in the 7th War Zone, and about the virtues and short-comings of Chiang Kai-shek and the Kuomintang. Those were all truly priceless lessons on matters most of which I had not even heard of. He said that I must know about such matters if I were to survive in the Chinese Nationalist Army. He certainly appeared to have taken to me like his own son just because I had given up a much better paid job in order to work for him; even in after years, the warm affection he had for me never at any time cooled off.

Lt.-Gen. Lee had taken a doctorate's degree in pharmacy in France before he became a professional soldier. I soon discovered that he was also a Chinese classical scholar and historian. His recollections and anecdotes on personalities and events covering the post-1911 Revolution era leading right up to the Japanese invasion of China were particularly fascinating. From the first time we met, Lt.-Gen. Lee had struck me as a true leader of men. In the course of time, I learnt to admire and appreciate him even more as a man of letters, a loyal friend, a faithful husband, a dedicated parent, and above all a man of virtue and a tireless fighter against corruption. I could not help noting the contrast in lifestyles between him and some of the high ranking officers in the 7th War Zone. Lt.-Gen. Lee lived a simple Spartan life with his wife and four young children. More than once I was invited to stay for dinner at his house, and could see and tasted for myself the simple meagre meals which he and his family took from day to day. Gen. Yu Hon-mou, for example, was known to have four wives all of whom lived in comfort and luxury. Yet Lt.-Gen. Lee's loyalty was such that I never heard him say one derogatory word against Gen. Yu. The two of them had apparently pursued their professional soldier's career together as sworn blood-brothers.

After the failure of the Kuomintang regime on the mainland in 1948, Gen. Yu followed Chiang Kai-shek and his armies to Taiwan. Lt.-Gen. Lee decided to do otherwise. Altogether disillusioned about Chiang Kai-shek and the Kuomintang by this time, yet unwilling to serve the Communist Party under Mao Zedong to which he had inherently been opposed, Lt.-Gen. Lee elected to take his family to Hong Kong instead in order to give his children a better education. Throughout his stay in Hong Kong until his death in 1989, he was content to live incognito and in utter poverty, maintaining his family and bringing up his four children on no more than the meagre pay of a school teacher. His wisdom in bringing his family to Hong Kong has long since been richly rewarded by the outstanding achievements of his children. Of his two sons, one is today an eminent Queen's Counsel (now Senior Counsel) practising at the local bar, while the other is a renowned neurologist and physician and a former lecturer at the university. One of his daughters, who read law late in life, is now a District Judge in New Zealand and the first Chinese to be so appointed. In 1971, after my son Denis had successfully taken his Oxbridge Examinations in England, he came home specially in order to study Chinese for a year before going up to Merton College at Oxford. Lt.-Gen. Lee was kind enough to come out of retirement to be Denis' tutor. To this day, Denis still takes pride in describing the many incomparable and interesting lessons he was fortunate enough to have received from his affectionate mentor.

When in 1943 I received the official documentation relating to my appointment, I was pleasantly surprised to find that Lt.-Gen. Lee had succeeded in getting the post of an English secretary to the 7th War Zone specially created for me. That was why my appointment had taken so long to materialize. I was given the rank of major in the Chinese Nationalist Army and was seconded to the Political Department to work under Lt.-Gen Lee. Indeed I could hardly have expected a more satisfying appointment, or hoped to have a better superior officer. As things turned out, however, I must confess that work-wise, my job left much to be desired. It was not without good reason that hitherto there had not been any English secretary appointed in the 7th War Zone, because there was no need for one. There was no English correspondence to be handled; there were few documents which had to be translated from day-to-day; and English speaking visitors to Headquarters who required the regular services of an interpreter were extremely limited in number.

For no more than a couple of weeks at the beginning of 1944 was I busily engaged in liaison work with a team of American aviation officers who visited the 7th War Zone to explore the possibility of setting up an airfield or two in the area. But the plan was soon abandoned because the marginal utility of such airfields could not justify the enormous cost. Besides, such airfields could not be safeguarded from the watchful eye of the Japanese air force and army. In 1943–4 there was a British Army Aid Group stationed in Qujiang headed by one Major Urquhart but I had no more than a few isolated and minor dealings with him. In fact my main and regular work as English secretary of the 7th War Zone consisted of listening to the news broadcast from the BBC three times a day, and thereafter in translating any material news item into Chinese, and circulating it among the different departments of the War Zone. After a while, I could not refrain from speaking to Lt.-Gen. Lee and asking for more work of any kind. In due course, he appointed me as deputy leader of a group of young officers, all about my age, who were responsible for war propaganda in the 7th War Zone through group singing, drama and sport. Unfortunately I could not sing at all while the dramatic activities of the group were severely limited by the extreme shortage of funds and play scripts. However, I did succeed in organizing a fair number of soccer, basketball and ping-pong competitions for the group, and getting the British Army Aid Group, the Provincial Government Civil Service, as well as my eldest brother's regiment to participate in them. At times I also tried conducting a few English classes for the officers of the propaganda group, but immediately felt handicapped by the shortage of books and other necessary equipment for teaching.

At the end of 1944, the Japanese army made one last effort to capture Qujiang. As a result, the headquarters of the 7th War Zone had to be evacuated. I was dispatched to Long Chuan in the East River area with a section of the propaganda group and a skeleton complement of the Political Department. Gen. Yu, Lt.-Gen. Lee and most of the senior officers and men of the 7th War Zone retreated into Jiangxi Province.

My younger brother Brian, who had shortly before been appointed

tutor to the four children of Lt.-Gen. Lee, was evacuated safely to Long
Nan in Jiangxi with the Lee family. My parents, sisters Winnie and
Rosalind, and sister-in-law Norma and her son Anthony on the other
hand all came from Qujiang to Long Chuan before branching off
northwards to an obscure village of no strategic importance whatever in
the hills some thirty to forty miles away called He Shi (鶴市), where it
was thought they would be safe from the Japanese army. There they all
stayed until the end of the war. My brother Ping Tsung was transferred
back from Chungking to the 7th War Zone at about this time. He rang
me up while I was in Long Chuan and gave me a very unusual although
by no means unpleasant assignment. A very attractive and charming
female medical student of Ling Nan University by the name of Wong
Wai Wa was one of the many evacuees from Qujiang to Long Chuan.
Ping Tsung made me promise to look after her and keep her company
while she was in Long Chuan. I could readily guess what that meant,
and was only too happy to carry out my brotherly assignment. Seeing
Wong Wai Wa regularly in Long Chuan pleasantly added colour to my
life and led to our becoming close friends. After the Japanese surrender
she returned to her folks in Canton and in due course she became Ping
Tsung's wife and my dear sister-in-law. My brother Pak Chuen in the
meantime fought the Japanese army to a standstill at Qujiang for two
weeks before being compelled to retreat into Jiangxi with what was left
of his command.

At this stage, the so-called 7th War Zone was in tatters, and what
remained of its army could easily have been completely wiped out by the
advancing Japanese. I can still remember the uncomfortable feeling my
fellow officers and I had in Long Chuan every day during this period
trying to anticipate where the Japanese army might be going next. There
were of course isolated units of the Cantonese army still remaining in
Jiangxi and in the East River Area. But they were so depleted and
demoralised that it was altogether doubtful whether they could give
battle to the Japanese at all if the latter chose to march against them.
But, thank heavens, the Japanese military obviously had their own
problems. They were heavily committed not only in many other parts
in China but also in the Pacific, as well as all over south-east Asia, and
their lines of communication were getting more drawn out and precarious
every day. As a result, they elected to stay put after capturing Qujiang,
and thus enabled the 7th War Zone Command to reorganize and redeploy
their beaten armies for yet further efforts of resistance.

It was in those circumstances that Long Chuan survived the following
six months in comparative peace and quiet. Once every ten days or so

during this period, I would hire a bicycle in order to ride the thirty to forty miles to He Shi to visit my parents for no more than a couple of hours each time before returning to my place of work. This was an altogether uneventful although anxious period.

At the beginning of August the first atom bomb was dropped on Hiroshima followed by a warning that unless Japan instantly surrendered, more such bombs would follow. Three days later the second bomb was unloaded on Nagasaki. On 15 August, Emperor Hirohito broadcast the unconditional surrender of Japan. My parents and the rest of the family almost immediately packed their belongings and returned to Hong Kong. I, however, had yet to go through another brief but exciting episode before I quit the Chinese Nationalist Army.

12 *The War Years (Part Three): Drama in Huizhou*

Within a week of the Japanese surrender, I was back in Qujiang. Qujiang was a sorry sight compared to what it had previously been. Everywhere partly burnt down or wholly destroyed buildings served as vivid reminders of the bloody battle which had taken place in the city less than a year before. Hardly any structure at the former site of the 7th War Zone H.Q. was left standing. At first opportunity I took a long walk to the northern outskirts where the British consulate had been situated. I was saddened to find the old consulate building and our family bungalow both completely gutted by fire.

At the special request of the Japanese, a select team of officers was dispatched from Qujiang to Huizhou (惠州) to monitor the formal surrender of the Imperial Japanese Army in the 7th War Zone which would in due course be presided over by Gen. Yu Hon-mou. Huizhou is one of the largest cities in the East River Area in Guangdong. It is about 100 miles to the east of Canton and 80 miles to the north-east of Shenzhen. During the war, it was in Huizhou that the biggest Japanese military depot in Guangdong was situated. After the war it was to Huizhou that the majority of the Japanese troops in the 7th War Zone had been conveniently withdrawn in order to facilitate a collective surrender. Immediately following upon the announcement of the Japanese surrender, Chiang Kai-shek had surprisingly declared Canton together with most of Guangdong to the west of Canton to be a part of the 4th War Zone headed by Gen. Chang Fa-kwei (張發奎). This effectively severed Guangdong Province into two separate halves, leaving only the eastern half from the Pearl River to the Fujian border under the 7th War Zone. Obviously Chiang Kai-shek had no desire to be confronted again by a powerful Guangdong Province led by a single war-lord such as Chan Chi-tang in the pre-1937 days.

In September 1945 I was one of the select team of seven members appointed to proceed to Huizhou. The others included a major-general, a colonel, and two junior clerical officers, all of whom were henchmen of Gen. Yu Hon-mou chosen from the staff members of the 7th War Zone Headquarters. Two lieutenants appointed by Lt. Gen Lee Yen-wor from the Political Department made up the rest of the team. I was included because representatives of the foreign press as well as English speaking observers were expected to be present. Of the members of the select team, only one of the two lieutenants was known to me. We had spent the previous year together in Long Chuan, and we both idolized Lt.-Gen. Lee Yen-wor. The colonel had been educated in Japan and spoke fluent Japanese.

On our arrival in Huizhou we were met by a Japanese reception committee consisting likewise of seven officers the respective ranks of whom corresponded exactly to those of our party. After the usual formalities, we were immediately conducted in a smart-looking bus to our quarters. These were situated in an isolated spot just beyond the city limits and no more than a stone's throw from the main Japanese headquarters. The road which led to our quarters and beyond was lined intermittently all the way by a long string of army barracks literally swarming with Japanese soldiers. I had never before seen so many of them. If Emperor Hirohito had not already broadcast Japan's unconditional surrender, I would most certainly have preferred to be elsewhere than in their midst. Their superb physique and discipline deserved admiration. This was the all-conquering Japanese Imperial Army which hitherto had hardly lost a major battle in China. Yet as we drove along in our bus, we were smartly saluted everywhere not only by all the sentinels on duty, but also by each and every soldier we happened to pass. Without doubt, they were obeying their emperor's order to the letter.

After settling into our quarters, we were told to wear our military uniform and pips at all times so that we could be readily identified. Apparently the Japanese had withdrawn all their soldiers from the city so that they could not guarantee our safety if we chose to venture into town, especially after dark. We were accordingly advised to remain in our quarters as far as possible for our own good. All along we were aware that Huizhou was infested with loyal communist followers of Mao Zedong who would just as readily snipe at the Chinese Nationalist Army as at the Japanese. In fact, for much of the time a three-cornered battle had been going on in many parts of the East River Area in the 7th War Zone involving the Japanese army, the Chinese Nationalists, and the Chinese Communists. Huizhou had in particular attracted the attention of the communists because of the huge Japanese military depot situated there.

As from the second day of our arrival in Huizhou, a number of unusual happenings took place. To begin with, the major-general and the colonel preferred to have their meals by themselves and not with the rest of us. In fact, after our arrival I seldom saw them. Time and again, when I tried to look them up in their respective rooms, I was surprised to find that they were not only not there, but also nowhere in our quarters. On two separate occasions, a Japanese military escort with transport arrived obviously by prior appointment to take the major-general and the colonel to visit the main military depot, which was situated some distance away. I was not invited to participate in or even informed of those visits. During the rest of the time, I had no inkling where they had disappeared to or what they were doing during their absence from our quarters.

In the meantime, masses of account books and other documents were delivered by the Japanese to our quarters, and even more followed in the course of time. On the instructions of the major general, those books and documents were all retained exclusively by the two clerical officers, who were in due course engaged in transcribing them into Chinese with the assistance of the colonel from time to time. Apparently those were account books and records relating to various items of arms, military equipment, and other supplies in the military depot. Despite the two lieutenants' readiness to help, their offer was declined. This was the more surprising because both of them had worked for some considerable time in the accounts and records section of the Political Department, and presumably had been appointed to the select team mainly for that reason. After a while, I could not help being made to feel that the three representatives of the select team from the Political Department were being deliberately kept out of whatever was going on; the two lieutenants said that they had the same feeling.

At the end of our first week in Huizhou, I developed a bad tooth. In the days which followed, it deteriorated into a swollen jaw as well. One morning, as I lay in bed nursing my toothache and swollen jaw, the two lieutenants went out for a stroll for want of something better to do. In their absence, the colonel came, for the first time, into my room. On the pretext of enquiring after my bad tooth, he started what appeared to be a friendly conversation. After a few innocuous preliminaries, he asked with great concern what I planned to do hereafter now that the war was over. Very tactfully he brought up the prospect of going abroad to further my studies. I naturally told him that pursuing my studies abroad was the one ambition I had always cherished, although it was extremely doubtful that my father had the necessary means after the war to enable me to realize that ambition. Thereupon, half-jokingly, he suggested that as English secretary of the select team from the 7th War Zone there was nothing to prevent me from commandeering a few river-going motor-driven large junks in Huizhou in the name of the British Army or the American Air Force, riding them into Canton under the flag of the 7th War Zone, disposing of them in the black market in Canton, and pocketing the proceeds of sale before returning to Hong Kong. In this way I would have more than enough money to pay for my education abroad. No one would be any the wiser once I sailed into Canton which was in the 4th War Zone, and no one would be able to interfere with the sale of the junks in Canton in the face of the flag of the 7th War Zone. Even if the authorities should by any chance discover what had happened after the event, he said, I should be happily pursuing my studies abroad by that time and be beyond their reach. It was the most atrocious, most ingenious, and most corrupt proposition I had ever heard. I was so shocked that I did not know what to say. Furthermore, not being able to tell immediately whether he was serious, or merely joking, or what he really had in mind when making such a preposterous suggestion, I decided in any event that it would be wisest to say nothing at all. After some embarrassing moments during which we both remained silent, he merely grinned, and said he sincerely hoped that I would not misinterpret his friendly intentions. Before he left my room, he added that I should surely give the matter some serious thought; that if he could be of any assistance to me, he would be only too happy to render it; and that he would talk to me again about the matter in a couple of days after I had thought about it. Those final observations of his most certainly did not sound as if he had been joking. Indeed, if his suggestion were to be taken up, his assistance and surely the connivance of the Japanese as well, would be necessary in order to commandeer the junks in Huizhou.

I was so shaken by the implications of this dialogue that I could not sleep at all that evening. I did not know whether to treat it all as a joke, or forthwith lodge a formal complaint with the major-general. Hitherto, it had been obvious that the major-general was much closer to the colonel than to me. In fact, I found it somewhat difficult to believe that the latter could have made the corrupt proposition to me without the former's prior knowledge.

On the following morning, on the pretext that I longed to have an early dim-sum breakfast for a change, the very first thing I did after washing-up was to invite my lieutenant friend to have morning tea with me in one of the tea-houses in town. On the way I could hardly wait to tell him what had taken place the previous day. Surprisingly he disclosed to me immediately that he himself had stumbled on an alarming discovery. Some if not all of the figures in the account books and records transcribed into Chinese did not tally with those in the corresponding Japanese account books. Furthermore at least two separate sets of account books in Chinese were being prepared from each of the Japanese account books, whereas only one of them was specifically addressed to the Commander-in-Chief of the 7th War Zone. Something sinister and dishonest was obviously going on behind our backs which might explain why the two lieutenants' offer to help with the account books had been refused. If so, the colonel's conversation with me could well mean that an attempt was being made to have me compromised. The lieutenant solemnly suggested that I must leave Huizhou immediately and return to Qujiang in order to report everything to Lt.-Gen. Lee. It would be too easy to knock off someone in lawless Huizhou and make it look like an accident. He even suggested that my toothache might be used to request a transfer back to Qujiang. Although he sounded a little melodramatic, he was far from unconvincing.

From the tea-house in town, I hurried back to our quarters and caught the major-general getting dressed in his room. I told him about my bad tooth, and my vulnerability to blood-poisoning and requested permission to ask Lt.-Gen. Lee forthwith to transfer me back to Qujiang for treatment. At first he queried whether the Japanese dentist at headquarters might not be invited immediately to treat my ailment. I tactfully declined the kind suggestion because the Japanese dentist would not know about my medical history and might further be handicapped by the language barrier. In no time an urgent wire was dispatched, and a couple of hours later Lt.-Gen. Lee had wired back to recall me back to Qujiang. I hardly waited before hastening on my way, electing to travel by boat upstream rather than by land despite the latter being much more expeditious. Both the lieutenant and I felt I would be safer travelling in the company of the many other fellow travellers on board. My excuse for the preference was that I would be more comfortable lying down because of my bad tooth and swollen jaw.

Back in Qujiang I immediately reported to Lt.-Gen. Lee everything that had happened in Huizhou. He took me to see Gen. Yu Hon-mou who merely said that the matter would be looked into in due course. In making my report, I fully realized that while the colonel obviously had much to explain regarding the corrupt proposition he made to me in Huizhou, I was unable to put my finger on anything against the major-general which could be said unequivocally to incriminate him. His frequent absence from our quarters and his denying the two lieutenants access to the account books were not in themselves incapable of innocent excuses. The duplication of the account books and the discrepancies in the figures were based solely on what the lieutenant told me, and could likewise admit harmless explanations. I was therefore much relieved when neither Gen. Yu nor Lt.-Gen. Lee even suggested I had too vivid an imagination or had over-reacted in the circumstances. Both generals knew better than I of course about the presence and activities of the communists in the Huizhou area. If any of the arms, equipment, or supplies from the Japanese depot was made available for sale locally, they hardly required to be reminded who the most likely purchasers would be.

In the meantime, civil war was already on the brink of breaking out. As a result units of Gen. Yu's army were already standing by to receive orders to march north and render support to Chiang Kai-shek. Ere long Lt.-Gen. Lee sent for Ping Tsung and myself to inform us that he would soon be going north to Quzhou (衢州) in Zhejiang Province (浙江省). He advised us that as the situation was looking altogether unpredictable, and neither of us could be of much help in a civil war, it would be in our best interest to return to Hong Kong instead, and seek an opportunity to go abroad to further our studies. This happily coincided with what had been occupying our minds in the immediately preceding weeks. Our home was in Hong Kong. We had only left it out of necessity and in order to render what little contribution we could to the war effort against Japan. Now that the war was over, our first thoughts were, inevitably, to go home. Unlike our eldest brother, we were not professional soldiers. Fighting a civil war was alien to us, and never a part of our plans at any time. However we did not want Lt.-Gen. Lee to feel we were eager to leave him. We were therefore much relieved that he should bring up the subject first.

At about this time, we also received word from home that the post-war Hong Kong government had invited applications for a number of Victory Scholarships to study in the United Kingdom. Applications had to be handed in before the end of the first week in December. While I was more than ready to apply for one of those scholarships, Ping Tsung had his reservations because he had set his mind on furthering his Economics studies in an American university, if possible. He said he would have to discuss the question of means with our parents after we got home. It was in those circumstances that we decided to accede to Lt.-Gen. Lee's suggestion to discard our military uniforms and return to Hong Kong, and happily told him so.

On the day we left Qujiang, Lt.-Gen. Lee shook our hands warmly as we bade him good-bye. Several times he said he hoped it was 'au revoir' and not 'good-bye'. Although none of us knew it at the time, our two families were destined to spend many more happy years together subsequently in Hong Kong.

13 A Very Merry Christmas

Christmas 1945 was a memorable occasion at Nos. 15–17 Upper Shelley Street. The occasion was, of course, also the 4th anniversary of the end of the Battle of Hong Kong. Our family had survived four years of war covering Hong Kong and the Chinese Mainland without having suffered any casualty; instead, we had been enabled to visit many interesting places, and to benefit from innumerable useful experiences. For these blessings we had truly to be thankful. Upon his return to Hong Kong, my father had resumed working in the Education Department where he was joined by SY Tong, the husband of my eldest sister Sheung Woon. The latter was a graduate of Downing College, Cambridge and a contemporary of Pak Chuen. Sheung Woon and her husband had spent the war years with their four young children in Macau, and had only returned to Hong Kong after the Japanese surrender.

At about this time, my father was more than happy to be advised that a fair amount of back pay as Senior Inspector of schools was due to him for the two odd years which he spent working at the British Consulate in Qujiang. It was expected to be more than sufficient to send brother Ping Tsung to an American university for his desired studies. Younger brother Brian and I had lost no time in sending in our respective applications to the Hong Kong government for a Victory Scholarship each. In the month of December 1945, we were both called upon to appear twice before the selection board chaired by the Director of Education, Mr Arthur Walton. This was promising, because among the many other applicants known to us, some were never interviewed, others only once, and only a handful a second time.

Meanwhile, sister Margaret, who had worked with Chinese

Intelligence all by herself at the Guangxi border throughout the war years, had been nominated by the Director of the Catholic Centre in Hong Kong for a Bishop Yu Bin scholarship to do a postgraduate course in the United States. Christmas 1945 was thus more than just an occasion for thanksgiving for the family. We were also filled with great hopes for yet better things to come.

In the months which followed, each and every one of those hopes of ours became a joyful reality. At the end of February 1946, Brian and I were named by the Hong Kong government as two of the seven Victory Scholars to be sent to the United Kingdom to pursue our studies. This was followed a little later by sister Margaret being awarded a scholarship to do a postgraduate course in journalism at St Frances College, Illinois in the United States. Finally my father's back pay came through in early summer, and Ping Tsung was able to apply for and gain admission into St Louis University in the USA to do a master's degree in Economics in the fall.

Before the long summer ended, all four of us were happily on our way to our respective destinations abroad.

14   *Merton College Oxford*

I wonder how many Chinese families have been represented for three consecutive generations at any college at Oxford. I feel singularly proud and fortunate that my father, I and my son Denis were all educated at Merton College, and cannot help hoping that our family tradition will, in the course of time, continue for yet more generations to come.

The circumstances which led to my father pursuing his studies in England at all were unique, to say the least. In 1912, he had embarked on a sea voyage from Hong Kong to further his education in the United States of America. An extremely poor sailor, he was confined to his bed almost as soon as the boat in which he was travelling left harbour and throughout the journey. It was only upon disembarkation at the end of the voyage that he discovered he had surprisingly landed in Liverpool in England instead of San Francisco in California where he had originally planned to go. Quite by chance, in Liverpool he met an old family friend who took him to Oxford to spend the weekend. That weekend visit by my father to the world-famous citadel of learning changed his whole life. For, upon arrival, he was so fascinated by everything he saw that he fell instantly in love with the place and decided to travel no further. Accordingly, there he spent the next two years learning the English language from private tutors, at the end of which he took his Oxford University Entrance Examination and happily gained admission into Merton College.

Founded in 1274, Merton is one of the oldest colleges in Oxford. Among other things, it is renowned for its well-preserved historic library and chapel as well as its fabulously beautiful garden in which the Oxford University Dramatic Society has over the years seen fit, time and again, to stage many a Shakespearean play. Merton was one of the first colleges in Oxford visited by my father in 1912 and had remained his favourite ever since. Apart from his Oxford education, my father was essentially a Chinese scholar. It was the natural poetical environment at Merton which inspired him to write many of his lovely Chinese poems while longing for home as an undergraduate. In later years, it was the distant lingering memory of Merton which prompted him to compose yet more captivating verses in Chinese this time while pining for Oxford instead, especially after I had followed in his footsteps to become a second-generation Mertonian in the family.

Getting admitted into Oxford University after no more than two years' private tuition was no mean feat for my father, bearing in mind that he could hardly speak or write English properly before he left Hong Kong. In 1916 he took his bachelor's degree in Political Economy at Merton, and was immediately summoned home after his graduation. Sadly my father never returned to England at any time, although to my knowledge, he dearly wanted to visit Oxford and Merton again in after years. It was most unfortunate that travelling by sea never agreed with him while flying perpetually frightened him.

In 1946, my father wrote on my behalf to his former tutor, Sir John Miles, who had by then become the Warden of Merton College. Sir John remembered his former pupil well. As a result I promptly became the second member after my father to represent my family at Merton. I was not required to take any entrance examination. Furthermore, an adjoining bedroom and sitting room, once occupied by my father on the second floor of one of the residential quadrangles in the college, was specially reserved for me. The casement windows in those rooms overlooked on one side a well-kept lawn in the quadrangle directly below, and on the other, most of the picturesque college garden. Beyond the high wall forming the external boundary of the garden, a part of Christchurch Meadows was also plainly visible. It was a magnificent view. Inside both rooms, the elegant half-length oak panelling on the walls was easily recognizable from the pictures which I as a child had seen standing constantly on my father's desk in our house at Nos. 15–17 Shelley Street in Hong Kong. I felt almost like homecoming when I entered those rooms.

I can readily recall the occasion when I first arrived at Merton College in October 1946. At the entrance to the Porter's Lodge which lay to the immediate left of the main gate, I was greeted by a tall, good-looking young man who appeared to be of about my age. As soon as he saw me, he said, 'You must be Yu from Hong Kong. You are Yu Wan's son, aren't you? And you are going to read PPE or is it History?' Yu Wan was of course my father's name, and he had written to Sir John Miles to say that I would be reading PPE or History. I could not help feeling flattered that this young man should know so much about me. Naturally I returned his compliment by asking his name and what he read. Thereupon he said his name was Norman Gibbs, and that he was my tutor! He added that my rooms were directly above his at Stubbans 3, and that he would take me there. I soon learnt that Stubbans was the abbreviation for St Albans Quad, one of the four residential quadrangles in the college in which students and tutors alike resided. '3' was the number of the particular staircase leading into the rooms from the quadrangle. Dr Norman Gibbs was a brilliant historian who had written a White Paper for the British government on the First World War, and in 1946 was in the course of doing another on the Second World War. In subsequent years he was duly appointed Professor of History of the Two World Wars. I could not help being a little taken aback by his disclosure that he was my tutor, because he did not look quite thirty to me. But he was friendly enough, and our relationship proceeded quite smoothly and happily from that day. I had no end of difficulty, though, with the essays I wrote at his behest during my first term in college.

When I embarked on my journey to England in 1946, I had not anticipated any difficulty in my studies. Of course Politics, Philosophy and Economics were all subjects about which I knew little or nothing. But that did not cause me any undue anxiety. PPE was, I thought, just the modern name for Political Economy which my father had apparently no difficulty in mastering. Unlike me, he had not had the advantage of a prior university education. Although I had heard of the exacting demands of the tutorial system and an honours course at Oxford, I had no reason to doubt my ability to cope. I soon discovered that I had not reckoned with a number of factors which worked to my disadvantage.

To begin with, for more than four years during the war I had not read or written anything in English. As a result, my command of the language had naturally suffered although I might not have realized it. Furthermore, I had always been a slow reader. This proved to be a telling handicap. At the University of Hong Kong before the war, I was accustomed to learning most of what I was expected to know from lectures. Only a very limited amount of consequential reading was expected, if at all. At Merton, for each of my essays I was required not only to peruse a large number of reference books, but also to formulate my own views after reading them, and be prepared to explain and justify those views if necessary. I had never experienced anything like this before.

Political Institutions and Modern European History were two mandatory PPE subjects. Dr Gibbs was my tutor for both of them. One week before my first tutorial on Political Institutions, I remember being told to write an essay on the relative merits and demerits of the respective British and French parliamentary and electoral systems, and being given a long list of reference books to read.

Hitherto I knew nothing about any parliamentary or electoral system whether of Great Britain, France, or any other country in the world. This was the first time I was asked to write an essay on a subject of which I was totally ignorant. Furthermore, I had never before been called upon to study the works of so many authors in the space of no more than a single week. As far as I was concerned, it sounded rather like one of those Herculean tasks assigned to FBI agents in the Mission Impossible Programme on television, save that my task was real.

After duly collecting some of those reference books from the college library and the majority of the others from the Bodleian, which was the university library, I got down to reading them almost straightaway. The first and the most voluminous of those works was all about the British parliamentary and electoral system. Ploughing through it was hard work which took me no less than three and a half days, because it was the first book in English I had read in almost five years, and its contents were entirely unfamiliar to me. Furthermore inexperience made me read from the first page to the last instead of only the material and relevant parts. The next work I tackled was the leading authority on the corresponding French system. Reading it cost me another two and a half days. Although at the end of this period, I was glad to have gained some knowledge on the subject of my essay, I was unfortunately left with but a single day in which to commit to writing what I had learnt from those two volumes. Accordingly, I decided that the remaining reference books would simply have to wait if they were to be read at all, and that I would lock myself in my rooms on the last day in order to write my essay. This was because since my arrival at Merton, I had made quite a number of friends. Being one of the only two Chinese in college, I appeared to be an undoubted attraction to some of the other students. As a result there was no shortage from day to day of callers at my rooms, whom I would have to keep out if I were to finish my essay in time.

There was no lock on either my bedroom or sitting-room door. Between my suite and the landing at the top of the staircase at Stubbans 3, however, there was an empty ante-chamber where my baggage, sports gear, and other spare belongings were kept. At the entrance to this ante-chamber from the landing was a thick oak door fitted with a sole handle on the inside, so that once the door was shut, there was no way to open it from the outside. This door had remained open at all times since my arrival. As this was the only door on which I could rely to keep out likely callers, I promptly closed it for the first time. I never expected that this would cause a somewhat unpleasant incident.

I had settled down at mid-morning on that fateful day to writing my first essay at Oxford. By mid-afternoon I was reasonably happy with the progress I had made when suddenly there was a spate of loud and persistent knocking on the ante-room door. In the morning, several callers had indeed also knocked on that door but only gently, and had all been turned away by my refusal to respond. In fact I was beginning to feel pleased with my own wisdom in sporting that oak door when the heavy knocking started. Soon the knocking became thunderous and continued for long periods. Human voices could also be heard. I was naturally annoyed by this inconsiderate and uncivilized behaviour, but eventually yielded to the continuous hammering, and reluctantly opened the door. To my surprise, I found Dr Norman Gibbs standing on the landing outside.

Before I could show my resentment against the persistent knocking, Dr Gibbs asked in a slightly unfriendly voice why I had caused that door to be shut. Somewhat sarcastically I replied, 'To keep undesirable intruders out, what else.' He ignored my sarcasm and made a quick tour of my two rooms before apologizing for the intrusion, adding that the college rules did not permit the oak door to be shut save and except on the night of the College May Ball(!), and that it was his fault not to have told me about it before. His apology and explanation naturally brought an end to that unexpected incident. All the same I could not help wondering what Dr Gibbs had expected to find in my rooms that afternoon.

On the following morning I duly attended at Dr Gibbs' rooms for my first tutorial. When I informed him I had managed to peruse only two of my reference books, he merely remarked that I would have to finish my reading during the vacation at the end of term. As I read out my essay, Dr Gibbs frequently interrupted me in order to express a contrary view to the many comments and conclusions of the two authors which I had reproduced in my essay. Yet, as soon as I signified my agreement with his contrary opinion on any point, he would regularly do a U-turn, and begin advancing equally logical arguments in support of the authors' views instead. Although I was made to feel ridiculous at times, the experience was an eye-opener and was most inspiring, and I quickly learnt to appreciate what tutorials at Oxford were calculated to achieve.

This priceless lesson hardly helped, however, to resolve my immediate personal problems. The difficulty I had with my reading and my writing could not be overcome overnight and continued to create problems for me week after week. It was not until the Summer term of my first year at Merton that I felt completely at home with the tutorial system at Oxford. During those initial months, essay writing was constantly an uphill climb which gave me an altogether trying time.

Fortunately, college life was not confined to writing essays and attending tutorials. There were other less taxing activities in college such as getting to know one another at breakfast and dinner in the dining hall, fraternizing in the Students' Common Room, and social gatherings for tea and supper in the students' respective rooms. Regular participation in the inter-college soccer, table-tennis and bridge games also enabled me to win quite a few friends among the many other players from both Merton and the opponent teams.

There was a medical student at Merton who at one time captained the Oxford University soccer team. I could not help feeling flattered when more than once he invited me to play for the university. I would of course have loved to be able to do so. Unfortunately members of the university team were required to pay their own fare whenever travelling by coach or train to play away matches. With my meagre scholarship allowance, I simply could not afford the expense of such regular travelling. Accordingly I had no alternative but to turn down his kind invitation time and again. It was also a pity that I could not row because that was easily the most popular sport other than cricket. Besides, in those immediate post-war days, bread, butter and sugar were all strictly rationed in college and only those who rowed for the college were given extra rations!

I must not forget to mention the pleasure of punting which was a perpetual attraction at Oxford for students, local residents and tourists alike, especially in the summer months. The scenic beauty all along the river Isis was quite out of the ordinary and nothing less than breathtaking at places. I would like, however, to add the word 'hazards' when referring to the pleasure of punting, because time and again I found myself frantically clutching my pole in mid-air before slowly and comically subsiding into the river after my punt had shot forward and left me behind.

Dining in college on the first two nights was quite an event for me. In 1946, Don Bradman of Australia was regularly hitting centuries in both Test and County matches in England, and his exploits were frequently the only subject of discussion at college meals. This was exactly what happened during dinner on my first evening at Merton as well as at breakfast on the following morning. As I had never played cricket in my life and knew hardly anything about the game, I naturally took no part whatever in the conversation at the dining table during those two meals. On the second evening, however, as soon as I sat down at the long dining table, I deliberately made a nasty uncalled-for remark about this legendary Australian cricketer in a more than audible voice which must have caught the ears of everyone sitting to the left and right of me as well as across the dining table. Just as I had anticipated, all conversation seemed to stop suddenly, and all heads were turned in my direction. A polite voice civilly enquired what had caused me to make that remark. Bulls-eye! I happily replied that it was because I knew nothing about cricket and as a result had not been able to get a word in at dinner the previous evening or at breakfast in the morning. There was stony silence for a couple of seconds followed immediately by uproarious laughter all around, and I quickly became the centre of endless friendly attention. Obviously at college a foreign student has sometimes to be aggressive in order to make friends.

While I was struggling with my essays at Merton, I could not help thinking of my younger brother Brian and wondering how he was getting on at Pembroke, Cambridge, and in particular, whether he had the same difficulty with his essays as I had with mine. We had a standing agreement that every vacation we would spend some time together alternately at Oxford and Cambridge. In this way we could regularly compare notes about college life as well as hold each other's hand when we missed our folks in Hong Kong. Flying home during vacation time was out of the question in those days. Those were joyful brotherly reunions which we found ourselves eagerly looking forward to every term. Very occasionally we would travel by train to spend the odd day sightseeing in London where our very good friend Simon Li and his wife Lillian would invariably treat us to some delicious Chinese food cooked by Lillian herself. Most of the time, however, Brian and I would each be on our own trying to catch up on our reading which had invariably fallen behind during term time.

Simon Li had travelled with us to England on board the SS Britannic and was then reading law at University College in London. In 1946–7 I never expected that ere long he and I would be eating Bar dinners together at Lincoln's Inn in London, or that in due course our paths would cross time and again in the law courts in Hong Kong.

15 Unique 1947 Friendship Ties

One summer morning in 1947, I returned to college to find the former Director of Education of Hong Kong, Mr Arthur Walton, who had awarded me my scholarship, waiting for me in my rooms. This was so unexpected that I was momentarily lost for words. With his customary charming smile he apologized for his intrusion, and explained that after arriving back in England the previous evening, he had on the spur of the moment taken the first train to Oxford in the morning to see how I was getting on at Merton. His manner was so overwhelmingly cordial and unassuming, and his handshake so very warm, that I was instantly made to realize that any official or other barrier hitherto dividing us had existed only in my imagination, and from that moment, despite the disparity in our age and our respective stations in life, a rare friendship grew up between us which has continued to this day. Although I was blissfully unaware of the good fortune which had befallen me that summer morning in 1947, this newly discovered friendship proved ere long to be of priceless assistance to me as a Victory Scholar.

Before Mr Walton departed on that occasion, he invited me to visit him the following weekend at Brightwell Rectory in Wallingford near Oxford where his parents lived. Accordingly I had lunch and tea with him the following Saturday at Wallingford where we spent a leisurely afternoon just chatting in the pleasant garden of Brightwell Rectory and basking in the glorious sunshine with which we were blessed that weekend.

Today, Mr Walton lives in a lovely cottage at Buckland Newton in Dorchester, a retired gentleman in his nineties. He had given up an outstanding career with the Hong Kong government in the late 1950s and retired prematurely as Commissioner of the New Territories in order to dedicate himself entirely to looking after his beloved wife Jean who was suddenly and permanently disabled by a neurological disease. Before Jean was thus tragically invalided, my eldest sister Sheung Woon, my brother Brian, I and our respective spouses had been invited almost every year to spend Christmas Eve with the Waltons. Arthur Walton and I write every so often to each other, and I visit him once in a while when I am in England.

In December 1946, at the Oxford Chinese Students' Union I met a lady undergraduate from Somerville College by the name of Mary Low. Her father was a Singaporean Chinese while her mother was English. At our next get-together towards the end of January 1947, she told me that her father, who was educated at Cambridge, remembered my father well from their undergraduate days and that he would like to meet the offspring of his old friend. Accordingly, my younger brother Brian and I were invited to spend a weekend with her family in Brighton at the end of the Hilary Term.

On the appointed day, Brian and I happily alighted from our train at the Brighton railway station expecting to be met. It was only after the train had left that we discovered that there were two train stations at Brighton and we had got off at the wrong one. We were thus left to find our way on foot to the next station through a whole labyrinth of streets and alleys encumbered with a dilapidated old-fashioned suitcase which we had inherited from our parents. To add to the excitement of the occasion, shortly after our long march began, the handle of the suitcase broke so that Brian and I had to take turns to heave it on our shoulders. Although we arrived at our destination completely dishevelled and feeling a trifle ridiculous, the warm reception extended to us by our hosts immediately put us at our ease and more than made up for our discomfort on the way. That weekend at the seaside resort to which the Lows treated us was the first real holiday in England for Brian and myself, and was not only most enjoyable, but also decidedly memorable.

The Lows were a happy, hospitable, devout Catholic family. Mary's father, Mr CM Low, who had tragically lost his eyesight, accepted his fate with courage and resignation, and was full of fun and laughter. Mrs Low, one of the most charming ladies I ever met, was always smiling and completely dedicated to looking after her blind husband and their three children. Mary was their eldest child. Suzanne, their second daughter, was in those days studying to become a nurse. Their son Peter was then in a Catholic seminary learning to be a Jesuit. In due course he became a member of the Jesuit teaching staff at Stonyhurst College in Lancashire where my son Denis went as a student in 1968. Tragically Fr Peter Low

SJ was drowned in the late 1970s while trying to save the life of one of his students after their canoe had capsized.

In after years, I saw the Low family again every so often both in Brighton and London; Mary, Suzanne, and their parents in turn more than once visited me in Hong Kong. Mary and I correspond regularly with each other to this day, while Suzanne still recalls how at the Merton Ball in May 1947 she waltzed with me until the early hours of the morning before breakfasting in an enormous marquee specially set-up on the lawn right below the windows of my rooms. Today Mary resides in an apartment in Brighton, while Suzanne and her husband live in France.

During my Brighton visit in 1947 an unexpected and unusual occurrence took place on the day after my arrival. Brian and I were cruising along the waterfront in an open-decker bus, when a pleasant young man sitting in front of us turned round to ask politely whether I was a student at Oxford. He apologized for eavesdropping but explained that he could not help overhearing a part of our conversation. Apparently he had often entertained dreams about pursuing his own studies at Oxford but never had the opportunity to do so. He introduced himself as James Roberts, an architecture student serving articles at the time in Birmingham, where I was subsequently invited to visit him in the summer. That marked the beginning of yet another warm friendship which has lasted to this day.

Jim, as he has been known to me ever since that encounter of ours on a bus in Brighton in 1947, was born in the same year as I. He was a victim of infantile paralysis as a child, and had to overcome many obstacles and handicaps in life before he qualified as an architect. Apart from his love for Oxford, he had been obsessed since his student days with the novel idea of designing and building a round multi-storey commercial complex which would overlook the whole of Birmingham in every direction. In the late 1950s, this architectural dream of his became a reality when he was commissioned to erect just such a building, after which he became one of the most fashionable architects not only in England but also in Europe.

James Wilson was my contemporary at Merton College who had returned from the war to do a PPE degree. We shared the same Economics tutorials both with Mr McDougall at Wadham and later with Mr Matthews at Merton. I remember well how I envied the ease with which he wrote his excellent weekly essays. We were also happy partners representing our College at bridge. After I became immersed in my legal studies in London, I did not see James again until he and his wife Julia came out to the Far East in the 1950s to set up a family business in Hong Kong for a number of years. Those were memorable years during which we met almost weekly to play family bridge and to sample a variety of Chinese food for which both James and Julia have always had a gourmet's deference. We have not lost touch again since.

Before they returned to the United Kingdom in the 1960s, James and Julia appointed me godfather to their eldest son Charles upon his baptism. Today Charles is a Commander of the British Navy. Proud as I am to be his godfather, I never cease telling Charles, whenever we meet in London, that I would not be consummately happy until I have a godchild who is an admiral.

Charles is the proud father of two extremely bright boys, who, aged respectively twelve and ten, have already inherited their grandparents' palate for Chinese food. My wife and I are singularly touched that in addition to serving the British Navy and his own family well, Charles spends a considerable amount of time attending to the care of handicapped children. We know well how much in need these unfortunate ones are of constant attention and daily help. We had one such daughter ourselves who was born spastic and had required special looking after from day to day until she was lost to us when she was ten.

My two sons Denis and Dominic both feel particularly attached to James Wilson among my many friends, Denis because of the Mertonian bond, and Dominic, who is based in London, because of the occasional generous gifts of vintage wines from James' cellar in his Wimbledon manor. My only criticism of James is that in his younger days he preferred playing hockey to soccer, and now he has taken to golf and not mah-jong.

16 Changes in the Wind

In December 1945, before the Victory Scholarship Selection Board in Hong Kong, I had made it known that upon the conclusion of my studies in England, I intended to return to work on the Chinese mainland. I could not obliterate from my mind the ignorance and poverty I had seen in China during the war years, nor could I forget the sterling example of Lt.-General Lee Yen-wor of which I had personal knowledge. Hence I elected to do a second first degree in PPE at Oxford. I reckoned that an insight into the various systems of government in other parts of the world and a sound knowledge of the basic principles of Economics would be more useful to me in pursuing such an intention than a postgraduate degree in one of the arts subjects I had studied at the University of Hong Kong.

My express wish to seek eventual employment in China raised not a few eyebrows among the members of the Selection Board, one of whom went so far as to suggest that as a Victory Scholarship candidate I might be cooking my own goose by not pledging my loyalty to Hong Kong instead. At this juncture, the Director of Education Mr Arthur Walton, who chaired the Selection Board, graciously intervened on my behalf. Holding in his hand the Gazette Advertisement inviting Victory Scholarship applications as well as the Terms of Reference of the Selection Board, he reminded his fellow members that the basis for the award of the Victory Scholarships was distinguishable from that for other government and departmental scholarships. He said the Gazette Advertisement expressly stipulated that there would be no strings attached to the awards, while the Terms of Reference stressed only the importance of past academic record and war service. He then turned to thank me for being so honest and frank with the Selection Board. To this day, I am convinced that Mr Walton's intervention on that occasion and his whole attitude towards the award of the Victory Scholarships must have played a big part in gaining for me one of those scholarships. In 1948, this conviction gave me fresh courage to seek his assistance and support in order to add legal studies to my academic plans.

This idealistic although ill-fated desire on my part to return to work in China had persisted throughout 1946 and for the greater part of 1947. Although I was not altogether happy with the many failings of the Kuomintang which I could not help witnessing for myself during the war years, I genuinely believed at the time that Chiang Kai-shek, if anybody, was the one man who could bring about the birth of a united, prosperous and progressive modern China in the post-war era. After all he had ably led a hitherto divided and poverty-stricken China against the formidable military might of Japan for eight long years and emerged victorious against the odds. Besides, he would hardly have been invited to meet Roosevelt and Churchill in Cairo in 1943, if I had been alone in my belief.

However, the civil war in China which had closely followed the conclusion of the Sino-Japanese conflict ran almost entirely contrary to expectations. Those who thought it would be short-lived and must end sooner or later in favour of Chiang Kai-shek could not have been more mistaken. Bitter fighting raged all over the country for more than three painful years between the respective Nationalist and Communist camps of Chiang Kai-shek and Mao Zedong. Despite their superiority in firearms, the former's much vaunted American trained and armed troops were outfought, outgeneralled and constantly overwhelmed by the latter's dedicated followers. By the end of 1947, the writing was already on the wall. It seemed that ere long a new leader and a new regime would emerge to rule the Chinese continent.

At about this time my father wrote to say there were obvious signs that Chiang Kai-shek was already planning as a last resort to vacate the mainland and move his government and his troops beyond the Formosan Strait to the sanctuary of the island fortress of Taiwan. In the circumstances, he could not help querying whether I too should readjust my own bearings for the future.

I was then in my fourth term and second year at Merton. I had completed a leisurely first year doing no more than one paper in each of the three foregoing terms but making up excellent ground during vacation time especially in the long summer. I was writing more easily, and had no more difficulty with my reading. I was tackling two papers for the first time in that term, which meant two essays per week, yet managing comfortably without feeling any undue pressure for the extra effort.

Those were both Economics papers. For my tutorials, I had to pay bi-weekly visits to a Mr McDougall of Wadham College since Merton College had as yet no Economics tutor of its own. I did not in the least mind doing so. Apart from being a renowned Economist in Great Britain and a respected adviser to the British Labour Government under Clement Atlee, Mr McDougall proved to be another excellent tutor. He made Economics seem such an easy yet interesting subject. With Dr Gibbs and Mr McDougall as my respective Politics and Economics tutors, I was thus counting on and eagerly looking forward to spending another two enjoyable years in the PPE School before returning to the Chinese mainland to lend a helping hand to the job of post-war reconstruction and rehabilitation.

The shock defeat of Chiang Kai-shek's armies in the civil war and the impending failure of his regime on the mainland, however, necessarily wrought havoc upon my future plans. As a professional soldier my eldest brother Pak Chuen had not only pledged his allegiance to the Chinese Nationalist Army but had fought many a pitched battle against Mao Zedong's Communist followers. I myself had been given the rank of an officer in the Chinese Nationalist Army during the war years. Furthermore, as a die-hard supporter of the Roman Catholic faith I was naturally opposed to Mao Zedong's professed Marxist doctrine. These factors could neither be erased nor ignored. Little wonder that my father should implore me altogether to forsake my original plan to return to the Chinese mainland and, instead, ponder the alternatives open to me including reading law especially with the view to becoming a barrister and practising at the Bar despite my previous resistance to the very suggestion. Very regrettably, it was already very late in the day to contemplate alternative courses of studies, bearing in mind that my scholarship was for no more than three years and almost one and a half had already expired. Having gone thus far, I could hardly abandon my PPE course. Even if I did so, I would not be any better off; it would only mean losing the benefit of the four terms already spent hitherto without anything to show for it.

The PPE course at Oxford was normally a three-year school. An undergraduate would be required at the end of the three years to take an examination consisting of eleven papers. After the war, an alternative course was introduced whereby an undergraduate in that school could elect instead to do a two-year degree of no more than eight papers. For someone with a three-year scholarship like myself, the shorter two-year course offered one other advantage. After taking my degree in two years, it would be open to me, if desired, to undertake some alternative course of studies in the remaining third year of my scholarship. When the matter came up for deliberation in December 1947, however, I hardly hesitated before opting for the shorter course even though the immediate result of this sudden late decision on my part, in effect, left me with only two remaining terms in which to cover the three outstanding papers and thus little opportunity for overall revision before my degree examinations in June 1948.

This decision was arrived at after due consultation initially with Dr Gibbs and subsequently with Professor Lawson of the Law School at Merton College.

17 *A Crucial Decision*

Until the late 1960s there had been no law school in Hong Kong. Thus, for more than one and a quarter centuries after the cession of this island to Great Britain as a colony, anyone from Hong Kong aspiring to acquire a law degree at a university or to qualify for the Bar would have to travel all the way to the United Kingdom and stay there in order to attain his objective. Naturally not many people had the means, the knowledge, the opportunity, or the desire to do so. As a result, for a long time the local Bar was extremely small in size, and the number of its local Chinese members was even smaller. It was only to be expected that very few of the Chinese inhabitants in Hong Kong in those days knew much, if anything, about the law, the study of law, and the practice of law. Until 1948–9, I was certainly not one of the privileged few who knew.

One main objective in choosing a profession must be to make a living from it. In Hong Kong, at least until the end of the last war, it was un-heard-of that a local Chinese barrister could make a name and a good living at the Bar. Besides, as far as I was concerned, not knowing what practising at the Bar involved, I had no idea what particular qualities a practitioner should possess in order to facilitate success, and whether I was blessed with any of those qualities. In short, the local Bar in those days offered no assurance whatever of a bright future and a comfortable living. It was hardly surprising that when in 1950 I was called locally and admitted to practise in the Courts of Hong Kong, I was only the eleventh name and the second Chinese in the list of practising barristers.

Notwithstanding this legal background, in the latter part of 1947 I found myself for the first time more amenable to my father's suggestion to read law than hitherto. Once the door to China began to close on me, the likelihood of having to earn my living in Hong Kong made me look upon the legal profession in a totally different light. With only one and a half years of my scholarship remaining, I could not help recognizing that the Bar was the only profession still left open to me, indeed if at all. Qualifying in any of the other professions was out of the question because of the time factor. Even if I wanted to qualify for the Bar, a number of obstacles remained to be surmounted. But those obstacles were relatively insignificant compared to what I would otherwise have to put up with if I should return to Hong Kong without the requisite qualification to enable me to practise in an independent profession.

The unfortunate fact was that for more than a century colonial discrimination had prevailed in Hong Kong and had dictated employment policies both in government and the private sector, and even after the war had persisted with few immediate signs, if any, of improvement in the overall colonial climate. Employees in Hong Kong were as a result conveniently classified into expatriates and non-expatriates. This was a clever and subtle distinction specially invented and relied on in all British colonies as an excuse to justify the inequity of the discriminatory policies pursued. In those days, top jobs in Hong Kong were reserved exclusively for expatriates, to whom, as a rule, also went most of the senior posts, while the non-expatriates, that is to say, the Chinese locals, were more often than not unjustifiably left out in the cold. Even if for any special reason, a non-expatriate was appointed to a senior post, he would nevertheless not be accorded the same emoluments and other privileges as those enjoyed by his expatriate counterparts.

My father, for example, was one of the few Chinese to be appointed Senior Inspector of Schools because of his Oxford education and his expert knowledge of the Chinese language. But he was never provided with any living quarters or housing allowance, long leave with pay, high cost of living allowance as well as other privileges to which each and every one of his expatriate colleagues was automatically entitled. The only leave which my father enjoyed was a two-day break each month called local leave, to which expatriates were equally entitled in addition to their long leave with pay every third year. Needless to say, my father was paid nothing like the same salary as his expatriate contemporaries doing the same job. It was especially ludicrous that while expatriates who passed various Chinese language tests specially provided for them would reap the reward of an immediate cash bonus plus additional increments in their salary and better prospects in their career, my father who was almost invariably their examiner got nothing for the job.

Against this colonial background in Hong Kong, I was keenly aware that unless I qualified to practise in an independent profession such as the Bar, once I returned to the colony, I would have to suffer the insult as well as the injustice of discrimination by seeking employment as a local recruit. Besides, unpleasant memories of my experience with the British Naval Intelligence Office during the war still lingered to haunt me, and hardly helped to reassure me of better treatment in the colonial environment of Hong Kong.

In consequence, in December 1947 I made immediate enquiries about reading for the Bar. In those days, unlike today, gaining admission into one of the four Inns of Court in London as a law student was comparatively easy. Anyone who had matriculated would be accepted. The Bar Examinations which the law student had to pass were in two parts. There was no maximum or minimum time limit within which either part had to be taken, provided that permission to sit for the Part II Examinations would only be granted after each and every one of the seven subjects in Part I had been successfully taken. Normally, three Bar dinners each year would have to be eaten for three years before a successful candidate who had passed both parts of his Bar Examinations would be accepted to be called. But after the war this requirement was regularly waived or relaxed for the benefit of those returning from the war. The Part I Examinations were held quarterly while the Part II Examinations half-yearly. Law lectures were organized and planned by the Council of Legal Education to prepare law students for their Bar Examinations. But those lectures were scheduled to help law students to qualify for the Bar in at least two if not quite three years. Thus they would be of little help to me since I was aiming at passing all my Bar Examinations in eighteen or even twelve months.

In December 1947, I had the choice of three alternatives. The first alternative was of course simply to carry on happily with my three-year course in PPE after which to return to Hong Kong and hope to find a decent job on the strength of my two university degrees. The second alternative was to abandon my PPE studies forthwith and proceed immediately to London, and after joining one of the Inns of Court, start eating bar dinners and preparing rightaway for my Bar Examinations. In so doing, I would have eighteen months in which to get through both Parts of those examinations. The danger of this alternative lay in the possibility that if at the end of the eighteen months I failed to pass my Bar Finals, I would have wasted all of my three-years' scholarship completely. On the other hand, this alternative offered me the advantage of a leeway of six more months for my legal preparations than in the case of the third alternative. In the third and final alternative, I would take a two-year PPE degree before trying to complete both parts of my Bar Examinations in the only remaining year of my scholarship. This entailed passing all seven of my Part I papers taken in whatever order not later than December 1948 in order to entitle me to sit for my Bar Finals in May 1949. In other words after my PPE degree examinations in June 1948, I would have a little more than five months in which to pass my Part I Examinations and after doing so, a little less than five months to surmount my Bar Finals test. It would of course also involve in the first place cramming for my PPE degree examinations in the only two remaining terms at Merton. It was an altogether audacious plan. But it stood to offer me an opportunity to end up not only with a PPE degree but also a professional qualification as a barrister.

Dr Gibbs was sorry to hear that I was contemplating an alternative course of studies at all. He could not help commenting on the commendable progress I had made in my second and third terms during which I did two European History papers for him. He further said that he had received complimentary reports from Mr McDougall of Wadham College on my performance in Economics. As a result he had been confidently waiting to see further progress on my part in the remainder of my three-year course. He pointed out to great effect that I was only two terms short of completing a two-year degree in any event, and saw no reason why I should not do that at least, and take my degree accordingly before switching to law. In other words, he was in favour of either the first or the third of the three alternatives open to me but not the second. As a fourth alternative, he did suggest that I might consider undertaking a one-year diploma course in some other choice subject after completing my two-year PPE degree. This would certainly add to the opportunities for alternative employment open to me upon my return to Hong Kong. However I did not find this suggestion at all attractive. I could not think of any subject which I would choose for such a diploma. Besides, I would rather do a full three-year PPE course instead. On Bar Examinations, he felt ill-qualified to offer any advice. Instead, he sent me to see Professor Lawson of the Law School at Merton.

Professor Lawson was another outstanding academic and a delightful individual with a keen sense of humour. In his days he had taken a First Class degree in both History and Law at Oxford before scoring yet another First in his Bar Finals. In later years he had elected to follow an academic career and was promptly appointed Professor of Comparative Law at Oxford. As to whether or not I should switch from my PPE course at all, he preferred not to give any advice. When referring to my second and third alternatives, he said Sir John Miles had told him that my father had an outstanding memory, and asked whether I had inherited my father's memory. I answered that most Chinese people had a good memory, and it would seem that I was no exception. He next asked whether I was good at mathematics. After answering him in the affirmative, I could not refrain from asking him in return why he had put those two strange questions to me. His reply was that law, like mathematics, was more or less logic, and that I would have to commit to memory a lot of new concepts and new terminology if I wished to complete my legal studies in a short time. Hence the importance of having a good memory and a logical mind. He himself had passed his Bar Finals in six months, after having been exempted from all his Part I Examinations although his task had been made considerably easier because he had previously spent three full years studying law at Oxford. His conclusion was that in my case he saw no reason why I could not complete all my Bar Examinations in twelve months with some careful planning and plenty of concentrated hard work. In the circumstances, he felt favourably disposed to endorsing Dr Gibbs' advice that I should first take my degree in PPE at the end of two years before aiming at qualifying for the Bar at the end of the third and final year of my scholarship. He said that the difference between spending eighteen months or one year in preparing for my Bar Examinations should not be unduly important if I was sufficiently dedicated to my task.

He was so dynamic and persuasive that after going into his room with an open mind, I came away completely convinced that the only sensible thing for me to do was to take a two-year PPE degree at Oxford before switching to reading law and qualifying for the Bar. I can still recall his particular words to me: 'If your father could pass his Oxford Entrance in two years, there is no reason why you could not qualify for the Bar in one.' Before I left him, he made me feel as if my problems were already over with the very flattering remark that he would be looking forward to finding my name among the successful Bar Finals candidates in May 1949.

18 *Wrangling with Officialdom*

My scholarship had been awarded originally to do a full three-year course in PPE at Oxford. The approval of the proper authorities was naturally required before I could switch from that course.

During my first term at Merton, a Mr Dussek wrote to inform me that the Colonial Office in London had taken over from the Education Department of the Hong Kong government the responsibility for all the Victory Scholars during their stay in the United Kingdom, and that he had been assigned specially to look after my general well-being and overall interest. A kindly gentleman in his sixties who had spent a number of years in the Far East before being recruited to work for the Colonial Office in London, he was an extremely conscientious and benevolent individual. Not satisfied with writing to me, he went to the trouble of travelling all the way from London to Oxford just for the day in order to satisfy himself that I had settled happily into my college. Meeting and knowing him was a real pleasure and a source of comfort. Before he departed, he told me to be sure to contact him if I needed assistance of any kind. Accordingly I wrote to him late in December 1947 to seek the approval of the Colonial Office for the change in plan I had decided on after seeing Professor Lawson.

Some days later, a reply came from the Colonial Office in London signed by a Mrs Anderson informing me that Mr Dussek had passed away in the summer and that she had taken over his job of attending to the welfare of the scholarship students from Hong Kong. To my dismay, she said that the permission I sought to read law was denied, without giving any reasons; furthermore, if I was still intent on taking a two-year degree in PPE, she had no objection but my scholarship would in that event be terminated at the end of my second year. I wrote back immediately seeking an interview in order to press my case. This was duly granted, and in the following week, I found myself in London appearing before a young woman who was stunning in her looks but even more stunning in the manner in which she conducted her interview with me.

Mrs Anderson had a thick file in front of her and was regularly turning over its pages and jotting down notes from it on a writing pad. As I entered her office and stood in front of the desk behind which she was sitting, she carried on with what she was doing and neither looked up nor even asked me to sit down, but merely said, 'I believe you have something more to say to me. Go ahead.' It was amazing that throughout the fifteen minutes she specified in her letter she would grant me, she never once turned her head in my direction or looked at me or took her eyes off this thick file she was poring and turning over in front of her. As I pleaded in vain for a review of my application for permission to read law as planned, she said time and again she did not think for a moment I would ever be able to do it, that I was only wasting my time and hers, and that she could see no cause for wasting government money in sponsoring and financing a course of studies which, according to enquiries made by her, nobody had ever completed or even attempted to complete in a single year. Her attitude was so unfriendly and her effrontery was so outrageous that I could not resist commenting no one had ever sailed to America either until Christoper Columbus did it. To which she replied she was in no mood whatever to argue with me. When I mentioned in particular that I had the blessing of Professor Lawson for what I proposed to do, she said that she had never heard of Professor Lawson and that in any event he did not represent the Colonial Office. At the end of exactly fifteen minutes, she literally dismissed me from her presence declaring that her refusal to allow me to read law stood, and that our interview was at an end because there were more important things requiring her immediate attention. I cannot recall a more infuriating and frustrating interview in my life.

This episode at the Colonial Office surprisingly left me feeling more outraged than disheartened. I have always loved meeting a challenge. On my way back to Oxford, I had plenty of time on the train for thought. At the end of the journey, I became more convinced and determined than ever that I must read for the Bar. I realized at once that in order to enable me to do so, the problem posed by Mrs Anderson must first be overcome, and this could not be achieved without the assistance of someone in a position of authority. Accordingly, I compiled a long letter to Arthur Walton, who had by this time been appointed an assistant Colonial Secretary. I explained why I was giving up my original intention to work in China and how at the 11th hour in consultation with Dr Gibbs and Professor Lawson I had arrived at the decision aiming to return to Hong Kong with not only a degree in PPE but also the additional professional qualification of a barrister. I readily acknowledged the stringent studies schedule I would have to meet and the formidable challenge I was required to surmount as a result of this audacious decision, but quoted Professor Lawson's expression of confidence in my ability to accomplish my task.

In no time, Arthur Walton wrote back to say that he would be happy to do everything in his power to help me attain my goal, although he was in no position to make promises, as the ultimate decision did not rest with him alone. After a little more than another two weeks of anxious waiting I was gratified to receive a letter signed by a Mr Oughton informing me that the Colonial Office, after due consultation with the Hong Kong government, would be pleased to reaffirm my three-year scholarship by granting me the necessary permission first to take a two-year degree in PPE at Merton College, and thereafter to read law in any of the Inns of Court in London in order expressly to qualify for the Bar within the remaining third year. I was of course delighted that the fight with officialdom was over and that I had won, although much remained to be done to render the victory worthwhile.

19   *End of Oxford Sojourn*

The summer break in 1947 and the month-long vacation following my second Michaelmas term at Merton had enabled me to catch up with all the necessary reading for the three Politics papers I did for Dr Gibbs as well as the two Economics papers for Mr McDougall. In the 1948 Hillary term, I tackled Philosophy for the first time. I also took on another paper, my third, in Economics. At the beginning of January 1948 a brilliant young scholar by the name of Matthews had been appointed Economics tutor at Merton. I found myself thoroughly enjoying working with him. As a result I even decided to do a fourth Economics paper with him in the Summer term. He was even younger than Dr Gibbs, and every tutorial spent with him was an education and a pleasure.

With my Philosophy paper, however, it was an altogether different story. In fact it proved to be a complete disaster. My tutor at Merton was a former Jesuit who was known to have reneged on his religious vows. I was a bigotted Roman Catholic in those days. The combination of those two factors probably caused me to be prejudiced against him even before we met. Perhaps for the same reason he was more inclined to making fun of me. He was always so very sarcastic that I was never able to relax in his presence but instead constantly struggling to ascertain what he really implied by everything he said. This never happened with any of the other academics I had met.

At our very first meeting, a most unfortunate altercation took place between us about Chinese philosophers and their teachings. I had to confess to having only a very limited knowledge of the subject, whereupon he inquired sarcastically whether I could genuinely be Chinese. I felt so offended that on the spur of the moment I asked him in return, 'As a philosophy tutor, which of the Chinese philosophers are you genuinely familiar with, if any?' He merely stared at me but gave no answer. Although I have never ceased to regret my impertinence since, the harm had obviously been done. After that occasion our tutor-pupil relationship not only never improved but instead went from bad to worse. Every tutorial I had with him was an agony. Every essay I wrote at his command was more or less ridiculed. Having one's essays criticized and contradicted happens all the time at Oxford. It is the manner and the spirit in which it is done which makes all the difference. I did not mind in the least being every so often shown to be mistaken or lacking in judgment in my Politics and Economics essays when for sound reason and in good spirit it was pointed out for my benefit where I could have improved on my efforts. But with my Philosophy tutor, every argument which occurred between us seemed to become personal as time went on. Unfortunately for me, he was so much better read that our confrontations were seldom fair and always one-sided. It was little surprising that ere long I fell victim to total indifference and lethargy in preparing for his tutorials which I literally loathed and dreaded attending. The inadequacy of my homework of course made me even an easier target for his sarcasm. It was a vicious circle. The only comforting thought in the end was that I was at least spared from having to do a second paper with this ex-Jesuit academic.

Very regrettably, in due course I had to pay a high price for this truculence and foolhardiness on my part. In my degree examinations, my sole Philosophy paper was unavoidably substandard in contrast to the rest of my papers whether in Politics or Economics. As every candidate was required to attain a minimum standard in each of the three divisions in PPE, I was not entirely surprised to be awarded only a third class; perhaps I ought to be thankful that at least I had not been relegated to a fourth. I could only hope that Dr Gibbs and my two Economics tutors were not unduly disappointed with my overall classification. Presumably they would be informed of the individual result of the several papers I had done with each of them.

In February 1948, soon after receiving Mr Oughton's letter, I had no difficulty gaining admission into Lincoln's Inn as a law student. In March I had even travelled to London to attend my first bar dinner in the company of Simon Li. I was to attend five more of those dinners with Simon before I was eventually called to the English Bar in January 1950.

Until the beginning of 1948, I had known not a word of Latin.

During my last two terms at Merton, however, Professor Lawson had arranged for a Latin specialist and retired law lecturer at Oxford to give me an hour of tuition in Latin every week. This was necessary, he said, to prepare me for my Roman Law paper in my Part I Bar Examinations to come. In due course, those sixteen hours of Latin tuition, thanks to Professor Lawson, proved to be a tremendous help in enabling me to cope with the many Latin tags and expressions in Roman Law.

My degree examinations ended early in June 1948. As soon as I had sat for my last paper, I took the first train to London. There were so many things which had to be attended to immediately. The first problem was of course to find myself suitable digs in which to live. I had been advised by the Colonial Office that after May 1948, my monthly allowance would be reduced by as much as 30% because it would no longer be necessary for me to pay the expensive college bills, called battels(!), for my de luxe rooms and tuition at Merton. So, I had to look around for an inexpensive residence. I was fortunate that another Hong Kong student who was about to return home made it possible for me to take over his fairly spacious and comfortable room on the first floor in two four-storey twin houses in West Cromwell Road. This was a private establishment kept and run essentially for students, and was no more than a five-minutes' walk from the Earls Court Tube Station. Breakfast and dinner every day as well as lunch on Sundays was provided with the room all for the incredible amount of only £2 10s per week! This was truly a welcome find, because my scholarship allowance in London was only £22 per month out of which I had to pay for my board and lodging, legal tuition, travelling, lunch, and every other item of expense.

Mrs Dignam, my landlady, was a very stern seventy-year-old widow who lived there with her daughter, her son-in-law, and a very vivacious eleven-year-old granddaughter with whom I got on extremely well. The son-in-law had come originally from Mauritius and was an accomplished cellist. In a beautifully-kept parlour on the ground floor of the establishment, there was a piano on which the old lady used apparently at one time to play. Despite its age, it was perfectly tuned. Because I could tinkle on the piano, I quickly became a friend of the whole family. Every now and again the son-in-law would request me to accompany him on his cello. At other times, I would delight the grandmother and the grandchild by playing some of their favourite tunes in turn. As a result I was accorded preferential treatment in more ways than one. I was the only resident in the establishment who was given free access into the parlour which was much better lit than my own room. This was a great help to my legal preparations in the evening. Besides, there was a huge desk in one corner on which I could lay out all my law and other books. I was also the only resident for whom Mrs Dignam and her family would take telephone messages. Naturally I was not only happy to live in those digs but soon became the object of envy of my fellow students in London. I hardly expected, though, that I would live there until the summer of 1950.

As soon as I had settled happily into No. 76, West Cromwell Road, I began preparing for my Bar Examinations literally with a vengeance. I cannot recall working harder at any other time as a student.

20 Reading Law at Last

I saw Professor Lawson several times after the first occasion, and each time he rendered me useful assistance and advice. After getting me a Latin tutor, he specially acquired for me, at a fraction of the price which I would otherwise have to pay, a complete selection of secondhand law books which proved to be indispensable to my preparations for the Bar Examinations. Furthermore, since the Council of Legal Education lectures took too long to be of help, he suggested that I should attend instead a crammer's course conducted by a firm of law tutors known as Gibson and Weldon which specialized in preparing students for their Bar Examinations. He said that Gibson and Weldon had consistently attained a high percentage of success in getting students to pass their examinations in especially quick time, which was what I needed, although they would hardly make a lawyer of me. 'Besides,' he added, 'most lawyers in any event only start learning their law in earnest after setting up practice'. It was certainly true in my case!

Accordingly, upon my arrival in London from Oxford, I made prompt enquiries in Chancery Lane where Messrs. Gibson and Weldon were situated. Unfortunately for me, they charged such exorbitant fees for their tuition by the subject as to be way beyond my means. I had no alternative but to write to the Colonial Office again requesting an additional subsidy for my legal tuition, feeling almost like a beggar in doing so. This was flatly turned down by the same Mrs Anderson. Unfortunately I had to let the matter drop, because even if I had wanted to pursue the matter further, by the time it was resolved, it would already be too late, since the Gibson and Weldon classes for the September examinations would by then have half concluded at least. The most unfortunate aspect of the matter was that unless I passed all my Part I subjects in time, I would not even be permitted to sit for my Bar Finals in May 1949.

Thus in June 1948, I had to brace myself to meet this additional new challenge of having to prepare for my Bar Examinations almost exclusively by my own effort, because the classes conducted at the Council of Legal Education were too slow while those at Gibson and Weldon too expensive. Eventually however I did attend the classes at Gibson and Weldon just for two subjects, namely, Roman Law in my Part I Examinations, and Private International Law in my Part II Examinations. I could not trust my scant knowledge of Latin for my Roman Law paper, and I was overawed by persistent reports of poor performance by many a Bar Finals candidate in Private International Law. As time was of the essence to my plans, I simply could not afford to take any unnecessary risks lest I might fail any part of my examinations. But paying for my tuition in those two subjects was all that I could afford.

The seven Part I subjects in those days were Roman Law, Criminal Law, Contract, Tort, Constitutional Law and Legal History, Real Property, and Trust. My initial reaction was to pick three comparatively easier subjects, namely, Criminal Law, Contract, and Constitutional Law and Legal History for the September sitting, and leave the remaining four for the December sitting. I was hoping that passing those initial three subjects in September would help to boost my morale and confidence for the more difficult sitting in December. On second thoughts, however, I decided to do exactly the opposite. In other words, I would take Roman Law, Tort, Real Property, and Trust in September 1948 and the others only in December. My reasoning was that those four theoretically more difficult subjects had to be tackled in any event sooner or later. The advantage of taking them sooner was that even if I should fail any of them in September, I would still have a second chance, and could take it again in December. In December, however, in no circumstances could I afford to fail any subject. Otherwise for me there would be no Bar Finals at all to be taken before my scholarship terminated in the following May.

So, the die was cast; I would aim at passing my Roman Law, Tort, Real Property, and Trust in September, leaving Criminal Law, Contract, and Constitutional Law and Legal History to be taken in December. Having thus laid my plan for my Part I Examinations, which I felt even Professor Lawson would have approved, I proceeded for the first time ever in my life to draw up a strict timetable for my daily routine to which I conscientiously adhered for the next ten months.

As from the second week in June 1948, every morning from Monday to Friday I would be at the Earls Court Tube Station not later than 8 a.m. I would read my Times on the crowded train on my way to Chancery Lane arriving there just before 9 a.m. I would settle down in my usual corner in the library at Lincoln's Inn at 9.15 a.m. and spend the rest of the morning there in the company of my law books, save and except when once a week I had to attend at Gibson and Weldon for my Roman Law class or when I chose to attend the odd lecture at the Council of Legal Education for some specific subject or reason. A break of no more than three-quarters of an hour at 1 p.m. every day would enable me to enjoy my sandwich lunch and perhaps stretch my legs walking around Lincoln's Inn in order to have some fresh air and to rejuvenate myself. I would return to my books by 2 p.m. and only leave the library at its closing hour at 5 p.m. Another hour by underground, during which I would happily peruse my Sports News and evening newspaper, would take me back to Earls Court. Back in West Cromwell Road, I would be just in time to listen to the BBC Broadcast at 6.30 p.m. in my room where I kept a small portable radio, before washing up for dinner in the company of the rest of the residents. After dinner, I would venture into the parlour with all my books and utilize the huge desk to compile notes from and revise what I had read during the day. At the stroke of midnight, I would retire to my room to listen to the midnight BBC broadcast before going to bed. On Saturdays, Sundays, and public holidays, I would take the morning off in order to attend to any outstanding domestic chores, but would spend the afternoon once again with my law books in the library of the Chinese Students' Union, of which I was a member, in Gough Street at Russell Square.

21   *Discipline Rewarded*

Until June 1948, I had known not a thing about Roman Law, Real Property, Trust, or Tort. To be ready by September 1948 for an examination in each of the four subjects was not in itself an easy assignment. Not having the benefit of any tuition in three of the four subjects naturally rendered it even more difficult. I had hoped to qualify for the Bar by May 1949 without fully appreciating the magnitude of what was involved. It was only after I began delving into my law books in the library of Lincoln's Inn that I recognized for the first time how tall the order was. The discovery was positively alarming. At the beginning of June 1948 my decision to attend the Gibson and Weldon classes for Roman Law was dictated essentially by my limited knowledge of Latin. In due course they not only secured for me a comfortable pass; they also enabled me to spend considerably more time preparing for the remaining three subjects. But most important of all was the insight they gave me into some of the methods of tuition employed by Gibson and Weldon in preparing law students for their examinations. In no time, I applied those same methods in the remaining three subjects to great advantage and with equally satisfying results.

My self-imposed timetable required me to read law every day for some ten to eleven hours during weekdays, and some six to seven hours during weekends and public holidays. Those seemingly unending long hours thus spent from day to day were not only oppressive but altogether demoralizing at times, especially when there was no telling whether the effort so expended would serve any useful purpose in the end. The constant concentration necessitated was naturally exhausting both physically and mentally. The unfamiliar legal concepts and new terminology which had to be understood, digested, and applied were a perpetual challenge. These daily testing efforts in cramming continued week after week for three full months until not infrequently I found myself dreaming in my sleep at night of whatever aspects of the law I had been pondering in the course of the day. Unbelievably, I even had occasional nightmares in the form of difficult law examination papers for which I was totally unprepared, and would invariably wake up in a cold sweat. June, July, and August in 1948 were inexorably trying months, as I made my initial acquaintance with the law. Often I had to exert all my determination just to carry on with the scheduled discipline and try not to think of the examinations to come. At the end of the period, however, I was at least grateful to be able to look back on my preparations for the September examinations with satisfaction and pride. Pass or fail regardless, I could not have done more in the circumstances.

Despite those months of solid work, I was still full of misgivings when I went into the examination hall in September 1948 for my Part I Examinations. This was my first venture into the law, and so much depended on it. Having to rely solely on my own reading for three of the papers, I could hardly foretell whether my sustained efforts in preparing for the impending examinations in those three papers had been misdirected or misconceived. By this time I was already resigned to worrying no more about my Roman Law. I simply trusted that the Gibson and Weldon tutor knew his job. His lectures were in any event excellent and most useful, and his confidence in getting his candidates through was infectious.

In the course of time, I was gratified to find that there were no ugly surprises in the examination papers for any of the four subjects. Even as I came away from the examination hall after each paper, I knew I had done enough to get at least a pass in Roman Law, Real Property, and Trust. Tort was the only paper which had caused me just a few anxious moments. After the results were announced however, I was surprised to learn from the clerk at Lincoln's Inn that I had passed even my Tort paper with consummate ease as in the other three papers. The consistency of my effort expended in the three preceding months had reaped its due reward. The premier test in law had been successfully completed and proven not to be insuperable. I could thus look forward with confidence to facing the second hurdle in December which in normal circumstances should be less difficult than the first.

Nothing else of significance occurred between September and December 1948. In December, I duly sat for my remaining papers in Criminal Law, Contract, and Constitutional Law and Legal History as planned, passing all three subjects without any anxious moments. Immediately upon the results being made known, I served the requisite notice to sit for my Finals in the following May. The second hurdle had likewise been surmounted according to schedule. The real test was, of course, still to come.

The Bar Finals in those days consisted of five papers which the candidate had to pass in the same half-yearly sitting. Each of the five papers was divided into two parts. Each part covered one separate subject. The ten subjects were (1) Private International Law; (2) Company Law; (3) Equity; (4) Conveyancing; (5) Evidence; (6) Criminal Procedure; (7) Civil Procedure; (8) Criminal Law; (9) Contract; and (10) Tort. The first seven were entirely new subjects. The last three were old subjects but the examination questions were expected to be more advanced. As in the case of my Part I Examinations, I attended at Gibson and Weldon for only one subject, namely, Private International Law, and prepared for all the others myself. The Part II Bar Examinations had always been looked upon as the real test for law students. Not so the Part I Examinations, from which the majority of the candidates who had already taken a law degree at the university would in those days be exempted at least in part. Thus law students seldom worried nearly as much about their Part I Bar Examinations as they did their Bar Finals. With me, however, the opposite was the case.

When I began preparing for my Part I Examinations in September, my initiation into the law was so abrupt and overpowering, and the amount of tuition and guidance available so minimal, that I felt at times as if I was swimming in a furious ocean with little notion of how far away shore was. After my Part I Examinations, however, my overall interest in law was so enhanced that I found myself actually enjoying my preparations for my Bar Finals as yet another welcome challenge so that the strict daily regimentation ceased altogether to be demoralizing or boring.

In April 1949, just one month before my Bar Finals, all my plans were in danger of being sabotaged. Constant travelling in the packed underground railway caused me to fall prey to a chronic nasal ailment. For several weeks I could not lie down without my nasal glands swelling so badly as to prevent normal breathing. Breathing by mouth necessarily left my throat dry and my lips parched. I could hardly sleep. At first the nasal drops which my doctor prescribed worked wonders. But soon I had to administer the drops regularly over shorter and shorter periods until it became necessary to get up almost hourly throughout the night in order to clear the congestion. This meant breaking up my sleep six or seven times every night which inevitably left me a complete nervous wreck. Needless to say, my concentration and my legal studies both suffered. For a short while I was so disheartened that I was minded to postpone sitting for my finals if only I knew how.

One day, out of the blue Dr Gibbs called at my digs in the late evening after having spent the day in London on business. He had dropped in primarily to see how I was faring in law, and, more particularly, to let me know the individual results of my several papers in my degree examinations. I had scored an alpha in Political Institutions, which obviously pleased him immensely, and a beta in each of the remaining papers other than Philosophy in which I could manage no better than a delta minus. This explained my overall third class grading just as I had expected. Dr Gibbs said that he had heard about my impasse with my Philosophy tutor, and hoped this would teach me a good lesson. He could not resist saying half-jokingly, 'The trouble with you Catholics is that you are either a renegade or a bigot!' Before he departed, he impressed upon me that I must in no circumstances defer my Bar Finals in May even if the Colonial Office could be persuaded to allow me to do so, because there was no way to predict what might happen next time. He said he regretted not having been of much help to me in my legal studies, but expressed the hope that this advice would make up for it.

Then a strange thing happened. I felt obliged to walk him to a somewhat distant bus stop where he would catch a special coach to return to where he was staying outside London. The brisk walk to the bus stop and back enabled me to breathe in the fresh night air for the first time in months. As a result, my nasal congestion was instantly better. Thereafter, I invariably took a long walk every evening in the area before going to bed. I managed to sleep longer hours, and soon could even do without the nasal drop altogether. My legal preparations were not interrupted again, and I had no problem passing my Bar Finals in May 1949.

22 Leisurely Year of Pupillage

In Hong Kong, until our first law school was established in 1969 which enabled us to produce our own members of the Bar, pupillage had not been an institution commonly known, or a prerequisite to a barrister, whether qualifying in the United Kingdom or Ireland, being admitted to practise locally. Since then, however, serving pupillage has become a requirement to qualify any barrister for practice in our courts.

In the early part of 1948, after I had been granted permission by the Colonial Office to read law, Professor Lawson asked me on one occasion whether I had thought of doing pupillage before returning to Hong Kong. Until then I had never even heard of such a thing as pupillage. Accordingly I told him so. In England, he explained, it was customary for every newly qualified barrister intending to practise to serve pupillage for a year after which to devil for his pupil-master for perhaps another year or two before setting up his own practice. He said that it was only while serving pupillage that a barrister learnt what to do and how to do it, because this practical knowledge and experience could not be acquired from the law books.

I told the professor that much as I would like to serve pupillage in England, there was no possibility for me to do so because my scholarship would terminate in any event after May 1949. His response was that it did not make sense for the Colonial Office to grant me permission to read for the Bar and yet deny me the opportunity to complete my training by serving pupillage. He added that a fellow bencher of his at Lincoln's Inn by the name of Burnett-Hall who was a contemporary of my father at Merton had indicated he would be delighted to take me as a pupil after my call. He said I should give the matter some serious consideration because Mr Burnett-Hall was well-established in the Chancery Bar and it would be a great advantage to have a pupil-master to whom one was personally known. On that note, however, our discussion ended. At that time, I hardly gave the matter a second thought. My greatest concern then was to get through my impending PPE degree examinations in the summer of 1948. Reading law, qualifying for the Bar, and more particularly, serving pupillage after call all seemed too far away to warrant any immediate attention.

After I had passed my Part I Bar Examinations in December 1948, I wrote directly to Arthur Walton setting out my position and quoting Professor Lawson's advice about the advantage of serving pupillage in London. I apologized for so presumptuously seeking an extension of my scholarship before my Bar Finals, but explained that I required time to lay early plans. Arthur Walton promptly replied in January 1949 to say that he would be looking forward to hearing the results of my Bar Finals in May 1949 before advising the Hong Kong government and the Colonial Office whether or not to accede to my request. He added, however, that in the event of my qualifying for the Bar within a single year as planned, the Hong Kong government would undoubtedly be proud that one of its students had achieved something never before even attempted after which there could be no realistic objection to my scholarship being logically extended for another year to enable me to complete my legal training.

In March 1949, I took the liberty of calling at the chambers in Chancery Lane of Mr B.C. Burnett-Hall as advised by Professor Lawson. As soon as my name was announced, Mr Burnett-Hall almost came charging out of his room to greet me. His opening gambit was, 'Why is Yu Wan not here? Don't tell me he has taken the wrong boat again and gone this time to America instead!' Obviously he still remembered how my father had landed in Liverpool in 1912 by mistake. Mr Burnett-Hall had read law at Merton from 1915 to 1917. While most other young men of his age were in those days of the First World War conscripted into the armed forces, he was specially exempted because of his fragile health and deplorable eyesight. My father was admitted into Merton in 1914 at the age of 24. Mr Burnett-Hall had gone to Oxford straight from school so that he must have been quite a few years younger than my father. In 1949 my father was 59 years old. So Mr Burnett-Hall could not have been other than in his early or mid-fifties at the most. But he looked much older. He wore thick spectacles, and his hair was already completely silvery. He was small in physical stature and stooped slightly. Despite his obvious sense of humour, he was a man of few words, although he kept asking about my father and wondering when they would meet again. Sadly, their intended reunion never took place. My father passed away in 1966 without setting foot on English soil again, while Mr Burnett-Hall outlived him by two years without ever travelling to the Far East.

When Professor Lawson mentioned that Mr Burnett-Hall had an excellent Chancery practice, I had no idea at the time what that meant. It was only after I had commenced my pupillage in his chambers that I discovered that my pupil-master specialized in company law, conveyancing, real property problems, family trusts, inheritance, and all such related matters. Although by 1949 he only very occasionally went to court, he must have had his share of litigation in his younger days, because for many years he was one of the joint editors of the White Book, that is to say, the Code of Civil Procedure in England. His experience in conveyancing matters in particular was universally acknowledged to the extent that he had been given the honorary title of Conveyancer of the Court. During my pupillage, Mr Burnett-Hall was kind enough to grant me free access to all his files, instructions, and other papers, which gave me quite an insight into many an interesting legal problem. This training was most useful when I started practice in Hong Kong in the early 1950s. In later years, after I became more often involved in criminal than civil cases, it was a standing joke between us that I must have learnt how to cross-examine witnesses and address juries from reading his opinions in chambers.

True to his word, after my Bar Finals in May 1949, Arthur Walton duly obtained for me an extension of my scholarship to enable me to do pupillage. This additional year in England proved to be the most relaxing and probably the most enjoyable of my four years spent in the United Kingdom. Although the humdrum routine of serving pupillage could in itself hardly rival the excitement of the many attractions of college life at Oxford, or the unique challenge of cramming in order to qualify for the Bar in limited time, it offered me, instead, complete peace of mind without pressure of any sort but with endless opportunity to enjoy the many attractions of the Metropolis. And all the while I was happily learning about the practice of law as well.

A surprise event took place in the second month of my pupillage which rendered my final year in London even more pleasurable than otherwise. A fellow pupil in our chambers who was another Oxonian invited me to take over from him the job of lecturing for two hours in the evening each week on Criminal Law and Contract at an institute in Kensington run for the benefit of clerks and other interested people.

Remuneration was at 2 guineas per hour. This meant almost 20 guineas per month. I could hardly turn down an offer which practically doubled my scholarship allowance. This new opulence enabled me to live almost like a prince. For the first time, I could afford to attend regularly at theatres and concert halls of my choice. Every now and again, I even went holidaying in various attractive parts of the British Isles which I had always longed to, but until then, could ill-afford to visit. My father used to tell me that half of one's education came from travelling. I certainly travelled more extensively during that fourth year of my scholarship than during the three previous years added together.

23 *Malayan Undertaking Contemplated*

Until 1950, Malaya (now Malaysia) had meant little more to me than the name of a long peninsula in Southeast Asia known to have a wealth of coconut trees, rubber plantations and tin mines, an unending summer all the year round, and a mixed population consisting essentially of Malays and Chinese as well as some Indians and Tamils. From childhood I had been aware that living in Kuala Lumpur, the capital of Malaya, was an aunt of mine who was one of the two younger sisters of my father. Her husband, Yong Shook-lin, a Malayan Chinese and a native of Kuala Lumpur, was educated at Emmanual College in Cambridge at about the time when my father was at Merton College in Oxford. After the First World War, he had come to Hong Kong and carried off my aunt as his bride back to his home town where they happily raised a family of one son and five daughters.

When I was about ten or eleven years old, my uncle and aunt had brought their young son, Pung-how, from Kuala Lumpur to visit us at Nos. 15–17 Shelley Street where they spent several weeks before returning to Malaya. Some four years younger than myself, Pung-how was at that time already noticeably extremely precocious, well-behaved, intelligent, and hard-working. For some strange reason he and I seemed to get on particularly well. The presence of my uncle was on the other hand a trifle inhibiting because he was always so serious, and spoke English most of the time. He was reputed to be a millionaire, and a very successful lawyer in Kuala Lumpur, although I hardly knew at the time what that meant.

In 1946, when my younger brother Brian and I were stranded for some two to three weeks in Singapore waiting for transport to take us to the United Kingdom, my aunt had travelled down from Kuala Lumpur with her four younger daughters to spend a couple of days with us. Her eldest daughter, Siew Chin, and her son, Pung-how, had, prior to our arrival, preceded us to England to pursue their studies. During my second year in England, I caught up with Pung-how in Cambridge where he read law at Downing College. I was only too happy to renew my childhood friendship with him. Since then, we have kept in close touch with each other. I also saw his sister, Siew Chin, very occasionally in London where she lived in a house of her own.

In August and September 1949, while I was serving pupillage in London, my father sprang a surprise on me. By this time Mao Zedong had firmly established himself on the Chinese mainland. It was anybody's guess whether his communist regime would honour China's unfair treaty obligations to the Western world and what would happen eventually to Hong Kong. With the lesson of the Japanese occupation still constantly on his mind, my father urged me seriously to consider practising law in Kuala Lumpur instead of Hong Kong after my pupillage. In so doing, he said, I could safely avoid being caught in Hong Kong again with the rest of the family as in December 1941, if fresh turmoil should visit the island colony. Furthermore I would, if necessary, be in a position to provide alternative sanctuary in Malaya for the family should emigration from Hong Kong become politically expedient.

The impact of this suggestion was so sudden that I naturally required time to turn it over in my mind. Before I arrived at any conclusion, my father wrote again to say he had, on my behalf, requested my uncle Yong Shook-lin to take me into his firm, and the latter had asked me to contact him directly myself. Although I hardly knew my uncle Yong Shook-lin, his friendship with my father had apparently dated back to their undergraduate days and continued through the years. In Malaya, unlike in England and Hong Kong, barristers and solicitors practised alike as advocates and solicitors, and there was no dividing line between the two professions. My uncle and his partner Tan Teow Bok had for some years been practising as advocates and solicitors in Kuala Lumpur under the firm name of Messrs Shook-lin and Bok.

While keeping an opening mind on this novel idea of a Malayan venture on my part, I felt obliged to ascertain how my cousin Pung-how felt about my joining his father's firm, because in normal circumstances he would presumably be doing likewise, and we might in due course have to end up as partners ourselves. Very tactfully and sensibly, Pung-how replied that delighted as he was to hear I was contemplating practising in Kuala Lumpur, whether I joined Shook-lin and Bok was strictly a matter between his father and his partner Tan Teow Bok on the one hand and me on the other, especially when he, Pung-how, would take at least another couple of years to complete his legal training, and until then, he preferred not to speculate what he might want to do.

Normally one would be slow to practise law in a foreign country rather than in one's home town. However until 1950 the legal scene in Hong Kong was as little known to me and my family as that in Kuala Lumpur. Besides, I had been away so long that the advantage of practising on home ground hardly existed. Instead, the system of a joint profession in Malaya, and the fact that Messrs Shook-lin and Bok was a well established law firm in Kuala Lumpur promised immediate financial security which practice at the Bar in Hong Kong could not guarantee. In post-war Hong Kong there was an acute overall shortage of office space in town. Finding suitable premises in which to set up chambers was therefore a big enough problem in itself, not to mention the considerable expense involved. Joining my uncle's firm in Kuala Lumpur would avoid all such related problems. The point that my father made about providing an alternative base for myself and the family also necessarily carried its due weight. Furthermore, there was no telling whether I could hold my own practising at the Bar in Hong Kong whereas in Kuala Lumpur my uncle and his partner would surely be there to show me the way whenever required.

In Malaya, I realized that I would be seeking acceptance into a new country, a foreign community, and a hitherto unknown society. Not being able to speak Malay was an obvious handicap although I could always learn. While my cousin Pung-how and I enjoyed great mutual respect for each other, my uncle and his partner were total strangers to me. Even my aunt was hardly better known.

Those were some of the thoughts foremost in my mind when I eventually summed up enough courage to enquire of my uncle Yong Shook-lin whether there was any room in his firm for another Oxonian lawyer. His partner Tan Teoh-bok was known to have been educated in Oxford. My uncle responded very briefly by welcoming me on behalf of his partner and himself to join Messrs Shook-lin and Bok and further inviting me to share his household as well at No. 211 Circula Road in Kuala Lumpur. Three more of his daughters had by this time gone to England for their education. Accordingly, he said, I could have the choice of any one of the many vacant rooms in his house. As far as I was concerned, this friendly invitation happily put the seal on my plan to practise law in Kuala Lumpur at the end of my pupillage.

24 Year of Mixed Fortune in Malaya

After an absence from Hong Kong of nearly four years, I was naturally glad to be reunited with my parents in the early part of July 1950. My father was a proud and happy man sitting in court on the day I was called to the local Bar. The acting Chief Justice Bill Williams officiated. An Irishman who spoke Cantonese without a trace of accent, he went out of his way in his speech of welcome to me to recall how kind my father as his Chinese examiner had been to him in his younger days. My joyful reunion with the family did not, however, last long. At the age of 28, I could hardly wait to get started in my legal career; besides, the call of Malaya was irresistible. Accordingly I set sail again for Singapore towards the end of August 1950, and in due course arrived in Kuala Lumpur by train in the first week of September 1950.

Despite my limited knowledge of Malaya, and my total ignorance of the Malay language and the Malayan way of life, I was convinced that my trip to Kuala Lumpur was a wise one, and that it would in the course of time lead to success and happiness in this foreign land in which I had planned to establish my new home. By this time I had become aware that in Kuala Lumpur my uncle Yong Shook-lin was not only a well-known legal practitioner but also a respected Legislative Councillor for the State of Selangor, and a past president as well as a current committee member of the powerful Malayan Chinese Association. As his nephew, I had no reason to think that I would not do well as a member of his law firm unless I was wholly incompetent. However, things did not work out the way I had hoped they would work out.

In 1950 the firm of Shook-lin and Bok was housed in an old-fashioned two-storey building in the heart of town. The clerical and other members of its staff took up the whole of the ground floor, while a creaky wooden staircase led to the respective offices of my uncle and his partner on the upper floor. I had a third room to myself while the only remaining room on this floor was used for storage. I was naturally gratified that a vacant office was waiting for me upon arrival. However my feeling of gratification ended there. In the days, weeks and months which followed I was surprised to find myself totally isolated throughout the day in my constantly empty office. Noticeably, I was never invited into my uncle's or his partner's room whether to meet any of their social callers or professional clients. Nor did either of them ever initiate me into any particular law-suit, commercial or conveyancing problem, or whatever other legal matter he might be handling. I was not assigned any work to do or given any file or other papers to read. At no time throughout my stay in Kuala Lumpur did my uncle or his partner ever discuss with me the business or clientele of the firm.

The law of Selangor in those days required a newcomer to the Bar to be registered with a recognized firm for at least six months and at the end of which to pass an examination on Malayan laws and procedure before he would be granted a licence to practise. At the time I thought that I was denied access to the files and clientele of Shook-lin and Bok merely because I had yet to obtain my practice licence. Accordingly I wasted no time before delving into the local ordinances and law reports in preparation for the statutory examination to come. Every day I spent hours reading up the local laws in my office at my uncle's firm. Every evening I did likewise at his residence at No. 211, Circular Road. It was almost a repetition of my Bar cramming days in London.

No. 211, Circular Road, where my uncle and his family lived, was an enormous house of two storeys situated in a high-class residential area just beyond the city limits of Kuala Lumpur in those days. I was accommodated in the only guest room on the ground floor. My uncle and his family all had their bedrooms on the upper floor, access to which was available via either one of two staircases, one in the hallway directly facing the main entrance, and the other, at the back of the house. After five of the children had gone to England, the only other member of the Yong family residing there beside my uncle and aunt was their remaining thirteen-year-old daughter.

My uncle never entertained. He dined early, and, after dinner, would invariably retire with my aunt to their rooms upstairs leaving me with the whole empty ground floor to myself. For a while I tried hard enough to make polite conversation or, alternatively, bring up subjects of various kinds for discussion which I thought might interest them, but soon gave up trying when my endeavours evoked little or no response. This absence of communication between us became progressively more marked and necessarily more embarrassing since we shared the same meals, lived under the same roof, and travelled in the same chauffeur driven car to and from my uncle's office and residence no less than four times each day. As the weeks and months went by, I could not help feeling more and more like an undesirable intruder whether in the offices of Shooklin and Bok or at No. 211, Circular Road.

In May 1951, I passed the statutory examination set by the Selangor Bar. Accordingly a standard notice was dispatched to advise Messrs Shooklin and Bok that I had qualified to take out a practice licence. When neither my uncle nor his partner took any notice of this, I was finally driven to conclude that there could be no further room for doubt or misunderstanding. The message was unequivocal, loud, and clear. My presence in my uncle's firm, and thus at his residence as well, was no longer welcome. I could only think that something must have happened to change my uncle's mind after he had written about a year earlier to welcome me to Kuala Lumpur. It was equally possible of course that he might not have approved of what he saw in his nephew upon arrival. Whatever the reason for his attitude, my pride and self-respect would no longer permit me to stay.

One great difficulty of mine was to explain to my father, indeed all of a sudden, why I was quitting my uncle's firm. I had not kept him posted of everything that had been happening from day to day since my arrival in Kuala Lumpur. It was impossible to do so by letter. On the contrary, I wrote to tell him that I was happily settling into my new environment and making steady albeit slow progress in my legal practice.

However, I was not going to give up my Malayan venture without a fight. Accordingly I contacted a total of five other law firms in Kuala Lumpur one after another in an attempt to find alternative employment. Ironically I had gone to Kuala Lumpur believing that being Yong Shooklin's nephew would give me an advantage. I soon discovered that it was more like a handicap. The representatives of those five law firms all instantly shied away in embarrassment as soon as it was discovered who I was and why I was looking for a job. One could hardly blame them for not accepting the risk of taking on the discarded nephew from Hong Kong of the Honourable Yong Shook-lin.

At the end of August 1951, I politely told my uncle that I was returning to Hong Kong for a brief holiday. I did not immediately disclose that my departure would be for good, although he might have suspected the truth. Back in Hong Kong, I convinced my father not without considerable difficulty, though, that for me to persevere as a guest who had overstayed his welcome in Kuala Lumpur would not serve any useful purpose. Only then did I write to bid farewell to my uncle and aunt and to thank them for their hospitality during the twelve months I spent under their roof.

My Malayan venture was naturally not one of the happier experiences in my life. I was grateful, though, that notwithstanding the ugly clouds which overhung this episode, two bright silver linings came shining through in the end. In 1953, my good friend and dear cousin Pung-how, the son of my uncle Yong Shook-lin, flew into Hong Kong out of the blue just to pay me a visit. In the previous year he had completed his legal training in England and returned to Kuala Lumpur. He took me entirely by surprise by inviting me to return to Kuala Lumpur to start a new law firm in partnership with him. Much as I appreciated his meaningful gesture, I told him after due consideration I did not think that as the only son he should turn his back on his father's firm.

After my uncle passed away in 1955, Pung-how once again sounded me out whether I would care to make a triumphant return to Kuala Lumpur perhaps as the senior partner of Messrs Shook-lin and Bok. This was a very generous and attractive offer indeed, because between 1953 and 1955, Messrs Shook-lin and Bok, reorganized and managed by Pung-how, had expanded beyond recognition to become one of the largest and best-known law firms in Malaya. Although deeply touched by his kind invitation, I myself had by that time made some headway at the Hong Kong Bar and much preferred to continue practising as a barrister in my home town than seek afresh to establish myself as a lawyer and advocate in a foreign land. Accordingly I thanked him again and told him so. But those two approaches of his most certainly further cemented our long standing friendship ties and brought us even closer to each other than before.

In 1970, Pung-how left Kuala Lumpur altogether and settled down with his family in Singapore. After filling various top posts and rendering innumerable invaluable services to the Singapore government in a variety of fields including Industry, Banking, Investments and Broadcasting, Pung-how returned to the legal profession when he was appointed first a Judge of the Singapore Supreme Court in 1989, and then Chief Justice in the following year. Currently he is still Chief Justice of Singapore and very much respected not only for the reforms he carried out and the improvements he rendered to the Singapore judicial system but also for numerous learned judgments he pronounced whether sitting in the first instance or in the Appellate Court.

The second silver lining in my frustrated Malayan venture took an entirely different form. During my first month in Kuala Lumpur I met a very friendly couple at church on a Sunday morning. Ignatius Tang and his wife Magdalene were very devout Catholics. They noticed that I had arrived in church and was leaving on foot, and kindly offered to give me a lift in their car. Naturally I was grateful to accept their offer because No. 211, Circular Road was a 45-minute-walk away. I soon discovered that the Tangs were originally from Hong Kong too and, further, that we had quite a number of mutual friends. In the months which followed they came to fetch me every Sunday to take me to church and thereafter breakfast at their home before sending me back to No. 211, Circular Road.

In May 1951, Magdalene's youngest sister Lucia Fung visited Kuala Lumpur with her mother, and I met her at the household of the Tangs. After returning to Hong Kong in the summer, Lucia and I continued to see each other, and after a whirlwind courtship we were happily united in holy wedlock on 23 February 1952. Today, we are the proud parents of two sons and two daughters, and the pampering grandparents of seven mischievous but delightful grandsons. If either of us had not been in Kuala Lumpur in May 1951, the chances were that we probably would never have met.

25 — First Chinese Crown Counsel

Homecoming in 1951 was not nearly as jubilant for me as in the previous year. There was precious little to celebrate. My Malayan venture had ended in disappointment and failure; my father was badly upset; and one whole year had been wasted without any headway being made in my profession. Instead, the future was fully laden with anxiety and uncertainty. Back home I had once again to pin my hopes on practising at the Bar where the prospects remained altogether unknown and unpredictable. The irony was that when I told my close friends and relatives in Hong Kong that I was unwanted in Kuala Lumpur and had been turned away, none of them would believe me.

As soon as I returned to Hong Kong, I caused extensive searches to be made for a suitable office in which to set up chambers. Everywhere I came up against a blank wall. In those days, not only was there an acute physical shortage of offices in town. Most of the buildings in town today had yet to come into existence, while all the pre-war buildings were subject to a tight rent control under the Landlord and Tenant Ordinance which was passed in May 1947. No existing tenant would voluntarily vacate or surrender premises for which he was paying only a ridiculously low statutory rent. Instead, enormous sums were invariably demanded for the transfer of any such existing tenancy. These sums were known as 'key money' and were illegal. But there was little that the authorities could do to prevent them from being constantly demanded and frequently paid. As I could neither afford nor was willing to pay any such 'key money', I was unable to find ready accommodation in town for my chambers.

As luck would have it, at about this time and quite by chance, I met at a cocktail reception the retiring Attorney-General of Hong Kong John Bowes Griffin who seemed to take an immediate interest in me. Apparently the Legal Department (as the Attorney-General's Chambers were known in those days) had been looking for a local barrister who could speak as well as read and write Chinese, and I was asked whether I would care to be the first Chinese Crown Counsel to be appointed. Until then, no Chinese lawyer had ever been employed or even considered for employment by the Legal Department. Obviously a new policy was in the making. As the Attorney-General was pleasantly direct and candid in his approach, I, too, preferred not to beat about the bush. I told him just as candidly that I was very interested, because I was not currently employed and was having problems setting up chambers. However I made it amply clear that I would not accept employment in the Legal Department save and except on equal terms with its expatriate members.

Bowes Griffin indicated that as far as he was concerned, this would not be an obstacle. Before a final decision could be made, however, other individuals and departments in government might have to be consulted. He failed to see, though, how government could justifiably deny me the best of non-discriminatory terms since the obvious purpose of appointing a Chinese Crown Counsel must be in order to enable bilingual services to be rendered which the other members in the department would be unable to provide. As he would be going on long leave in a day or two, Bowes Griffin said that in his absence the matter would have to be finalized by the acting Attorney-General George Strickland, to whom I was specially introduced by him later in the same evening.

Bowes Griffin and George Strickland were both educated at Oxford and obviously approved of the college tie which I was wearing. The latter, in particular, became seemingly even more enthusiastic than the former to have me join the Legal Department after discovering that I was as keen a bridge player as he was. Indeed in due course we played many an exciting game against each other. He was a first-class bridge player as well as lawyer.

In the weeks following our initial meeting, George Strickland took me out to lunch more than once and each time invited me to commence working for him rightaway without waiting for officialdom to approve formally my terms of service. He specially mentioned that the Registrar of the Supreme Court Mr Christopher D'Almada and the Director of Public Health Dr Yeo were two of the locals who had been appointed on expatriate terms. He revealed that the police had been pressuring government to appoint a bilingual Chinese Crown Counsel to facilitate a better understanding and working relationship with the Legal Department. In the past years, both the crime rate and the number of criminal trials had steadily and alarmingly risen, thereby considerably increasing the workload of police officers briefing non-Chinese speaking members of the Legal Department. It was obvious that he was fully aware of the understanding which had taken place between Bowes Griffin and myself. He did not expect any hitch to my being granted expatriate terms by government and went so far as to hint that the appointment of a Chinese Crown Counsel would very likely lead, in the course of time, to the appointment of a Chinese Supreme Court Judge and perhaps even a Chinese Chief Justice, and that in the circumstances I would be the most likely candidate for such eventual appointment.

He was so friendly yet persistent that it was difficult to insist on first receiving a written confirmation of my appointment on my terms before I commenced work. Accordingly I found myself instantly posted to the prosecution section of the Legal Department in the latter part of 1951. Indeed this unexpected opportunity to launch my legal career surprisingly as a member of the Colonial Legal Service was by no means unwelcome, especially when as a Class One officer I was led to assume that appropriate government living quarters would be provided with my job. Living quarters was of course one of the distinguishing features in the employment of all expatriates, and a bone of contention for non-expatriates in the first place. Towards the end of 1951, it was also a consideration of particular paramount and urgent importance to me for a personal reason. Lucia Fung and I had been dating regularly after our return from Kuala Lumpur to Hong Kong. At about this time, she had a choice of furthering her education in Australia or going as personal secretary to her father on a round-the-world cruise. In either instance, we appreciated that long separation could easily spell an end to our romance. So, after due consideration, we decided to get married and duly fixed our wedding day some two months hence for 23 February 1952. Naturally, the implied promise of government quarters played a part in prompting our wedding fixture.

Imagine how I felt when in December 1951, after working for almost a month as Crown Counsel, I was advised that the Public Services Commission had rejected the Attorney-General's representations to grant me expatriate terms. The primary reason given was that otherwise the floodgates would be open to similar representations from other local employees. I was thus to be paid no more than a minimum flat salary without any high-cost-of-living allowance, living quarters, housing allowance, long leave with pay, or any one of a long list of miscellaneous pecuniary as well as other privileges and benefits to which all expatriate officers were automatically entitled. I instantly notified George Strickland in writing of my immediate resignation, indeed if such was strictly necessary since I had yet to be formally appointed.

Earlier on the news of the appointment of the first Chinese Crown Counsel had made headlines in all the local newspapers and created quite a stir in Hong Kong. It would seem that my resignation so soon thereafter created a similar stir at least in government circles. Surprisingly, the Chief Justice Sir Gerald Howe immediately and specially sent for me, and at a private interview in his chambers pleaded with me to hold up my resignation at least until after the arrival of the new Attorney-General Arthur Ridehalgh. He told me that the two of them had successfully championed a similar cause for the locals in Nigeria, and offered to do the same for me. I could hardly say no to this kind offer especially when I had no immediate alternative employment and could ill-afford to give up my job just weeks before my scheduled wedding. It was in those circumstances that I acceded to his suggestion, and as a result remained as Crown Counsel eventually for a whole year despite being paid considerably less than my expatriate colleagues and accorded none of their many privileges. This was because the new Attorney-General Arthur Ridehalgh did not arrive in Hong Kong until October 1952. Yet another Oxonian he was an extremely considerate and thoughtful chief and a very sound and hardworking lawyer. He too had the excellent habit of taking his subordinates out in turn to lunch. My only complaint whenever I lunched with him was that out of deference to him I invariably had to consume at least a couple of pink gins before the meal, and would inevitably suffer for the rest of the afternoon. Spirits, wines, and alcohol of any kind simply did not agree with me.

In due course I was told that the new Attorney-General Arthur Ridehalgh and the Chief Justice Sir Gerald Howe duly went to Government House on no less than three separate occasions in an attempt to persuade the Governor to intervene and grant me expatriate terms. Apparently they were whole-heartedly backed by the police force which had had by this time a good taste of working with a bilingual Chinese Crown Counsel and could hardly do without it. However it was all to no avail. The Governor would not intervene; the decision of the Public Services Commission was allowed to stand; and colonial discrimination continued to reign supreme. The net result was, of course, that in December 1952 I finally quit government service. I shall always be grateful, nonetheless, to Sir Gerald Howe for having thus vainly endeavoured to champion my cause and in particular for his encouraging parting words. 'I am sorry I failed,' he said, 'leave by all means. Government will no doubt regret losing you. Go into private practice. I am sure you will never look back.' He was right. Happily I never looked back.

I would like to believe that the fight against colonial discrimination which I started alone by my resignation in 1951–2 had not been entirely in vain. Shortly thereafter government introduced a new housing policy whereby instead of living quarters, cheap loans, to be repaid only after long periods, were made available to its non-expatriate employees to enable them to build and acquire housing units for themselves. This was an enormous bonus and a signal first victory for the locals. In 1958, the Senior Non-Expatriate Officers' Association was formed and the fight against colonial discrimination continued thereafter year after year. Concessions in one form or another were won from government from time to time although progress was inevitably slow. In recent decades, as a result of the impending termination of British rule, more and more non-expatriates have been appointed at last to senior and even top posts in government. The gap between expatriate and non-expatriate terms of emolument was also noticeably and continuously narrowed. While it was comforting to trace the gradual disappearance of colonial discrimination in Hong Kong these past decades, it is singularly ironical that shortly before the reversion of the territory to Chinese sovereignty, a High Court Judgment should have been awarded against the former Colonial Government for discrimination against its expatriate employees as a result of its so-called localization policy of very recent years. Localization policy was of course yet another term conveniently coined and introduced by the British Colonial Government. What the non-expatriates had been fighting and hoping for all the while was for no more than equitable and equal treatment with the expatriates, and not for any policy specially favouring the locals. Indeed at no time had the non-expatriates ever sought any such favour, nor had the British Colonial Government ever granted them any. Perhaps even more surprisingly, there was no appeal from the said judgment.

Unlike the twelve months I spent in Kuala Lumpur, my year as Crown Counsel was far from wasted. As a result of constantly advising the police on crime, I acquired a rare insight into police methods and police procedure as well as goings-on in police stations. This proved to be of great assistance to me in my subsequent criminal practice at the Bar. From appearing almost daily in court, I was also learning about court etiquette, court craft, and court ethics. There were three other Crown Counsel apart from myself in the prosecution section of the

Legal Department but I seemed to be the only one constantly engaged in court. There was one particular month in which I conducted no less than a dozen full-fledged criminal prosecutions while my three expatriate colleagues lounged in the department enjoying their leisure. I did not in the least mind, though, being made to work overtime, because I was keenly aware of my limited court experience and welcomed the opportunity to familiarize myself with criminal law and practice. If government had not been treating me fairly, it had at least unwittingly rendered me a useful service.

I cannot help recalling an amusing incident which took place one day while I was working late in the department after returning from a long full day in court. One of my expatriate colleagues could not refrain from interrupting me as he watched me poring over my file. 'I don't understand why you are working so hard,' he said. 'Try to remember that in government service non-feasance is no bar to promotion while misfeasance is. Therefore the less you do, the smaller the chance of a misfeasance being committed, and the better the chance of promotion!' This gentleman was indeed notorious for doing precious little in the department. Yet in due course his non-feasance did not in fact prevent him from being appointed a judge in the Supreme Court before he retired.

Throughout 1952, just because I was the first and only Chinese Crown Counsel, the local newspapers somehow never failed to give me more than my due share of publicity whenever I appeared in court. The constant reporting of my cases caused my name to be better known than otherwise not only to the general public but also to the local legal fraternity. This publicity probably more than made up for my hitherto long absence from Hong Kong. As a result, when I commenced private practice at the local Bar on 1 January 1953, I did not have to wait long for my much needed early briefs.

26 No. 9 Ice House Street Also Known as Holland House

Sir Oswald Cheung QC is one of my oldest friends. I first met him at a teenage party in 1937 when he was introduced to me simply as Ossie. I have since called him by no other name. In the following year we joined the University of Hong Kong both as freshmen in the Faculty of Arts where we attended various lectures together until the Japanese attacked Hong Kong in December 1941. During the war years, Ossie and I spent time separately in different parts of the Chinese mainland although for a short while we met up again in Guilin (桂林) in Guangxi Province (廣西省). After the war Ossie read law at University College in Oxford at about the time when I was at Merton. Later we saw each other frequently in London when we prepared for our Bar Examinations at Lincoln's Inn.

Ossie returned to Hong Kong when I was in Kuala Lumpur. In 1952, he was practising at the local Bar and had his chambers at Alexandra House. In those days, members of the Bar in Hong Kong all practised individually in single rooms of limited dimensions. When he heard that I was finally quitting the Legal Department but had nowhere to go, he very generously invited me, at great inconvenience to himself, to share his room at Alexandra House as a temporary licensee until I found alternative accommodation for myself.

Ossie's kind offer was the best thing that could have happened to me. The shortage of office space in town was then as acute as ever. Not only was I enabled to commence practice at the Bar forthwith; as licensee, my name and particulars had to be supplied to Hongkong Land (i.e. The Hongkong Land Company Limited) which was the registered owner of Alexandra House as well as many other office-buildings in town; as a result I came to know its estate manager, a Mr G. Graham, who promptly put me down on the priority list of professional waiting tenants of his company. No more than a few months later I was offered and happily accepted the tenancy of a tiny room on the fourth floor of another office building then owned by Hongkong Land, namely, No. 9 Ice House Street, commonly known as Holland House because of the presence of a Dutch bank on its ground floor.

This room measured less than one hundred square feet. Although it hardly satisfied even my basic requirements, I was nonetheless grateful to be spared from further imposing on my good friend Ossie. Besides, it gave me a proud feeling, after endless searching in vain, to have at last a place of my own, however modest, to which I could smugly refer as my chambers. I can still recall throwing a small and exclusive party in this little joint to celebrate the occasion even though there was barely standing room for half a dozen guests.

I occupied this fourth floor cubicle for a little over a year before I moved upstairs to Room 711B which was a bigger and better room on the seventh floor of the same building. There I carried on with my legal practice for the next thirty odd years without interruption. In 1987, Holland House was pulled down for redevelopment, and has since been replaced by a new building renamed No. 9 Queen's Road Central. Accordingly I moved my chambers to Bond Centre (now renamed Lippo Centre). By that time, however, I no longer accepted briefs to go to court. Thus, except for the short period when I was with Ossie in Alexandra House, my private practice at the Bar had taken place exclusively in Holland House.

Ten years have since gone by. To this day, whenever I traverse that locality whether on foot or by car, fond memories are still rekindled of the happy, busy days I spent on that historical site where No. 9 Queen's Road Central now stands. There, on the unforgettable seventh floor, for more than three decades I invariably pondered my briefs, wrote my opinions, drafted my pleadings, interviewed my instructing solicitors and lay clients, prepared my submissions, and armed myself with case law before going to court. Pursuing this regular routine day after day over such a long period of time inevitably created a sentimental attachment to the venue which could not easily be displaced. Indeed Holland House had at times seemed like a second home to me.

My activities at Room 711B in Holland House were multifarious and far from limited to my legal practice. In the mid-1960s, I was appointed by the Governor, Sir David Trench, as a member of the first ever University Grants Committee in Hong Kong. Michael Davies of

Jardine Matheson & Co. Ltd. and T.K. Ann of Winsor Industrial Corporation Ltd. were the only two other members. The membership of that committee has since grown considerably over the years. Normally the function of such a committee is to act as a buffer between government and the university on finance as well as all other related matters. In the mid-1960s, apart from the overall question of subventions, the immediate additional tasks of the three-men committee of which I was one were two-fold: (1) monitoring the smooth amalgamation of three pre-existing academic institutions, namely, Chung Chi College, New Asia College, and United College, into a second university to be called the Chinese University, and (2) supervising the creation of a new Faculty of Social Sciences and Law in the University of Hong Kong. Among other things this meant the establishment of a law school for the first time in the history of Hong Kong.

For me, this responsibility of overseeing the formation of the law school was particularly welcome and satisfying. Ever since 1948 when I first became interested in the study of law, I had been publicly and privately advocating the need for Hong Kong to have a post-secondary law course at the university. Otherwise people in Hong Kong desirous of reading law and qualifying as lawyers, especially as members of the Bar, would have to go to the United Kingdom in order to do so. It was amazing that until the mid-1960s the Hong Kong government had not seen fit to provide this facility to read law for the local population.

I cannot help recalling the many long hours I, as a member of the first University Grants Committee, spent with Dafydd Evans upon his initial arrival in Hong Kong as Foundation Professor of the Law Department at the University of Hong Kong. Shortly thereafter he was followed by John Rear and Bernard Downey, two of the law lecturers. In due course the planned law department came officially into existence in 1968. In the following year the first batch of local students was admitted to read law as a post-secondary course of studies at the University of Hong Kong.

I was naturally overwhelmed with pride and satisfaction to see the law school for which I had been clamouring for some twenty years become a reality. In the years which followed, it gave me further gratification to maintain a close relationship with the Law Department of the University of Hong Kong even after I had retired as a member of the University Grants Committee. I hardly expected, though, the far-reaching effects this was to have on my chambers in due course.

In the latter part of 1973, Kenneth Kwok, one of the first law students at the University of Hong Kong, came, after completing four years of legal studies, to serve pupillage in my chambers. He was specially sent to me by courtesy of his mentor John Rear. In the following year Kenneth Kwok made history as the first local law graduate to be called to the Hong Kong Bar. I was given the privilege of moving his call. He was not however my first pupil. He was preceded by Marjorie Chui, a law graduate of London University, who in 1972 had completed her last three months of pupillage with me at Room 711B.

Other law graduates from the University of Hong Kong who followed in the footsteps of Kenneth Kwok to serve pupillage in my chambers included Mok Yeuk Chi, Patrick Chan, and David Yam, all three of whom also served a substantial part of their respective terms of pupillage in the chambers of Denis Chang before the latter was admitted to the Inner Bar. After 1974, my chambers were extended from time to time to include respectively Room 712, Room 713, and finally Room 702A, all in Holland House. Kenneth Kwok and Mok Yeuk Chi shared chambers with me in Holland House throughout that period until we finally moved to Bond Centre in 1987. After his pupillage, Patrick Chan remained in my chambers as a practising member until 1987 when he was appointed a District Court Judge. Marjorie Chui likewise practised in Room 713 for a while before she accepted appointment as a magistrate and eventually retired as such. Two other contemporaries of Kenneth Kwok and Mok Yeuk Chi at the University of Hong Kong, namely, Herman Poon and Mary Kao, also practised in our chambers at different times for short periods. Needless to say, in addition to those already mentioned, a large number of other law students and graduates also spent time in our chambers from time to time. Some were mere summer students, others served pupillage with one or other of the members of our chambers.

My son Denis returned from England in 1983 and has since remained a member of our chambers. Susan Kwan first came to Room 711B as a summer student like so many others. In due course she served her pupillage mainly with Andrew Li but also partly in London. However after completing her pupillage she elected to rejoin our chambers as a member. Last but not least Kitty Cheng also practised for a number of years in our chambers before she was appointed by the Hong Kong government as an Assistant Legal Adviser in 1991.

Today, Kenneth Kwok, Mok Yeuk Chi, Denis Yu and Susan Kwan still happily share chambers on the mezzanine floor of New Henry House. There they have been kind enough to reserve a special room for my exclusive use even though I have given up my practice certificate.

Susan Kwan is currently the Honorary Secretary of the Hong Kong

Bar Association. My son Denis and I had likewise filled that post at different times. Ironically, many years ago I was even elected Vice-Chairman of the Association for two terms at a time when its constitution did not provide for such an appointment. Kenneth Kwok also served for some years on the Bar Committee. We are truly a proud and happy family. Had it not been for my appointment to the University Grants Committee, this exceptional family of mine might never have come into existence.

Kenneth Kwok was called to the Inner Bar in 1993. Both Patrick Chan and David Yam were elevated to the High Court Bench shortly before the reversion of the territory to Chinese sovereignty.

After 1 July 1997, Patrick Chan became the first ever Chief Judge of Hong Kong under Chief Justice Andrew Li.

27 *My Family and the Bar*

My family has had an intriguing history in the study and practice of law. In the days of the First World War, my father had enlisted as a law student at Gray's Inn in London, but before he got any further with his legal education, unforeseen circumstances compelled him to return to Hong Kong thus effectively putting an end to any likelihood on his part of pursuing his career at the Bar. My eldest brother, Pak Chuen, on the other hand, took his Law Tripos at Pembroke College in Cambridge in the early 1930s, and was in due course called to the English Bar at Inner Temple in London. But apparently he had done so entirely out of deference to my father's wishes having neither any desire nor intention to put his legal knowledge into practice. True enough, after the episode at Cambridge and Inner Temple and for the rest of his life, he consistently followed a professional soldier's career, and never gave any thought to practising law. When I matriculated in 1938, Hong Kong was still a long way from having its first law school. At one stage, it was doubtful whether I could afford my post-secondary education even at the local university, not to say reading law in England. For me, before the war the question of qualifying as a barrister simply did not arise. In 1946, however, after my acceptance by Merton College, my father repeatedly urged me to read law with the view to making my living at the Bar. Obviously he dearly wished one of his sons to accomplish what he himself had been denied the opportunity of doing. For valid reasoning at the time, I elected instead to read PPE. Yet no more than twenty months later, I ended up cramming for the Bar in the last lap of my scholarship as if my life depended on it. If I had only heeded my father's advice initially, I would have been spared much of the toiling and sweating while preparing for my Bar Examinations all on my own at Lincoln's Inn.

Strange as it may seem, history almost repeated itself when, in 1975, my son Denis had to decide what to do next after graduating at Merton in English. At the time, I gladly invited him to join me at the Bar. I pointed out that my chambers, my staff, and my library would all be there to welcome him when he qualified. Instead, he chose to become a chartered accountant, and proceeded to qualify as such in near record time. However, after working for several years in London with the firm then known as Thompson McLintock & Co., (now Peat Marwick McLintock) Denis surprisingly came to the conclusion that practising as a barrister would suit him better than as an accountant. Accordingly he went back to school to read law and was in due course called to the English Bar at Lincoln's Inn. In 1983, he was admitted to practise in the Courts of Hong Kong, and has since happily remained in practice at the local Bar as a member of his father's chambers. It is a little ironical that of the three generations of my family, Denis and I who had each in turn cold-shouldered the law originally, and undertaken instead an alternative course of studies, should be the ones who ended up practising at the Bar.

At a time when little was known at large by the people of Hong Kong about the study and practice of law, I owed it to my father for initiating me into an otherwise altogether alien profession in which I duly found success and happiness. The influence of his long-professed interest in the Bar and his repeated prompting could not be overlooked. If he had been less persistent, the Bar might never have entered into my calculations in choosing my ultimate career. It would seem that I have similarly influenced Denis into changing his profession despite a flying start in accountancy. He says that his interest in the Bar was kindled as he sat in court on one occasion listening to one of my cases. He has never regretted his decision to join the legal profession or his father's chambers. The story of my family and the Bar is indeed not without its romance and its twists and turns. It was my father who had started our connection with Merton College and, indeed, the law. What a pity he did not live long enough to witness his grandson Denis holding the family flag high at his alma mater as well as the Bar. It would undoubtedly have given him endless satisfaction and pride.

After my father retired from government service in the 1950s, his health sadly began to fail. He gradually lost the use of his legs, and after a while had to be helped in order to be seated from day to day in his favourite armchair. During this period I spent most of my weekends with him until he finally faded altogether and passed away in 1966. It was tragic that in his retirement and ill-health, he had no hobbies or other activities to kill time and surprisingly few friends for company. Soon I was more than gratified to discover that he dearly loved hearing about my court cases and thoroughly enjoyed discussing them with me. My father read his newspapers avidly every day. From some of the questions he raised with me, it was obvious that he had retained a lively interest in the law and the Bar and fully apprehended every reported detail in all my cases. I would like to believe that discussing them with him did not just keep his mind more agile and alert; it obviously also pleased him to be consulted by his son in his own profession. Ere long these discussions became our favourite pastime and regular weekly routine. Surprisingly my father was not the only one who benefited from them because not infrequently I found that his enlightening impartial views accurately mirrored those of the court which I could readily turn to my advantage.

Those were very happy intimate occasions I shared with my father in the twilight of his life despite his fast deteriorating health. I cannot recall spending so much time singly and joyously with him during any other period. In after years I have often indulged in the belief that the progress, however limited, I made in the first fifteen years of my practice at the Bar did not altogether disappoint the expectations of a proud parent before he passed away. Nonetheless, I cannot help suspecting that my father must have gone to his grave wondering why his son had not applied to take silk and become a QC, that is to say, a Queen's Counsel.

28 *The Institution of Silk*

The institution of Silk is almost as old as the Bar itself. By creating a class of members with a higher ranking status called Queen's Counsel, it has had the effect of dividing the profession into a Senior and a Junior Bar. The Senior Bar, sometimes described as the Inner Bar, comprises exclusively those former members of the Junior Bar who have been appointed Queen's Counsel, while the Junior Bar is made up of the remaining ordinary members.

By convention, members of the Junior Bar of not less than ten years' standing can apply to be appointed Queen's Counsel so as to be admitted to the Senior Bar. The convention is known as applying 'to take silk', an expression derived from the fact that a successful applicant dons a silk gown and waistcoat in court which distinguishes him from his hitherto fellow ordinary members of the Junior Bar who wear only common stuff gowns. Consequently Queen's Counsel are frequently and conveniently referred to in everyday speech simply as 'silks'.

In England, applications to take silk are made to the Lord Chancellor. In Hong Kong, applications hitherto have been to the Chief Justice. Appointments of Queen's Counsel are made by Letters Patent, signed, in England by the Queen, and in Hong Kong, formerly by the Governor on behalf of the Queen, subject to an oath of loyalty being taken, after which the appointees will be entitled to the privilege of having the initials QC appearing after their name. However, the relationship between a silk and royalty does not thereby extend beyond his oath of loyalty, his appointment by Letters Patent, the name Queen's Counsel, and the deployment of the initials QC.

With the reversion of Hong Kong to Chinese sovereignty on 1 July 1997, naturally no more appointments of Queen's Counsel will be made in the territory; the very title will be anomalous. However legislation was enacted on the eve of the reversion to retain the institution of silk locally by replacing the name and status of Queen's Counsel with that of Senior Counsel hereafter. In future Senior Counsel in the Special Administrative Region of Hong Kong will simply be appointed by the Chief Justice after consultation with the Chairman of the Bar Council and the President of the Law Society. Queen's Counsel hitherto practising as such in our courts will be enabled to practise as Senior Counsel hereafter.

I can hardly wait to see whether Senior Counsel so appointed hereafter will want to have the fatuous initials SC appearing after their name. Legislation has also provided for the appointment of Honorary Senior Counsel in future. I hope I will be forgiven for saying that even though the name Queen's Counsel is not strictly what it purports to be, at least it has its attractions; Senior Counsel, like Senior Citizen, regrettably is neither colourful nor impressive, while Honorary Senior Counsel in my humble view borders on the ludicrous. For the benefit of the Chinese public of Hong Kong, it has been proposed to translate Senior Counsel into Chinese as 資深大律師 meaning barrister of vast experience. It may be a little difficult to lend oneself to this proposed translation. To say the least, it reflects unfairly on members of the Junior Bar many of whom are certainly no less experienced.

Although my father was never called to the Bar, as a law student at Gray's Inn he must have been familiar with the scenario involving the Senior and the Junior Bar. Somehow he and I never touched on the subject of taking silk notwithstanding the frequent and regular legal discussions we held in the latter part of his life. As far as my professional status was concerned, however, there was little doubt where his expectations lay.

When, on the eve of my departure from the Legal Department, my son Denis arrived in this world in December 1952, my father, as head of the family, named him 國充 (Quok Chung). At a time when the Chinese mainland was plagued by poverty and destitution left behind by years of historic wars both civil and otherwise and aggravated by teething problems of a new regime, my father appeared to be expressing a wish thereby to see his mother country both rich and prosperous. Surprisingly he went out of his way in addition to spell out, no doubt for my benefit, and indeed that of his grandson, the English romanization of those two Chinese characters, namely, Quok Chung, the initials of which are Q.C.

This latter gesture by my father, meaningfully timed at the commencement of my practice at the Bar, could only imply an earnest desire and hope on his part to see, in due course, a Queen's Counsel appointed in the family, primarily no doubt in the person of his son, but perhaps in the course of time in the person of his grandson as well.

If this surmise was correct, very regrettably my father was doomed to disappointment at least where I, his son, was concerned. The unfortunate aspect of the matter was that ever since my student days at Lincoln's Inn, I have held views regarding the institution of silk which must have differed from those of my father, judging from his choice of initials for my son Denis. Personally I have never entertained any desire or intention to be appointed to the Senior Bar. I have always felt that if I am to be known or at all remembered at the Bar, I would like it to be for what I have achieved without having to apply for recognition of such achievement. To this day, my only regret is that I did not have the courage to convey those feelings to my father. It would at least have lessened any disappointment he might have felt about his son never rising above the status of the Junior Bar.

I am only too aware that those views and feelings of mine are distinctly unconventional and shared only by a minority at the Bar. Attaining distinction and recognition in one's profession is rarely unwelcome, especially if it also promises financial gain. It is hardly surprising that the tradition of taking silk has been customarily looked forward to by members of the Bar as a coveted event in their career. A Queen's Counsel not only instantly becomes a renowned and awe-inspiring lawyer in the public eye because it is suggested by the very name, but is also entitled to charge higher fees. Little wonder that right through the ages there has been no shortage of applicants to be so appointed.

The mere fact that I had no desire for such appointment does not in any way imply criticism of those who feel otherwise about this long-standing customary practice at the Bar. It is just that I felt unable myself to accept or follow such practice. I hold great respect for many of the silks whom I know and with whom I have come into contact professionally. I admire them for their expert knowledge of those aspects of the law in which they specialize, their professional competence, industry, advocacy, and judgment, of which I have personal knowledge and experience. However my admiration and respect for them would not have been any less if they had remained among the rank and file of the Junior Bar as I have done. Only the public could possibly conclude that a lawyer compels greater respect for the sole reason of being a Queen's Counsel.

When application is made for silk, the following procedure applies. In England the Lord Chancellor invariably consults with noted members of the judiciary in the particular sphere of the law where the applicant is known to practise, while extensive investigations are not infrequently conducted among various cross-sections of the legal community. In Hong Kong the Chief Justice in the past decade at least used to appoint an ad hoc committee, that is to say, one specially named for the particular purpose, to assist and advise him in deciding whether or not to grant any such application. The members of this committee would include a judge from the Court of Appeal, one High Court judge, the Attorney-General, and a representative each from the Bar and the Law Society.

It will be seen, whether in England or in Hong Kong, that approval of applications for silk is based, not on any accepted standard or objective test, but on the subjective opinion of a number of individuals consulted who may or may not have personal knowledge and experience of the respective applicants' professional competence and expertise. Since these applications necessarily relate to the applicants' practice record spread over ten or more years, even if there exists some personal knowledge and experience, it cannot be expected to extend over the whole ten-year period, so that judgment thereon must perforce be founded, at least to some extent, on reputation and belief. Consequently, until and unless such an accepted standard or objective test can be found and applied, the quality of the appointments of Queen's Counsel made is bound to vary considerably from time to time. Perhaps this explains why sometimes there are almost as many members of the Senior Bar milling around who do not command the respect of their peers as those who do.

Admittedly laying down such an objective standard or test would by no means be easy. However this is no excuse for disregarding the need for it if the institution of silk is expected to command uniform respect. Had there been any such standard or test, those who hold unconventional views such as mine might feel differently about taking silk.

Speaking for myself, I fail to see any need to divide the profession into a Senior Bar and a Junior Bar, save perhaps for egotistic reasons. Nor can I be reconciled to the notion and practice whereby a professional man can be enabled to distinguish himself in his profession by personally applying for elevation to a higher ranking status. If his reputation is so well-established and readily supported by known record, what further need is there to apply for public recognition unless the purpose is to advertise his success and expertise to the public. In my days and indeed for a very long time hitherto, even professing to be a barrister-at-law in one's visiting card would be contrary to the etiquette of the Bar. Yet from time immemorial, members of the Senior Bar have been advertising their higher ranking status as Queen's Counsel by adopting the initials QC after their name.

In the medical profession before a general practitioner can hold himself out as a specialist in any particular field, he will be required to pass various stiff examinations set by acknowledged specialists in those fields. Hence the examinations set by the Royal College of Physicians, the Royal College of Surgeons as well as other recognized institutes. The Bar seems to be the only profession in which members can apply to have themselves elevated to a higher ranking status based on a number of years of successful practice. It would be interesting to see the reaction of other professions to a suggestion that doctors, architects, engineers, and accountants could apply to be similarly appointed to a higher ranking status in their respective professions after ten or more years of successful practice, and be enabled to dress with a recognized difference in public in order to distinguish them from their professional colleagues.

The following two events which took place a little while ago may be of interest. I sincerely hope that I shall be forgiven for recounting them. The etiquette of the Bar requires any member intending to take silk to notify those whose names appear ahead of his in the Bar list. Over the years I have received many a letter of such notification. On one occasion a long-standing and family friend of mine at the Bar for whom I have always had the greatest respect and admiration as a fellow practitioner wrote to me in the following terms; he said that while 'as an acknowledged legend' in the profession I had no need for further recognition, he was only 'a humble mortal' and therefore had decided to follow the customary practice of applying to take silk. While his legendary reference was no doubt unduly flattering, although I am sure he meant well, he was unnecessarily modest about himself, because he was one of the best-known and most successful members of the local Bar. Rightly or wrongly I took his apologetic and over-kind remark to imply that he did not altogether disagree with my well publicized views and feelings about the institution of silk.

The second event took place one morning in the Robing Room of the Supreme Court when the place was packed with lawyers and full of noise and activity. In the midst of this commotion, a remark was heard to be made by one of our silks referring to a particular absent member of the local Junior Bar as being 'definitely silk material'. I could not explain why, but at the time the said remark struck me as being particularly condescending and I spontaneously laughed aloud. Not surprisingly there was a momentary hush in the packed room, at the end of which a London silk who knew me well and who has since been appointed to the Court of Appeal in England said in a meaningful voice, 'I see your point, Patrick. What indeed is silk material!'

D.A.L. Wright[1] is one of my best friends at the Bar. An Irishman who came to Hong Kong in 1947, he has hardly left the island since, except when he ventures across the harbour for racing or golfing. He was not only a first-class lawyer and advocate, but also easily the most popular, the best liked, and a universally respected member of the local Bar. He has made more friends than most people in this multinational community of Hong Kong. I first met Leslie, as he is commonly known to all his friends, in 1950 shortly before I went to Kuala Lumpur. At the time he had his chambers in Marina House (now Edinburgh Tower). It was the practice in those days for all newcomers to the Bar to pay respect calls on every member previously called in the Bar list. Almost from the moment I introduced myself to him in his chambers, Leslie and I became friends. That friendship seems to have grown warmer each year as time went by. My Irish name, our mutual Irish friends in Wah Yan College, and our common interest in horse-racing have probably all played a part in cementing that friendship, one of the many happy features of which is that neither of us has ever wanted to apply for silk. I have always found it particularly comforting that Leslie, of all the others, should be one of the minority at the Bar who like myself evinced a singular lack of enthusiasm to become a member of the elite echelon of the Bar.

Over the years, Leslie had served regularly on the Bar Committee, and from time to time rendered invaluable advice and services to the Bar Association. In 1994, he was most deservedly voted a Life Member of the Hong Kong Bar Association for his sterling example and priceless contribution to the Local Bar. I was more than flattered and surprised to receive a similar contemporaneous award. Until then only the late Leo D'Almada e Castro QC who founded the local Bar Association had been so honoured. In 1996, Sir Oswald Cheung QC, the late Brook Bernacchi QC, and Albert Sanguinetti were likewise made Life Members. The last named was another member of the local Junior Bar who, like Leslie and myself, was never interested in taking silk.

As of today, of the four surviving Life Members of the Hong Kong Bar Association, surprisingly only one is a silk.

---

1. Mr D.A.L. Wright sadly passed away on 22 February 1998.

29 *Looking Ahead*

Now that 1 July 1997 has become a date in history, and Hong Kong has at law and in fact reverted to Chinese sovereignty, the world must be waiting to see whether, and if so, how far this novel idea of 'one country, two systems' is going to work out. To me, it seems that the very idea itself signifies nothing less than a healthy political as well as ideological acknowledgment of differences while allowing them to coexist in harmony. Such acknowledgment is the basis and beginning of democracy. Being an optimist, I cannot see how, given free rein and with the best of intentions, it can fail to produce the most desired of results, barring unexpected adverse factors setting in to render that harmony untenable. I hope that the passing away of patriarch Deng Xiaoping who initiated this novel idea will not prevent its adoption and perhaps further development on the mainland.

Especially for lawyers and Hong Kong belongers like myself, one of the most gratifying aspects of the Sino-British Declaration must necessarily be the undertaking to perpetuate the system of jurisprudence hitherto applied in Hong Kong, because so little is known about Chinese law and its practice. It was therefore not in vain that the Basic Law was drafted and adopted. This represents the codified law to be administered in the territory. Once this codification is accomplished, I find myself looking forward to a new era in the legal history of Hong Kong to be ushered in by the departure of the British Colonial Government and the setting up of the Special Administrative Regional Government. My reasons for so looking forward are strictly non-political.

Our system of jurisprudence has hitherto closely followed that in England. Not so our system of judicial appointments. In England judges are all appointed from and represent the best of the Bar. In Hong Kong, for more than a century and a quarter, a totally different system applied; during this period, our judges were invariably appointed from the Colonial Legal Service which was a separate entity from and had nothing to do with the local Bar. It comprised members who had joined the service as Magistrates or Crown Counsel in one or other of the British colonies or other parts of the British Commonwealth, and had worked their way up the hierarchical ladder.

It was not until 1977 that the first member of our local Bar was appointed to the High Court Bench although two such appointments had been made to the District Court Bench in 1973. This appointment in 1977 appeared, however, to be no more than a token concession to the local Bar because in the years which immediately followed, the only additional High Court appointments made by the Colonial Legal Service were from the English Bar instead.

I myself was offered appointment to the High Court Bench by three different colonial Chief Justices, namely, Sir Ivo Rigby in 1970–1, Sir Geoffrey Briggs in 1973, and finally Sir Denys Roberts in 1979. But on each occasion our dialogue broke down as soon as I insisted on being granted equal terms with the expatriate judges. I was thus denied the privilege of ending my legal career on the Bench in the manner that members of the English Bar commonly cap a successful practice.

Although in the last decade or so of British rule, there was a distinct welcome change in our judiciary with an appreciable number of appointments of members of the local Bar to the High Court and District Court Bench, it was unbelievable that varying degrees of distasteful discriminatory terms of employment still prevailed, noticeably in the District Court and the Magistracies, to the very end.

It is against this background that I have confessed to looking forward to the incoming new era in our legal history after 1 July 1997. The conclusion of colonial rule in Hong Kong will surely mark the end of discrimination once and for all, while in the award of judicial appointments, especially in the High Court, the local Bar will no longer be overshadowed hereafter as hitherto by the Colonial Legal Service, and will at long last be enabled to follow the practice in the United Kingdom in having such appointments made altogether from among the best of its practising members.

Having said all that, I must make it known that notwithstanding the imperfections of the Colonial Legal Service, and discrimination apart, we have had not a few eminent colonial judges for whom members of the local Bar have had the greatest respect. Names such as Mr Justice

Gould, Mr Justice Mills-Owen, Mr Justice Huggins and Mr Justice McMullin immediately spring to mind and were only a few examples. They not only were first-class lawyers, but constantly manifested the best of judicial temperament and attitude when holding court.

The strength of the legal system in any territory depends of course on more than the mere appointment of judges from the Bar. When I was called to the local Bar in 1950, there were less than a dozen practising members, mainly because until 1969, the British Colonial Government had not seen fit to make a single law school available in the territory to produce even a reasonably sized Bar, not to say an adequate number of members for recruitment into the judiciary. We all know of course that law schools do not merely teach law as a subject and produce lawyers as a profession but also play an indispensable part in educating the public better to understand and appreciate the rule of law. Today there are two separate law schools in the territory. It is hardly surprising that unlike in the days of my admission, the Hong Kong Bar is now more than 600 strong, and ought certainly to be healthy enough to provide the necessary recruits for our judiciary. It may be commonplace to observe that the importance can hardly be over-emphasized of the need to maintain a high academic standard among our law students from whom alone a steady flow of able and competent members of the Bar can be expected. It is only by sustaining a strong and adequate local Bar that the territory can count on having a respected judiciary.

Many years ago I was a member of the language committee appointed to investigate for the first time the feasibility of using Chinese in our courts. I was then of the view that whereas Chinese could conveniently be used in proceedings involving purely factual disputes, there was no way it could replace the English language in arguments and submissions on law. Today I am still of the same view.

As someone who can lay modest claim to being bilingual, I cannot help being keenly aware of the many legal concepts and terms under our system of jurisprudence which have no corresponding equivalents in the Chinese language, so that even the best of translation cannot do full justice to some of the thoughts and ideas they are calculated to convey. As arguments and submissions as well as learned judicial decisions in law necessarily involve explorations into the limitations of such concepts and terms, Chinese is hardly a suitable language in which to conduct these inevitable exploratory exercises. Furthermore case law and legal precedents as well as textbooks on law all form an essential part of our system. As there is no practical possibility of translating all law reports and textbooks in English into Chinese, it is difficult to imagine how legal arguments and submissions can adequately and properly be placed before the court other than in the English language.

It is not unnatural and hardly surprising, especially now that Chinese as much as English has been declared to be an official language in Hong Kong, that voices have been heard from members of the overwhelmingly Chinese public favouring a greater and perhaps even an exclusive reliance hereafter on the Chinese language in our legal proceedings. For the reasons set out in the preceding paragraphs, it is my view that until and unless a better system of jurisprudence can be found to replace our Basic Law, the English language can never be entirely dispensed with in our courts. On the contrary, I sincerely hope our law students will make sure that they possess as much an adequate command of the English as the Chinese language if they wish to become competent legal advocates and practitioners. Indeed it is not in vain and for good reason that bilingualism has been specifically provided for in our Basic Law.

After 1 July 1997, the authorities on the mainland must be watching over us with even greater interest than ever. In upholding the rule of law in this territory, let us do our special best to demonstrate not only the proficiency of the system of our jurisprudence but also of the overall new network of our law schools, our legal profession and our judiciary system operating for the first time under a Chinese Chief Justice appointed from the local Bar. It would be a most worthwhile reward if as a result of our example other regions on the mainland can be persuaded to borrow a chapter or two from our book and adopt the same as their own.[1]

---

1. In February 1998 Chief Justice Andrew Li was reported to have made it known that steps are being considered to upgrade the terms of employment of all local judges and magistrates in the territory to the level of the expatriates. If and when this upgrading materializes, it will put an end at last to the colonial discrimination left behind in our judiciary by the British colonial government.

Patrick (right) and family in 1933

Ping Tsung, Brian, Josephine, Margaret and Patrick in Coronation Terrace, 1926

Patrick as Portia in Merchant of Venice *produced by Fr Sheridan SJ at Wah Yan College, 1936*

Patrick in military uniform in Qujiang, 1944

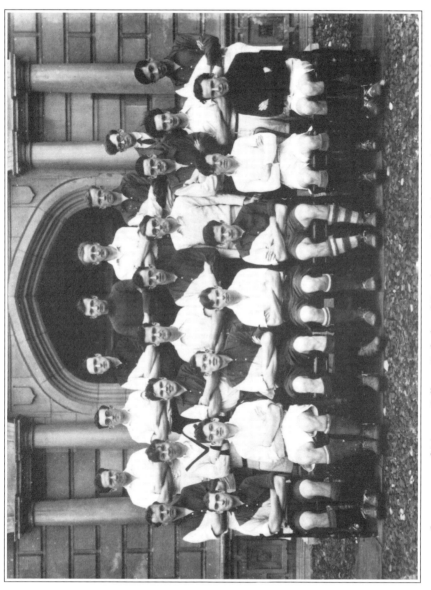

Soccer teams of Merton College, Oxford and Peterhouse, Cambridge outside Peterhouse, 1947

Patrick on a punt at Oxford shortly before he fell into River Isis

Called to English Bar in January 1950

*Patrick and Lucia emerging from the Catholic Cathedral in Canie Road
after their nuptials on 23 February 1952*

Patrick and Lucia at home in Bowen Mansions in April 1997

Patrick and Lucia, their four children and respective spouses, and their seven grandson at Bowen Mansions, April 1997. The only absentee was their son-in-law Dr Richard Cauldwell in Birmingham University.

Part Two

Introduction

The following is a collection of actual court cases in which I was involved as Counsel. To the best of my recollection and belief each account accurately reflects what took place in and out of court at the time. These eight cases are chosen primarily because each of them differs somewhat from the majority of run-of-the-mill criminal trials, and can be said to have a distinct flavour of its own. I have not included any civil case because civil procedure is a trifle technical and complicated, and makes tedious and laborious reading. Civil cases also take up too much space and are hardly suitable for inclusion in a work such as this.

To the lay mind, especially of a Chinese, a person charged with a criminal offence can only be either guilty or innocent. Under our system of jurisprudence, however, there is more often than not a third alternative. In any criminal trial, unless and until a person is found guilty beyond reasonable doubt on the evidence presented, he will be entitled to be discharged as being 'Not Guilty' of the offence with which he stands charged. The question of whether he is innocent simply does not arise because at law every person is presumed to be innocent until the contrary is proven. I hope these cases will help the lay reader to understand better one of the cardinal principles in our criminal law.

I have named these eight cases separately and individually, and added a few observations of my own at the beginning and conclusion of each of them, which, I hope, will further enhance their interest.

1 The Case of the Suicide Pact

There are those who believe in the jury system, and there are those who do not. I have no reservations about belonging to the first camp.

It is not without good reason that the jury system has survived the test of time in so many parts of the world. Its strength lies essentially in the fact that so long as humans cannot avoid misjudging or being biased from time to time, it is far less likely for all the members of a jury acting jointly to err than a single judge.

However, this view is not always shared by judges, some of whom have no faith whatever in juries. One particular judge in Hong Kong, who is no longer with us, said publicly more than once that if he had had his way, he would have abolished the jury system altogether. He was known to have thrown down his wig and stalked out of court whenever, contrary to his expectation, a not guilty verdict was returned by a jury in his court.

In the 1970s, he was a member of the law reform committee. Just because he disapproved of the jury's verdict in a civil law suit involving the law of passing-off, in which he was not even the trial judge, he immediately set about amending the relevant provisions in the Code of Civil Procedure governing jury trials. As a result, it is almost impossible nowadays to have a jury trial in our courts in ordinary civil cases other than libel actions.

It seems that it had never occurred to this particular judge that he was only human and could have been wrong instead of the jury in at least some of the instances where they had disagreed with him.

Besides, the overwhelming majority of our witnesses, especially in criminal trials in Hong Kong, are Chinese who give their evidence in Chinese. Although in those days the only official language of our courts was English and all evidence given in Chinese had to be translated into English through a court interpreter, the advantage which a bilingual juror must surely enjoy over an expatriate non-Chinese speaking judge in being able to put a proper interpretation on crucial intonations or inflections of Chinese speaking witnesses could hardly be over-emphasized.

I am not pretending for a moment that juries have not returned strange verdicts. They have. But so have judges. In my experience, there are certainly no fewer perverse verdicts pronounced by judges than juries.

On the other hand, I would be the first to concede that there is also no shortage of judges who approach the law with the greatest humanity and sensitivity. The case I am going to write about is a good example.

This was one of my earliest cases. I can no longer recall the name of my client, or the year in which the relevant events took place. But I shall long remember the hearing date, which was 27 December, the trial judge who was Mr Justice Wicks, and the jury of three men and four women in the case.

The Legal Aid Department had not yet come into existence in those days. Unrepresented criminal cases in the High Court were assigned by the Chief Justice to members of the Bar by rotation as Pauper Cases, and I was assigned as defence counsel in this case.

The defendant was a married woman in her late thirties, and the loving mother of a nine-year-old son. She worked in a toy factory, while her husband was a cashier in an import and export firm.

This small family was a reasonably happy one, until the husband began taking drugs. First, he lost his job as a result, and could not find another. To replace his lost earnings in order to maintain the family, the defendant took on an extra job in the evening washing dishes and helping to clean up generally in a restaurant.

Unfortunately, this did not altogether resolve her problems. The husband's unemployment continued, and so did his craving for drugs. He forced her to pay over the greater part of whatever she earned to enable him to satisfy his craving, and in the course of time started to abuse her unless she came up with more money for him.

As time went on, he became more and more violent and demanding, and she, less and less able to cope with him. When one day he threatened her with a knife to make her agree to be a call girl in order to provide yet more money for him, she could not withhold her misery any longer, and confided in a friend of hers in the factory where she worked.

To the defendant's utter amazement, her friend revealed that she was experiencing a similar fate in her family. The mother of a six-year-old son, she, too, was being maltreated by her husband who would beat her unless she gave him every dollar she earned to buy drugs. Recently he had similarly tried to force her to stoop to prostitution just to provide him with more money.

This was indeed beyond forbearance, and the two women decided to end their misery by committing suicide together in a hotel room.

Each woman wrote a parting letter to her son, explaining what had caused her to take this tragic step, apologizing for not being able to look after him any more, and expressing the hope that he would grow up to be a better man than his good-for-nothing father.

They then locked themselves in the hotel room, and each consumed a full bottle of insecticide. Their moaning and groaning after drinking the poison attracted the attention of the hotel staff, who broke open the door, and rushed the two women to hospital.

The defendant surprisingly survived, but her friend died.

In those days, if two people agreed to enter into a suicide pact, and one of them died, the survivor would be chargeable with murder. Hence the trial in this instance.

It might seem hard to charge the survivor of a suicide pact with murder. But the circumstances of suicide pacts could vary substantially.

This state of the law would be more than justified in those cases where one party would benefit materially from the death of another, and would thus be motivated to persuade the latter to enter into a sham suicide pact, so that by surviving, the former would be enabled forthwith to collect that benefit, e.g. a scheming young heir luring his rich and sick old uncle to enter into a suicide pact with him.

However, in the absence of any such sinister motive, one might expect the law to follow a different course.

In those days the death penalty for murder was mandatory. In appropriate circumstances the Governor could, of course, either commute such death penalty to a gaol sentence, or even grant an executive pardon for any conviction and sentence.

Before the trial, prosecution counsel Graham Sneath invited me to consider advising my client to plead guilty to the charge, as there did not appear to be any defence. In that event, he promised that he would secure an executive pardon for her from the Governor.

I thanked him on behalf of my client, but told him that I would prefer to try to get her acquitted on the charge, because I genuinely felt she should not have been prosecuted in the first place.

Graham Sneath regretted that whether my client should or should not be prosecuted was unfortunately no longer a decision within his power to make. All the same, he wished me and my client the best of luck in the case, adding that his promise to secure an executive pardon for the defendant would still hold good even if the jury should return a guilty verdict against her.

Graham Sneath had read law at Cambridge, and was a former colleague of mine in the Legal Department. He was a brilliant lawyer and advocate, and a gentleman of great integrity with a keen sense of justice. He took silk in 1962 and was appointed Solicitor General in 1966. He would undoubtedly have in due course become an outstanding Attorney-General, if in 1970 he had not had to go on early retirement for personal reasons. He subsequently took up a senior academic appointment in the Faculty of Law at Bath University in the United Kingdom, which he held until shortly before his death at the beginning of 1995.

The foregoing dialogue between Graham Sneath and myself told me two things. First, the decision to prosecute my client in spite of the tragic circumstances of the case had obviously been made by his superior officer Mr Alastair Blair-Kerr who then headed the prosecution section of the Legal Department, and to whom no doubt the Attorney-General must have delegated the prerogative power to decide whether or not to prosecute. Second, opinion within the department was obviously divided as to whether this decision had been rightly made.

After her discharge from hospital and pending trial, the defendant was detained at the Lai Chi Kok Remand Prison for Female Prisoners, where I visited her on two separate occasions. The first visit was undertaken with the primary object of meeting her, and scanning the material facts of the case with her to make sure that nothing had been overlooked on which the eventual result of the trial might hinge. This was duly done.

Although the defendant could tell me nothing new in connection with the case, I was happy to learn that a Jesuit priest had visited her time and again both in hospital and at the remand centre, and had succeeded in inspiring in her a totally fresh outlook on life.

Apparently, he had prevailed on her husband to accept treatment for his drug addiction at one of the government clinics, and arranged for periodic visits to be made by a Catholic social welfare officer to the defendant's home to attend to some of the more immediate needs of her nine-year-old son.

It was evident that despite the tragedy which had overshadowed her life hitherto, the defendant's tender feelings for her husband still lingered, so that she readily welcomed the news of his willingness to submit to treatment. She also found warmth and comfort in the knowledge that at any time she secured her release from gaol, a suitable job would be waiting for her at one of the Catholic institutions.

It would certainly appear that her vain suicide attempt and all these subsequent happenings had given the defendant new courage to grapple with the harsh realities of life, as she kept asking me when she would be allowed to go home and be reunited with her son.

I had considerable difficulty explaining to her the nature and gravity of the offence with which she stood charged, and consequently, why no bail could be granted.

She was at a loss to understand why she should be charged with murder at all, as her attempt at suicide was aimed merely at putting an end to the misery and pressure to which she had been subjected, and she had never intended any harm to come to anybody, especially to her dear unfortunate friend.

Now that she had returned from the brink of death, she was very disturbed to hear from her fellow inmates at the remand centre that she would be hanged if convicted, and hastened to inquire of me if that was correct. I assured her that although the penalty for murder was indeed death by hanging, she had in fact already been promised an executive pardon in the event of her being convicted.

Overall, however, the defendant was evidently much more concerned with the welfare of her son than for herself. She was full of remorse for her deceased friend, for whose demise she felt morally responsible.

She was such a loving mother and devoted wife, and such a simple decent woman that my heart truly bled for her. Thus at the end of the day, I was more determined than ever to plead on her behalf for an outright acquittal from the jury, and to win the backing of the trial judge for such plea, notwithstanding the strict letter of the law.

Before I left her, she made me promise to visit her son and see her again before the trial commenced.

Accordingly, I paid her a second visit as promised no more than a couple of days before the trial, just to let her know that I had seen her son, that he was reasonably well looked after, that he loved and missed her very much, and wanted her to know it.

The trial itself took no more than the greater part of one hearing day. There was no dispute between the prosecution and the defence on the evidence. The jury was told the story of the respective tragic lives of the defendant and her friend, and the unfortunate chain of events which led to their being found unconscious in the hotel room. The two letters left behind by the two women for their respective sons were produced in court and relied on by the prosecution as evidence of their common intent to commit suicide.

I asked no question of any of the prosecution witnesses. Nor did I object to the production of the two farewell letters to the two sons. In fact I was counting on the prosecution to produce them. As the defence called no evidence, Graham Sneath elected not to address the court again after having already outlined the prosecution case at the commencement of the proceedings. So the time arrived for me to speak up on behalf of the defendant.

I began by reminding the jury how the devotion and loyalty of the defendant to her family had only been rewarded by her husband's cowardly and despicable attempt to make her a prostitute, thereby forcing her to resort to suicide as the only escape from her misery and misfortunes.

Tragic and touching as those incidents were, none could match the impression made on the jury by the letter which the woman had left behind in the hotel room for her son. She was obviously no scholar. Nor would her letter qualify as a literary work. But this fact only served to underline its simple heart-wrenching appeal, because every line in it was genuinely packed with feeling, and every word had obviously come from the very depth of her heart.

As I read out this moving message of lingering love and impending farewell from a devoted mother to her beloved son, slowly, deliberately, and in my best voice, a hushed silence noticeably descended upon the court, and all of a sudden, I felt so charged with emotion myself that I had to pause momentarily in order to avoid losing control of my composure. It was not surprising that tears could be seen streaming down the cheeks of at least two of the four women on the jury.

I ended my address on the following note:

'Members of the jury, you may well find it surprising that this unfortunate woman, namely my client, should have been brought to court at all especially after what she had gone through in life. Of course, the Attorney-General is acting well within his authority in charging the survivor of a suicide pact with murder, as he has done in this case. Likewise on the undisputed evidence you would be perfectly entitled at law to find my client guilty of the charge before you. If you should do so, I would have no complaints. But first, let us ponder what this woman is supposed to have done to deserve being convicted of such a serious crime. The sum total of her alleged criminal conduct amounts to no more than that she and her friend had endured more hardship and humiliation than they could bear, and that they had decided to end their misery by taking their own lives in order to be spared from being forced to stoop to prostitution by, of all people, their own husbands. Can it be your wish to add further to her already innumerable misfortunes by having her condemned and stigmatized as guilty of murder for that mere attempt at suicide? Yesterday was Boxing Day. I hope, members of the jury, you have had a happy Christmas as I have. In a few days' time, you and I will be celebrating the arrival of a New Year. Let us try in our joyful moments to remember to be generous with those who are less fortunate in this world, such as my client, who is now in your hands as to whether she would be found guilty of murder or whether she could go home a free woman without a conviction on her slate. His Lordship here is well-known for his charity, and his constant regard and great sympathy for the underprivileged. But if you should find the defendant guilty as charged, he would be required by law and would have no alternative but to impose the death sentence on her irrespective of his own feelings in the case. It is only fair to let you know that in that event, Mr Sneath here has already very kindly indicated to me that he intends to advise the Governor to grant her a special executive pardon in respect of her conviction and sentence. But securing such an executive pardon would inevitably take time. She would thus have to return to gaol just to wait for officialdom to restore her freedom in due course. Meanwhile, the New Year would have come and gone, and while the poor mother lounges unnecessarily alone in custody, her nine-year-old child would have to make the best of everything at home without her love and care, and with only his drug addict father to attend to his domestic as well as other needs. I would be so much happier if you would let my client go home today to be reunited with her young son forthwith so that together they could welcome the arrival of a New Year and perhaps a new life altogether.'

Following upon my address, Mr Justice Wicks summed up the case very briefly to the jury.

Mr Justice Wicks had been a chartered surveyor before he was called to the Bar and eventually became a High Court Judge. He was known to be a very kind man, and was in particular renowned for his humanitarian outlook on life. The knowledge that the case would be heard before him had played no small part in my refusal to advise my client to plead guilty to the charge. I was banking heavily on his sympathy for the poor woman to back up my plea to the jury for an acquittal. As things turned out, he did not disappoint me.

Mr Justice Wicks not only told the jury that he agreed with every comment of mine in the case. He expressed positive regret that the Attorney-General had seen fit to charge the defendant at all. He directed the jury that although on the undisputed evidence the proper verdict in accordance with the strict letter of the law would be 'Guilty' as charged, no one could question their exclusive right to return an alternative verdict if they thought it would be more appropriate in the exceptional circumstances of the case. In other words, he left it altogether open for the jury to return a 'Not Guilty' verdict.

Not surprisingly, after the briefest consultation on the bench with his fellow members, the foreman of the jury announced a unanimous verdict of 'Not Guilty' in favour of the defendant who was accordingly acquitted.

Immediately after the defendant was discharged, all seven jurors walked over to our side of the court to wish both the defendant and myself a happy New Year, and my client, in particular, a joyful reunion with her son and the best of everything to follow. As the court adjourned, Graham Sneath also came over specially to offer me his congratulations. He then turned to tell the defendant that although she was lucky not to have been convicted, he was more than pleased with the outcome of the trial.

Needless to say, the defendant was gratitude itself, as far as I was concerned. She tried to find words to express her thanks, but simply choked with emotion as she held my hand.

I cannot recall any other suicide pact survivor being charged during my thirty odd years of practice in our courts.

In the aftermath of the case, I wrote and spoke to the Director of Social Welfare to make sure that the best would be done for my client and her son, as well as for the son of the deceased woman. I am happy to say that Mr Justice Wicks and Graham Sneath both did likewise.

The law was changed somewhat in 1963. Today the survivor of a suicide pact would only be chargeable with manslaughter. I would reiterate that the crux of the matter appears to me not to be whether the charge should be of murder or of manslaughter.

The prerogative vested in the Attorney-General to decide whether or not to prefer or proceed with a charge against a defendant is a discretionary power which necessarily implies that the manner in which it is to be exercised must depend on the particular circumstances of each case.

I simply cannot visualize the circumstances of any suicide pact in which the survivor could be more deserving than my client in the aforementioned trial to have the Attorney-General's discretion exercised in her favour in not preferring a charge at all.

Obviously I was not alone in holding this view. To say the least, Graham Sneath's offer of an executive pardon even before the trial, Mr Justice Wicks' summing up in the case, and the jury's instantaneous verdict at the end of it were all unmistakably resounding echoes of that view.

Last but not least I welcomed with open arms the happy ending to the very sad real life story in that trial, not only as a possible new landmark in the life of my client, but more particularly as a complete vindication of the jury system in which I have always placed such great faith.

2 — *The Case of the Midnight Court*

Jimmy's Kitchen is a restaurant in Hong Kong with an essentially Caucasian cuisine, situated on the ground floor of South China Building, No. 1 Wyndham Street. It may not be the favourite meeting place of gourmets and billionaires, but it is inexpensive, and commands a menu with a great variety of dishes including some with a Malaysian, Indian, as well as Chinese flavour, which entitles it to boast of a wide patronage and great popularity among the residents of Hong Kong.

I am still a regular patron of Jimmy's Kitchen at its current location, but I must say I remember it best as an elite little place in the 1950s of no more than a dozen tables, with a cockloft, that is to say, a small elevated area at the back of the restaurant reserved for regular patrons and accessible only via a wooden staircase.

In those days, it was situated at Theatre Lane facing Queen's Theatre, and was part of China Building. It was then wholly owned by one Leo Landau, who used to go round the tables every day cracking jokes with and recommending the best dishes of the day to his guests and regular patrons.

Immediately after the last war, it was one of the few places in the colony where fresh oysters were served. I remember only too well the regular luncheon meetings I had with my lawyer friends the late Leo D'Almada e'Castro, QC, Leslie Wright, and the late Frank D'Almada at Jimmy's. Those gatherings would almost invariably take place in the cockloft on Fridays.

Friday was chosen for two reasons, primarily because those were slack and leisurely days for the Bar and the legal profession at large, and every weekend would be a long one commencing from Friday afternoon, so that even an additional glass of wine or two at lunch would do no harm to anybody. Furthermore, fresh oysters were regularly flown into Hong Kong from Australia every Thursday afternoon, and Jimmy's would invariably have the best ready for its guests on the following day.

In the early and mid-1950s, among the dozen or so practising barristers listed in Hong Kong at the time, Leo D'Almada e'Castro, QC, John McNeil, QC, Leslie Wright, and Brook Bernacchi practically monopolized all the civil work in our courts.

As a newcomer to the local Bar, I had no real cause for complaint because as a result of their preoccupation with the more lucrative civil litigation, I was seldom short of briefs to appear in the criminal jurisdiction of our courts.

Frank D'Almada was a solicitor with an enormous criminal practice to whom I owed quite a number of my earlier briefs. He was a very popular member of the legal profession who alternated between practising as a solicitor and sitting as a magistrate. The latter eventuality was due to the fact that there was a distinct shortage of legally qualified magistrates in those days, and as a favour to the government, a number of legal practitioners in the private sector accepted temporary appointments as magistrates from time to time in order to help clear up the huge arrears of accumulated hawkers' summonses, parking summonses, as well as other normally uncontested matters in the magistrates courts. Contested cases would of course be adjourned to be heard by permanent magistrates.

At one of our Friday gatherings, Leo Landau came to our table, and offered free liqueurs for all of us. As we sipped our coffee and his liqueur, he said he had a favour to ask and a proposition to make.

Apparently, his cook boy Kam Yee Fai had been arrested, and charged with wounding with intent to cause grievous bodily harm. Leo Landau said he would like one of us to defend him, looking first at Leslie Wright and then at me.

Leslie Wright immediately suggested I was the man he wanted, because he was not particularly fond of jury trials. Frank D'Almada said he assumed that his firm would be required to instruct me for the defence, and asked further whether Leo D'Almada should also be retained as leading counsel in the case. To which Leo Landau replied with some embarrassment saying that it would be too expensive. What he had in mind was simply to treat us to a couple of free luncheons at the conclusion of the case.

Frank D'Almada thereupon said in that case he would see to it that a competent articled clerk of his was detailed to look into the facts and assist me in preparing the defence.

Accordingly, we parted on the understanding that Frank D'Almada's firm would instruct me to defend Leo Landau's cook boy, at the conclusion of which there would be a couple of succulent meals waiting for us at Jimmy's.

The competent articled clerk promised by Frank D'Almada turned out to be Helen Lo, the daughter of Hin-Shing Lo, a well-known magistrate. Helen Lo was not only an able budding lawyer, but also a talented opera singer in both Cantonese and English, and a competent horsewoman, whom I knew well. Hin-Shing Lo and my father were contemporaries at Cambridge and Oxford respectively during the First World War, and long-standing good friends. I was of course more than happy to have the assistance of Helen Lo in preparing the defence.

I heard no more about the case until shortly before the mid-autumn festival, when Helen Lo told me that our client Kam Yee Fai had already been committed for trial before a judge and jury in the Supreme Court, and that she was sending me a complete set of the depositions of the witnesses taken before the magistrate. After reading the depositions, I rang Helen Lo to arrange a meeting at the Victoria Remand Prison with our client.

The prosecution case could be summarized as follows. Kam Yee Fai had worked for some years for Leo Landau at his residence in MacDonnell Road, where he reported for duty every morning at about 7.30 a.m., prepared breakfast, lunch, and dinner, and washed up in the evening before leaving. There was also an amah who lived in and attended to the domestic chores of the household from day to day.

Several months before his arrest, Kam Yee Fai had gone to visit his sick father in Shanghai after recommending his friend, Yau Yiu Tim, to replace him. Upon his return to Hong Kong, he asked to be reinstated. But Yau Yiu Tim refused to quit. As a result there were quite a few unpleasant confrontations involving not only the two of them but also the amah and Leo Landau.

Prior to Kam Yee Fai's departure for Shanghai, he and the amah had been lovers. In his absence Yau Yiu Tim had replaced him not only as Leo Landau's cook boy but also as the amah's paramour. That naturally added spice to their dispute over the job.

Leo Landau took the stand that the triangular love affair was none of his business. As Kam Yee Fai and Yau Yiu Tim had both served him well, he left it to them to sort things out themselves.

Unfortunately that was exactly what the lovers were unable to do. As a result there were repeated appearances by Kam Yee Fai at MacDonnell Road. Each of those occasions led inevitably to an unpleasant exchange of angry words and mutual recriminations.

The amah would not commit herself to either of the two men, maintaining that they were both her friends and were being very silly over the whole affair. This certainly did not help to resolve the stalemate.

On the night of the alleged offence, Kam Yee Fai had turned up again at MacDonnell Road and asked to see Leo Landau shortly after 8 p.m. Leo Landau was entertaining a number of guests that evening. Accordingly he told Kam Yee Fai to call again at some other time. Instead of leaving, however, Kam Yee Fai proceeded to the servants' quarters, where Yau Yiu Tim and the amah were just preparing to serve dinner.

Shortly thereafter, there was another row between the two men and the shouting and recrimination was clearly audible throughout the house.

Leo Landau naturally went to the servants' quarters, and ordered Kam Yee Fai to leave at once, threatening to send for the police. At this juncture, Kam Yee Fai allegedly turned to Yau Yiu Tim, accused him of stealing his woman as well as his job, and warned him to watch his step thereafter. The time was then about 8.30 p.m.

The dinner party ended shortly before midnight.

After cleaning up, Yau Yiu Tim left Landau's residence, took the short cut as usual from MacDonnell Road, down the footpath alongside the Peak tram railway in order to get to the Peak tram terminal.

As he was walking along the footpath, he was attacked by someone from behind, felt a sharp pain near his waist, and fell to the ground. When he sat up, he said he could see Kam Yee Fai running away down the footpath towards the terminal and disappearing.

Yau Yiu Tim was bleeding badly and so decided not to give chase. Eventually he too made his way to the terminal, where a policeman gave him first-aid before sending him to hospital.

In consequence, Kam Yee Fai was arrested on the following day at his home in Shaukiwan, whither he claimed he had gone immediately after being told by Leo Landau to leave. He denied having threatened or attacked Yau Yiu Tim.

Upon examining Kam Yee Fai's person, and the shoes and clothes he had worn on the previous evening, the police found a recent blood smear on one of his shoes, which was however too small for testing or grouping. It was not possible even to determine if it was human blood.

Leo Landau did not know enough Cantonese or Shanghainese to say whether Kam Yee Fai had or had not threatened Yau Yiu Tim that evening, although he confirmed that the two were shouting at each other at the top of their voices. That was why he saw fit to order Kam Yee Fai to leave, as he had guests in the house whom he did not wish to upset.

The amah was not very helpful to the prosecution case. Although she confirmed that there had been disputes between Kam Yee Fai and Yau Yiu Fai, she said she did not know what it was all about. Furthermore she said that she did not hear Kam Yee Fai threaten anybody that evening.

That, then, was the sum total of the evidence against Kam Yee Fai; apart from someone from the Public Works Department, who merely produced a plan of MacDonnell Road, the footpath and the Peak tram terminal. Yau Yiu Tim had no difficulty reading and fully understanding this plan, and duly marked on it the spot where he said he was attacked and stabbed.

It sounded to me like a straightforward case of a jilted lover stabbing his rival, and I could not help wondering what defence Kam Yee Fai could put up other than a bare denial.

Alibi? Unlikely, because Kam Yee Fai lived alone and it would be difficult to find corroborative evidence. He had told the police he had gone straight home from MacDonnell Road and almost immediately to bed.

Mistaken identity? The two men were close friends and knew each other very well, so that any suggestion of mistaken identity was not likely to be well received.

Feigning the attack was out of the question, because the medical evidence was unmistakable. In fact, Yau Yiu Tim was immobilized and hospitalized for nearly three weeks.

Thus the thought did cross my mind to enquire whether Kam Yee Fai was prepared to admit the charge, and plead for leniency from the trial judge.

However as soon as Kam Yee Fai saw Helen Lo and myself at the Victoria Remand Prison, he burst out against Yau Yiu Tim saying how could anyone be so wicked and ungrateful. He had made it possible for Yau Yiu Tim to take up his job at a time when the latter was out of work and money, and was badly in need of employment. Instead of appreciating this assistance rendered to him, Yau Yiu Tim had refused to give Kam back his job in accordance with the clear understanding they had arrived at prior to Kam's departure to visit his sick father in Shanghai. Furthermore, Yau Yiu Tim had taken advantage of his absence and stolen his woman, meaning the amah at Leo Landau's residence, and had now falsely accused him of such a serious criminal offence. He alleged Yau Yiu Tim must have planned to implicate him in order to keep his job and his woman.

I could see instantly there was no point in asking Kam Yee Fai to consider changing his plea. Apart from denying the charge however, he could not help us at all otherwise with the defence. He had heard Yau Yiu Tim say at the committal that the stabbing took place after midnight along the footpath leading to the Peak tram terminal. He said that he would not dream of waylaying anybody at all, especially after midnight, because he was a timid man and particularly feared the dark. If we did not believe him, we could confirm it with Leo Landau, or the amah, or even Yau Yiu Tim.

I asked Kam Yee Fai only one question before we left him. The blood stain on his shoe: was he aware what it was and how it got there? He said that as he was a cook boy it could easily have been chicken blood or even strawberry ice-cream. I politely told him that while I would not know whether it was chicken blood, there was no way it could have been strawberry ice-cream.

I must say that Kam Yee Fai's suggestion that the blood stain might have been strawberry ice-cream demonstrated what a naive and stupid man he was. It hardly augured well if he had to go into the witness box to give evidence and submit to cross-examination. On the other hand, the simplicity with which he spoke, and the vehemence with which he accused Yau Yiu Tim of treachery, was impressive.

The next thing I decided on was to visit the scene of the crime.

The case had already been set down for hearing on the Tuesday following the mid-autumn festival long weekend. As the actual date of the mid-autumn festival happened to fall on a Sunday, the following Monday had been declared a public holiday to make up for the occasion. That visit of Helen Lo and myself to the Victoria Remand Prison had taken place during the week before the festival date, so that there were only a handful of working days left before the trial.

I suggested to Helen Lo that in order to make our visit to the scene of the alleged offence altogether worthwhile, it must be undertaken after midnight, just in case some otherwise unimportant but related incidence might turn out to be important after all. Helen Lo was most reluctant to venture out after midnight, and said so. Out of deference to me, however, she eventually agreed, but only as a result of a compromise suggestion proposed by me.

I had promised to take my wife and children on the Peak tram on Sunday evening to go to the Peak around midnight in order to watch the festival lanterns and to celebrate the mid-autumn festival there, as many people customarily did in Hong Kong every year. So, I asked Helen, would she come along, and have supper with us on the Peak after visiting the scene of the alleged offence, thus killing two birds with one stone. Put to her that way, Helen Lo said she could hardly refuse.

On the Sunday evening two days before the trial, I drove my family shortly before midnight to the Peak tram terminal compound half way up Garden Road. Helen Lo was already there waiting for us. We all caught the next Peak tram, but whilst Helen Lo and I got off at the very first stop at MacDonnell Road, my wife and children proceeded on to the Peak to wait for us to rejoin them.

From the Peak tram station where we alighted, Helen Lo and I went down to MacDonnell Road, and there took the footpath which ran almost parallel to the Peak tram railway, and walked along it all the way back to the terminal, keeping a careful lookout for anything of significance throughout our little walk.

In those days, there were a large number of big tall trees almost lining the whole length of the footpath which ran alongside the peak tram railway from the terminal to MacDonnell Road. The thick foliage of those trees provided ample cover for users of the footpath from the hot sun in the course of the day. The St John's Apartments had not yet been erected, so that the peak tram's terminal was a much more desolate spot at the time than it is today, especially in the evening. Most of those trees were subsequently cut down and disappeared, when the St John's Apartments were built and the Helena May Institute was redeveloped.

Apart from the foregoing premises, however, there was very little difference then in the general outlay in that area.

At the end of the little experiment which Helen Lo and I carried out at the footpath, neither of us was any wiser than before as to how best to proceed with the defence. The only conclusions arrived at were that there were few people along the footpath at that hour, and visibility was fairly good.

There was an unexpected turn of events on the following Tuesday, on which date the trial was originally scheduled to commence. The trial judge was suddenly taken ill, and the case had to be adjourned for fresh dates to be fixed. The original dates had not been appointed to suit my diary, because the court had not previously been notified that I was appearing for Kam Yee Fai. But when in due course fresh dates were fixed, I particularly asked for and was given certain specified dates of my choice, the reason for which will be made known to the reader shortly.

Between the adjournment of the original hearing dates and the fixing of new dates, another of our foursome luncheon dates took place at Jimmy's Kitchen.

On this occasion, I took the liberty of asking Leo Landau, perhaps somewhat improperly, as he was a prosecution witness in the case (although it was done with the knowledge and consent of prosecution counsel) whether Kam Yee Fai was known to be afraid of the dark. To which he replied, somewhat bemused, that indeed he was. He added that Kam Yee Fai was particularly afraid of ghosts, and would usually ask to leave his apartment slightly earlier than usual whenever there was little or no moon, because he would invariably avoid taking the short cut via the footpath, but would instead walk the whole distance of MacDonnell Road, down Garden Road to the Peak tram terminal. This of course bore out what Kam Yee Fai had told Helen Lo and myself at the Victoria Remand Prison.

The trial in due course took place on the rescheduled dates before Mr Justice Gregg. Prosecution counsel was Dermot Rea.

After the prosecution case had been outlined to the jury, Leo Landau was called as the first witness. He told the court that Kam Yee Fai and the amah had been working for him for some time. Several months ago Kam Yee Fai left for Shanghai, and was replaced by Yau Yiu Tim. When he returned, he had asked Yau Yiu Tim in vain for his job back. Each time this would end up in a row between the two men. On the night of the alleged offence, there was another such confrontation to the extent that Leo Landau had found it necessary to threaten to call the police. He had retired to bed shortly after midnight immediately following his guests' departure. The next thing that happened was the arrival of the police at his apartment at about 4 a.m. the next morning, to inform him that Yau Yiu Tim had been stabbed, and to ask him for a statement.

Dermot Rea then asked him to identify in turn, Kam Yee Fai, Yau Yiu Tim, and finally the amah employed by him.

In cross-examination, I asked Leo Landau to confirm, which he readily did, that Kam Yee Fai was a very mild and timid man, who was afraid of the dark, to the extent that on occasions, he would rather walk the whole distance of MacDonnell Road, down Garden Road, than take the short cut via the footpath to the Peak tram terminal. Leo Landau added that he regretted not having adopted a more positive attitude in the dispute between Kam Yee Fai and Yau Yiu Tim, and given the job back to Kam Yee Fai, who had been employed by him for so long. On the other hand, he said that Yau Yiu Tim was definitely a better cook, and he had no knowledge of any previous understanding between the two men requiring Yau Yiu Tim to quit upon Kam Yee Fai's return from Shanghai.

The amah of Leo Landau was a pretty young woman, who had obviously enjoyed playing the two cooks against each other. Under cross-examination, she denied having been the woman of either of them, or the cause of their repeated quarrels. She had heard no threat uttered by Kam Yee Fai, and furthermore said she was more than surprised to hear that Kam Yee Fai would stab anyone at all, because he had always been such a timid and mild man, who was known to be afraid of the dark, and would frequently avoid taking the footpath to the Peak tram terminal. She said both men were good friends of hers, and she did not mind which of them she worked with. She said that on the evening of the alleged offence, Kam Yee Fai was wearing a dark Hawaiian shirt and dark trousers.

The plan of MacDonnell Road, the Peak tram terminal and the footpath was then agreed upon and tendered as evidence by consent, thus leaving Yau Yiu Tim as the only remaining witness to be called for the prosecution.

Yau Yiu Tim turned out to be a somewhat aggressive man, who obviously felt rather sure of himself. He admitted that he had been out of work for a little while until Kam Yee Fai suggested that he should take his place at Leo Landau's home, but denied that there was any understanding or agreement that he should quit when Kam Yee Fai returned. In fact he said Kam Yee Fai had told him it was more than likely that he would not be returning to Hong Kong. He admitted that he was fond of the amah, and that they were lovers. He said he did not know whether or not Kam Yee Fai had previously been her lover. He denied having stolen Kam Yee Fai's woman. He said the many rows he had had with Kam Yee Fai were all because Kam Yee Fai wanted his job back, and he saw no reason why he should oblige him.

Yau Yiu Tim's account of the assault and stabbing at the footpath was very brief. He was suddenly grabbed by someone from behind, after which he felt a stinging pain in his side, as he struggled and fell. At one stage, he said he saw Kam Yee Fai's face when he struggled to sit up after being stabbed and falling to the ground. But later, under cross-examination, he corrected himself and said he never saw Kam Yee Fai's face, but only saw his back as the latter ran away. He admitted that he was in great pain as he struggled to sit up, and his main thoughts were to have his wound treated. Once again he identified the spot marked on the agreed plan of the layout in the area where he said he was attacked and stabbed.

I asked him how far his attacker had run away, when he sat up and saw his back. He said he could not say offhand. I asked whether that man was as far away from him as I was from where I stood. He was then standing in the witness box while I stood behind counsel's table. He thought for a while and agreed. I asked the trial judge to note that this was a distance of some twenty-five to thirty feet, which prosecution counsel readily agreed.

Yau Yiu Tim concluded by saying that he had no reason to make false accusations against Kam Yee Fai, and that he genuinely believed that it was in fact Kam Yee Fai who had stabbed him. On that note, I sat down. That completed the prosecution evidence.

I should mention that in the course of the trial, I had had a couple of quick conferences with Kam Yee Fai in the Supreme Court Building, and had decided on a number of things with him. After Mr Justice Gregg had given his usual advice on the three alternatives then open to the defence, I informed him that Kam Yee Fai had decided to remain silent and to call no evidence.

Mr Justice Gregg enquired whether that meant I was closing my case. I replied yes, save that before doing so, I would request him and the jury to visit the scene of the alleged offence. He asked whether that was necessary in view of the very clear official plan of that area already admitted by consent. I said that it was very, very necessary because I was asking for the visit to be made that same evening at midnight.

Mr Justice Gregg was obviously surprised, and initially very reluctant to grant my application, saying that it was ages since he last ventured out after midnight. Eventually he said he felt obliged to grant it, adding however that he hoped I knew what I was doing, because he would be very very unhappy if nothing important turned on the unusual proposed nocturnal undertaking by a court of law. I assured him he would not be disappointed.

Helen Lo could not refrain from asking me, as the court adjourned, what mysterious trump card I had up my sleeve, as her previous visit with me to the scene had produced nothing of significance. I said she would find out soon enough.

The application for the visit was made at mid-morning on the third day of the trial. Transport was immediately organized by the judge's clerk for the judge and jurors, and a time was fixed for everybody to meet again shortly before midnight at MacDonnell Road, where the steps led to the footpath.

Thus at the agreed hour, everybody involved in the case duly attended at the designated spot in MacDonnell Road. This included all the jurors, the judge, the judge's clerk, the court interpreter, Kam Yee Fai, Yau Yiu Tim, prosecution counsel, Helen Lo and myself. I was carrying my usual brief case.

As soon as the judge's clerk had ascertained that everybody was present, I led the way down the steps followed by the trial judge, his clerk, the court interpreter, and the jurors, in that order.

Shortly after the descent down the steps, I could hear a small murmur from those following me, **because it was pitch dark**.

It was the end of the lunar month, just as it had been on the evening of the alleged offence, and there was no moon whatever. This was the reason why I had particularly asked for those rescheduled dates.

I had brought along with me in my briefcase a fair number of electric torches which I produced and handed over to the other members of the party in order to light up the footpath. Not only was there no moon, but the thick foliage of the trees also completely shut out any possible light from the stars.

When we reached the spot marked on the agreed plan of the area where Yau Yiu Tim said he was stabbed, I requested that the electric torches be switched off, which was promptly done.

The court interpreter was the fourth member of the party walking behind me, and about fifteen feet away. I asked him whether he could see me at all. I should mention that I was wearing my court suit, which was no darker than the Hawaiian shirt and trousers Kam Yee Fai was wearing on the night of the alleged offence. He answered emphatically and without hesitation — 'NO!'

I asked the judge and jury to note the distance between the court interpreter and myself, and his answer to my question. The foreman of the jury thereupon volunteered the comment that visibility did not extend to beyond three to five feet from where he stood.

That brought an end to our nocturnal visit, but not before I had thanked Mr Justice Gregg for granting my application, to which he responded with a happy grin of satisfaction. I also thanked the jury and everybody concerned for taking part in the visit, and for being so patient with me. One of the jurors in turn thanked me for being so thoughtful as to bring the torches.

On the following morning, I asked the court interpreter to confirm with the lunar calendar that the date of the alleged offence had been at the very end of a lunar month. This was duly done. I thereupon formally closed the case for the defence.

As the defence had called no evidence, prosecution counsel elected not to address the jury a second time. I then made a very short speech to the jury simply inviting them on the evidence to acquit Kam Yee Fai, confident that the trial judge would back me up all the way after the visit to the footpath the previous evening.

This was followed by Mr Justice Gregg's summing-up, in which he directed the jury, inter alia, just as I expected, in no uncertain terms, that after the very enlightening and useful experience of the previous night, they should have no difficulty whatsoever in dismissing the claim of Yau Yiu Tim that he could identify his attacker as Kam Yee Fai, by just looking at his back at a distance of twenty-five to thirty feet and running away, when the visibility at the material spot at the material time could not have exceeded three to five feet.

The jury duly responded by forthwith returning a unanimous verdict of not guilty against Kam Yee Fai, who was duly acquitted and discharged.

Helen Lo was at one stage furious with me, because I had obviously visited the footpath again on a moonless night in her absence, and had kept it from her, which was exactly what I did. But she forgave me readily, when I reminded her that she had said she hated going out into the wilderness after midnight. She said she should have realized there was a full moon at mid-autumn festival, which rendered the visibility then better than otherwise. She further asked me how I first came to think of the limited visibility at the venue when there was no moon. I replied, 'Elementary, my dear Watson; Kam Yee Fai had told us that there were occasions when his fear of the dark would lead him to avoid travelling along the footpath, and Leo Landau and the amah had both confirmed it!'

After she qualified, Helen Lo had a very successful practice as a solicitor, and ended up as a district judge. Tragically, however, leukaemia in the course of time robbed us all of a very competent judge, and me, in particular, of a very good friend.

In the aftermath of the case, Leo Landau dismissed both Yau Yiu Tim and the amah, and employed a new cook boy and his wife to serve him in his MacDonnell Road residence. He decided he could not afford to have any more trouble arising out of the triangular love affair, even though Yau Yiu Tim was truly a first-class chef. As far as Kam Yee Fai was concerned, Leo Landau felt he had already done more than his due in getting lawyers to defend him on the wounding charge. But he did not forget to treat the four friends to two sumptuous luncheons, as promised, as well as Helen Lo and myself to an excellent dinner.

3 The Case of the Murder Trial without the Corpus Delicti

Just in case the reader knows as little Latin as I do, *Corpus Delicti* is the Latin for 'dead body'.

It must be difficult to imagine a murder trial without a dead body. The reason is simple. Murder is the unlawful killing of a human being with malice aforethought, and a dead body is the handiest evidence to prove death.

Secondary evidence such as photographs of the dead body might be just as good, provided that they had not been doctored or tampered with, but there must still be a dead body in the first place.

Jurists have often asked or been asked whether there could or should be a conviction for murder without the *Corpus Delicti,* because in the absence of the dead body one can hardly be satisfied beyond reasonable doubt of the death of the victim.

I suppose the answer must be in the affirmative, for circumstantial evidence of death can be just as conclusive, although there is always the danger of witnesses giving such evidence being unreliable, inaccurate or mistaken. A dead body speaks for itself and no such danger exists.

In the United Kingdom, a very long time ago, there was a notorious case in which the alleged murder victim reappeared some time after the trial very much alive, but tragically not before the person accused of his murder had been convicted and hanged.

In the days of the trial about which I am going to write, the death penalty in Hong Kong for murder was mandatory, so that a wrongful conviction would necessarily lead to a wrongful hanging.

Although the death penalty has now been abolished, irreparable damage can still result from sending a man to gaol for a murder which he did not commit, or which did not even take place.

One fine morning in 1957, as soon as a cargo boat SS Foochow sailed into Hong Kong from Shanghai, the captain of the ship immediately summoned the police to place one of his seamen by the name of Cheung Yam San, under arrest for murder.

The alleged victim of the murder was another seaman on the same ship by the name of Kong Ching Tong.

On the day the ship left Shanghai, Kong Ching Tong had failed to report for duty at his station. When his absence was reported to the captain, Cheung Yam San was immediately sent for, as he was the person last seen with Kong Ching Tong.

Before the captain, Cheung Yam San appeared to be extremely emotionally upset, and readily confessed to having killed Kong Ching Tong. He was patently remorseful, because the two of them had been close friends.

Cheung Yam San further disclosed to the captain that he and Kong Ching Tong had been involved in smuggling gold over a period of time.

In recent months, he said, Kong Ching Tong had altogether declined to account to him in respect of not only the profit made, but also the capital invested, despite Cheung Yam San's repeated requests to put an end to their joint venture. This had led to numerous heated arguments and violent quarrels.

On the day in question, another unpleasant confrontation involving the two men had taken place in their cabin. This led first to a scuffle, followed by Kong Ching Tong seizing a knife and threatening Cheung Yam San with it. Thereupon Cheung Yam San instinctively grabbed an iron bar in the room. The next thing he remembered was that Kong Ching Tong had been hit heavily on the head, had collapsed to the floor and remained motionless thereafter.

The ship had by this time just begun to move on its voyage from Shanghai. Realizing that Kong Ching Tong's failure to report for duty would shortly be noticed, Cheung Yam San immediately dragged Kong Ching Tong's body from the cabin to the side of the ship and threw it overboard to avoid discovery.

As soon as Cheung Yam San had done this, he began too late to regret it and was utterly overcome with emotion. He was still in a state of shock when he appeared before the captain.

Upon an inspection being made, the knife, the iron bar and signs of blood in the cabin and along the trail leading to the side of the ship, were found.

On arrival in Hong Kong, the captain recounted to the police what he had been told. Cheung Yam San was consequently taken ashore into police custody and in due course charged with murder.

In answer to the charge, Cheung Yam San made another lengthy confession to a police inspector, repeating more or less what he had told the captain, and saying how sorry he was to have killed his friend in a moment of anger.

The murder charge thus hinged almost exclusively on the two confessions made by Cheung Yam San: the first to his captain, and the second to the police.

Cheung Yam San had already been committed for trial before a judge sitting with a jury in the Supreme Court, when I received a phone call from Denis Remedios of Messrs D'Almada Remedios & Co. (Solicitors) to retain me as defence counsel in a very interesting murder trial, he said, in which no *Corpus Delicti* was recovered.

Denis Remedios had then newly qualified as a solicitor, and that was going to be his first jury trial.

After we had both perused the relevant depositions, Denis Remedios came to discuss the case with me in my chambers. We readily agreed that the best chance would probably be to aim at a knock-out victory by having the two confessions dismissed in a successful *voir dire*. Without the two confessions being admitted as evidence, there would be no case against our client.

A *voir dire* is an inquiry conducted by the judge at the request of the defence in the course of a trial in order to ascertain whether a confession by a defendant in a criminal case was made freely and voluntarily, or had been elicited as a result of threats or force or undue influence or fraudulent or other unfair inducement. At law, only a free and voluntary confession so found by the trial judge would be admissible as evidence against a defendant.

But first, there must be the necessary material instructions to support the application for a *voir dire* to be held. Accordingly, Denis Remedios invited me to go with him to the Victoria Remand Prison to have a conference with Cheung Yam San, and we duly went.

Regrettably, however, at our meeting with Cheung Yam San in the Victoria Remand Prison, any hope we had entertained of ruling out Cheung Yam San's two confessions, and thus the murder charge itself, were immediately dashed.

In answer to questions put to him by Denis Remedios and myself, Cheung Yam San told us that neither his captain nor the police nor anyone else had used any force or undue influence or any other unfair means to coerce or induce him to make those confessions, which were entirely free and voluntary.

A simple, uneducated, but extremely honest man, Cheung Yam San was still finding it difficult to get over the killing of his friend. He realized only too well that, in the face of his two confessions, defending him was by no means an easy task, but still besought us to do the best we could for him.

To explore whether there was an alternative defence, I specifically asked Cheung Yam San, whether he had in fact struck Kong Ching Tong in self-defence, because in his two confessions he had mentioned Kong Ching Tong seizing a knife.

Once again however, this effort of mine came to nothing, as Cheung Yam San's immediate and spontaneous reply was that Kong Ching Tong had never really attacked him with a knife, but merely looked threatening holding it in his hand.

I asked him why in that case he had struck Kong Ching Tong at all with the iron bar. He said that he was infuriated by Kong Ching Tong's flat refusal to answer questions about their joint gold venture and altogether lost his head. As soon as he saw Kong Ching Tong reaching for the knife, he had instinctively grabbed the nearest thing to hand, and hit out without thinking and hardly realizing what exactly he was doing. Everything had happened in a matter of seconds, he said, and it was at least in part spontaneous reflex action on his part.

At this stage, a sudden thought nonetheless occurred to me. I asked Cheung Yam San where he had hit Kong Ching Tong with the iron bar. 'His head,' he said. I asked him where on the head, and he indicated a spot between one of his eyes and his ear. I urged him to continue. He said there was a thud. He saw blood. Kong Ching Tong collapsed to the floor, and did not move again.

I reminded him he had said he had killed the man, and asked him why he had said so. His reply was that it was a heavy blow, Kong Ching Tong did not move again after collapsing to the floor of the cabin, and so, he naturally assumed he was dead.

I asked him the all important question what had made him assume Kong Ching Tong was dead. He repeated his earlier answer and added that even if he had not in fact died from the blow, he most probably would have drowned after being thrown overboard, unconscious, and with that sort of wound on his head.

I paused before asking him next whether he had felt Kong Ching Tong's pulse at any time. He answered in the negative.

I asked him further if he took the trouble to check whether there was any breath left in him. He replied that it had never occurred to him to do so, especially because there was so little time and everything had happened so quickly.

Before Denis Remedios and I left the Victoria Remand Prison, I told Cheung Yam San that at the trial I would like him to go into the witness box and tell the court exactly what he had just told me. I said he must not try to be clever and must limit himself to telling the truth.

It did not take long before the case came on for hearing. The trial lasted no more than a couple of days. I did not challenge any part of the prosecution case, and asked a limited number of questions only of the captain of the ship and the police inspector who had charged Cheung Yam San with murder.

I asked the captain whether his ship was still in harbour and Shanghai was still in sight when Kong Ching Tong's absence was reported to him. His answer in each instance was 'very much so' because the ship had only just begun to move.

I asked him what time of the day it was then. His reply was 'About mid-day'. 'Was visibility good?', I inquired. 'Extremely' was the answer. Likewise the weather. I asked whether he remembered if at that time there were boats, sampans, or other vessels moving about near his ship. He answered, 'Of course'. 'Many?', I asked. 'Indeed', he answered. Could he see the people and what they were doing on those boats and vessels? 'Easily and clearly', he added.

I asked him how long after his ship began moving before Shanghai and the smaller vessels went completely out of sight. He paused momentarily, before answering that he would have thought at least three-quarters of an hour.

I asked him whether by that time he had already sent for and interviewed Cheung Yam San. To which he replied that he had many things to attend to when a ship left port, so that he had to keep Cheung Yam San waiting a little while before interviewing him. 'How long?' I asked, and he replied, 'Probably a little over an hour'. 'By which time Shanghai had gone out of sight?', I asked. 'Naturally', he replied.

My questions to the police inspector were simply to establish the fact that Cheung Yam San had been completely spontaneous, straightforward, and co-operative, in answering all questions put to him relating to the case.

In passing, I would like to mention that both the captain of the ship and the police inspector appeared a little surprised, and perhaps even disappointed, at the nature and mildness of my questions.

Perhaps they too, must have realized that the two confessions of the defendant practically made up the whole of the prosecution case. Thus, they might have been expecting the defence to attempt to have them thrown out on the ground of either undue influence or pressure being brought to bear on Cheung Yam San. However, that was not to be.

After the prosecution case ended, and the trial judge had given his usual advice on the three alternatives open in those days to a defendant, Cheung Yam San elected, as advised, to give evidence on oath in the witness box.

His evidence was more or less a repeat of the two confessions he had made respectively to his captain and the police. When I asked him why he had struck Kong Ching Tong with the iron bar, where he had struck him, why he said he had killed him, why he thought he was dead, and whether he had felt Kong Ching Tong's pulse or breath at any time, his answers were exactly the same as those he gave to me at the Victoria Remand Prison.

Cheung Yam San was an impressive and a straightforward witness, and obviously made a good impression not only on the jury but also on counsel for the prosecution as well as the trial judge, because none of them asked him any questions.

I called no other evidence and accordingly closed the case for the defence.

This was followed by prosecution counsel Dermot Rea's final address to the jury. An extremely competent advocate, Dermot Rea emphasized that Cheung Yam San's own admissions in this case constituted the best evidence against him.

Dermot Rea said that in his experience he had never before come across a case in which a defendant was heard to have confessed, not once, nor twice, but as many as three times to killing the victim of the alleged murder with which he stood charged.

In this case, Cheung Yam San had admitted first to his captain, then to the police, and finally in Court, that he was responsible for the death of Kong Ching Tong.

He had not only explained why but also described how he had killed his victim. Furthermore he had added with rare honesty that Kong Ching Tong must at least have otherwise drowned after being thrown into the sea unconscious and obviously badly injured.

Therefore, Dermot Rea said, the jury should have little or no difficulty in concluding that Kong Ching Tong must have met his death one way or the other, and that accordingly Cheung Yam San was guilty of murder.

In turn I addressed the jury, and likewise laid stress not only on

Cheung Yam San's evidence, but also on that of the captain of the ship, and the police inspector, and in particular on the following aspects of the case, namely:

(a) Cheung Yam San was obviously a truthful witness as the jury could see for themselves.

(b) He had indeed confessed more than once to having killed his friend, but that did not prove that the latter was necessarily dead. The court had now heard that he had felt neither the victim's pulse nor his breath, and only thought he was dead because of the heavy blow, the bleeding head, and the fact that he had not moved again after collapsing to the floor of the cabin.

(c) Without anyone having checked Kong Ching Tong's pulse and breath, to say the least, the possibility should not be overlooked that he might merely have passed out as a result of the blow to the head, and remained unconscious between the time of the blow, and the dumping of his body overboard.

(d) In those circumstances, what happened to him after he was thrown into the sea was anybody's guess.

(e) There was no evidence to suggest that the injury to his head was necessarily fatal, or that anyone dumped overboard with such an injury must drown.

(f) Furthermore, at the time when Kong Ching Tong was thrown overboard, the ship had only just begun to move. According to the captain, even when the absence of Kong Ching Tong from his station was reported to him, the ship was still very much in harbour, and moving amidst many other vessels and much traffic. It was broad daylight; the time being about midday. The weather at the time was extremely good; so was visibility.

(g) The captain said he could see the people and what they were doing in the other vessels easily and clearly, so that it would not be unfair to assume that the same was true vice versa. In which case the dumping of Kong Ching Tong overboard could easily have been seen by the people in the other vessels. If so, there was nothing to prevent him from being picked up, especially in good weather, and thus saved from drowning at least.

(h) In the light of this possibility, and in the absence of proof that his head injury must bring about his death, it could hardly be said to have been proven beyond reasonable doubt that Kong Ching Tong must have met his death one way or the other.

(i) I cited the unparalleled tragedy of the very old English case in which the alleged murderer was hanged before the alleged murder victim re-emerged unharmed. The danger of such a tragedy being repeated in our case could hardly be overstressed.

I ended my submission on the following note:

'True, we have not heard anything from or about Kong Ching Tong up-to-date since he was thrown overboard. But this could be due solely to the so-called Bamboo Curtain cutting off all communication between Hong Kong and Shanghai. In any event, Cheung Yam San has been in custody since his arrival in Hong Kong, and no more than eight weeks have elapsed since his ship left Shanghai. Neither he nor the local authorities could in the circumstances realistically be held responsible for having failed, or be expected, to provide us with any further information about the death or otherwise of Kong Ching Tong, or his current whereabouts if he is still alive. For all we know, at this moment of time while we are busy deliberating here today on this case, he may still be recovering from his head injury in hospital in Shanghai, or perhaps even roaming the streets there in perfectly good health. All I am asking of you is to decide, whether on the evidence before you, it would be unreasonable to believe that he could still be living today as a result of what had happened.'

After the collapse of the Chinese Nationalist regime under Chiang Kai-shek in 1948, and until the introduction in the early 1970s of the so-called Ping-Pong policy of Zhou Enlai, which more or less reopened the door to China to the rest of the world, the Chinese mainland was virtually curtained off from almost all news media for more than two decades. During this period, little or nothing was known about the happenings from day to day in most parts of China. There was no way, for example, for Hong Kong to make contact with Shanghai, whether officially or otherwise, to inquire about the whereabouts or well being of someone such as the alleged murder victim Kong Ching Tong. Hence the worldwide use of the expression Bamboo Curtain to distinguish it from the Iron Curtain in Eastern Europe.

Mr Justice Gregg summed up the case extremely fairly. He told the jury that on the evidence they might feel there was a reasonable doubt as to whether Kong Ching Tong must necessarily have met his death from the head wound or from drowning, or whether he might still be alive. In which case, they must give the benefit of the doubt to the accused.

After a long deliberation lasting some nine and a half hours, the jury returned a unanimous verdict of 'Not Guilty' to the charge, and Cheung Yam San was duly acquitted and discharged.

4   *The Case in Which the Crown Failed to Prove That Gold Was Gold*

All that glitters is not gold. My son Denis, who is a fellow member of my chambers, tells me that the original saying was 'All that glisters is not gold.' Be that as it may, curiously that could be said to be the defence in a case of mine in or about 1960.

In the years which followed the end of the Second World War, many parts of Southeast Asia were embroiled in either civil war, teething problems in self-rule, or other forms of political disturbances.

During this period Hong Kong was one of the few places in this area which could boast of a stable government, the rule of law, and a growing population which was hardworking, intelligent, enterprising, and happily non-political.

Furthermore, its excellent harbour facilities, low taxation, free foreign exchange, and ready accessibility not only to the Chinese mainland, but also to the rest of Southeast Asia all served to contribute immensely to its rapid growth as a business and trading centre in the post-war era.

As a result, for the first time in the history of Hong Kong, foreign capital poured in, and new banks were regular additions to the local financial institutions. The ever-increasing turnover in the hitherto altogether humdrum local stock exchange was almost a new daily experience, and every so often, reached what were historic heights in those days.

Because of the worldwide fear of inflation, gold was the constant favourite subject matter for hedging, hoarding, and/or speculation, and many a fortune was made or lost each day in lawful as well as illicit trading in this commodity alone.

This was the background against which a fairly large consignment of a metal, believed to be gold, was allegedly imported in very unusual circumstances into Hong Kong, and became the subject matter of a somewhat intriguing court case.

At the time the law governing the importation of gold into Hong Kong was contained in an Order-in-Council made by the Governor in 1947, which provided that no person shall import gold into Hong Kong without a permit.

It further provided that 'gold means gold bullion, gold coin, or articles made wholly or partly of gold'.

Any gold so imported would be liable to forfeiture upon application made to a magistrate. Before 1947, no such licence was required. Likewise, no such licence is required today.

The relevant facts of the case were as follows. Some time in 1959, local customs officers, no doubt on information received, boarded a ship which had just arrived in Hong Kong, and seized some 25 bags of granulated sugar declared as such in the goods manifest of the ship and earmarked for delivery to a local company.

When the bags were opened and examined, they were found to contain also a large quantity of metal in varying shapes, forms, and sizes, amidst the sugar. The metal, which looked like gold, had obviously been melted and poured into the sugar in its molten form, and solidified again into the pieces found inside the bags.

A chemical test for gold carried out on the metal pieces proved positive. As a result, application was duly made to a magistrate to have the said metal pieces forfeited.

The case was set down for hearing before the late Mr Hin-Shing Lo at the Central Magistracy in Arbuthnot Road. I was instructed by Messrs M.K. Lam & Co. (Solicitors) to oppose the application, and to move the court for the return of the metal pieces to the local company, to which the bags of sugar had been manifested for delivery.

I first met the late M.K. Lam in London in 1948, when he was preparing to sit for his Solicitors' Finals, and I for my Bar Finals.

After our return to Hong Kong, we set up private practice at about the same time and he used to send me the odd brief now and then.

He was the sole proprietor of his firm at the time when he came to see me about the case in question. After apprising me of the relevant facts of the case, he asked me what I thought our chances were of successfully resisting the application for forfeiture. My response was that on the face of what he had told me, the case did not sound like an attractive proposition either legally or morally, because the facts revealed an obvious attempt to evade the law.

He queried whether there was any loophole in the relevant law of which we might take advantage, and requested that I look into the matter. On this note we parted.

A couple of days later I told him in conference that in my view, the relevant legislation could have been better drafted, and that in its current state, the authorities might have difficulty bringing the case in question within the prohibition intended against unlicensed importation of gold into Hong Kong.

Thereupon he made me a strange proposition. He asked me whether in view of my opinion, I would waive my usual brief fee, and agree to accept a share of the metal pieces, but on a contingent basis.

In other words, he was suggesting that I be remunerated not in monetary fees but in the form of an agreed percentage of the subject matter of the application, but only if the application for forfeiture was dismissed. In the event of the application succeeding however, I would of course have to be content with no payment of any kind whatsoever.

He added that he was making this suggestion only because of the optimistic note reflected in my advice. He further explained that as far as he was aware, assuming that the whole consignment had in fact consisted exclusively of solid gold, it would easily be worth some four to five million dollars in the open market, and a reasonable percentage thereof would far exceed many times my usual brief fee.

I felt obliged to remind him immediately that our system of jurisprudence would not permit remuneration on a contingent basis, and furthermore would not permit payment of fees in the form of a percentage of the subject matter of the forfeiture application, as in this case; any lawyer seeking or receiving such remuneration could be struck off the rolls.

He appeared to be somewhat taken aback by my response, and said that if that were the case I would best forget he had ever proposed it.

In due course the application for forfeiture came up for hearing in 1960. Michael Morley-John appeared for the Hong Kong government and I for the local company opposing the application. The only issue before the Magistrate was whether the metal pieces were or were not partially or wholly gold.

The seizure of the 25 bags of sugar containing the metal pieces was admitted. Michael Morley-John thereupon proceeded to call the only other evidence in support of his application, namely, the government chemist, Dr E. Edgely, to describe how under his supervision the following experiment was carried out.

Those 25 bags with all their contents were initially submerged in boiling water until the sugar and all other soluble elements had disappeared, leaving only metal pieces. These metal pieces were heaped together, from which a reasonably sizeable sample was taken at random. A further smaller and handier sample was taken at random from the first sample. The smaller second sample was then melted and eventually became a metal alloy. A chemical test was finally carried out on the said metal alloy, the result of which showed that it was at least partly gold.

Under cross-examination, Dr Edgely agreed with me that the contents of the sugar bags comprised a mixture of sugar and metal pieces. What remained after the disappearance of the sugar was a mixture of metal pieces. Likewise the first sample was a mixture of metal pieces. Similarly the second sample. The metal alloy emerging from the melting of the second sample was, however, a compound.

He further agreed that whereas in a mixture the constituent parts retained their separate existence, qualities and elements, this would not be so in the case of a compound, which would have a new existence altogether after the integration of its original parts.

Michael Morley-John called no other evidence in support of his application and accordingly closed his case.

I proceeded thereupon to call Professor Alan Greene to give evidence on behalf of the local company.

Professor Greene, who had taken a First Class Honours degree in English at Merton College, Oxford, was then the head of the English Department of the University of Hong Kong.

He told the court that according to his knowledge of the English language, gold bullion meant pieces of gold of standardized form, shape and weight accepted internationally as a means of exchange; gold coin meant standardized specimens of money for circulation and/or collection, which bore denominations, origins, and other particulars of the mint; and articles were objects, which had been subjected to a manufacturing process for domestic or commercial usage.

When shown some of the metal pieces recovered from the sugar bags and exhibited in court, he had no hesitation whatever in saying that in no way could they be said to be either gold bullion, or gold coins, or articles of gold. He concluded that if gold was proven to be present in any one of such pieces, he could not describe it in any way other than as a metal piece containing gold. He was not cross-examined.

Thus at the conclusion of the case, his evidence stood unscathed, intact, and unchallenged, and remained as the only evidence on record in connection with this aspect of the case.

I called no other witness.

After closing my case, I submitted to Hin-Shing Lo that as the relevant Order-in-Council had the effect of penalizing anyone who disobeyed it, its provisions must be strictly interpreted. Furthermore the word 'means' in the statutory definition of gold, as contrasted, say, for example, with the word 'includes', rendered that definition necessarily exhaustive.

Accordingly on a strict interpretation of the definition of gold as provided in the Order-in-Council, the metal pieces before the court did not come within the meaning of either gold bullion, gold coins, or gold articles as defined by Professor Greene, and thus did not fall within the prohibition laid down in the said Order-in-Council, and were accordingly not subject to forfeiture.

The application must therefore necessarily fail.

I further submitted to Mr Hin-Shing Lo that even if the court should rule against me on the first part of my submission, the result of the chemical test carried out under the supervision of the government chemist showed no more than that one or more of the metal pieces in the second sample which went to make up the emerging metal compound must have contained gold.

But it proved nothing against the rest of the metal pieces whether in the first sample or the principal heap, because, notwithstanding the chemical test, what the rest of the metal pieces contained remained altogether unknown.

Thus, at best, only the metal compound would be liable to forfeiture, if at all.

At the end of my submission, Mr Hin-Shing Lo adjourned the hearing, and in due course in a written judgment upheld my submission on both points made, holding that

(a) the applicant had failed to bring the metal pieces recovered from the sugar bags within the prohibitive definition of 'Gold' provided in the relevant Order-in-Council, and the application to forfeit must fail; and

(b) in any event, the applicant had only succeeded in proving that the metal compound emerging from the second sample contained gold. Thus only this alloy would be liable, if at all, to forfeiture, but not the rest of the metal pieces.

However, in the light of (a), any application for forfeiture even in respect of the compound must also fail. Accordingly, he ordered that the whole of the metal pieces be returned to the local company opposing the application for forfeiture.

Mr Hin-Shing Lo was undoubtedly one of the most colourful judicial personalities in Hong Kong of all times. He had read law at Cambridge, and was called to the English Bar at Middle Temple.

Shortly after he returned to Hong Kong in the 1920s, he created quite a sensation by taking a policeman to court for wrongfully putting a hand on his shoulder. Although he was awarded only nominal damages for assault and battery, he nevertheless made headlines in all the local newspapers for several weeks during and after the case.

He was also a renowned philanthropist. Time and again, he was known to have imposed a fine on some poor hawker for causing obstruction in the street, and then proceeded to pay the fine on his behalf, while warning him that next time he would not be quite as fortunate, and would have to pay a heavier fine himself.

It was always a pleasure to appear before him, because he was courtesy personified in court, and never failed to treat counsel to an excellent cup of his special coffee during the mid-morning adjournment.

He was a keen racing fan, and a great story-teller. His best story of which I have personal knowledge was how on one occasion he had lost money in every race, until the last one of the day, when the horse he backed won in a photo-finish at odds of eighty to one — only for him to discover that he had thrown his winning ticket away together with all his losing ones.

Somewhat surprisingly, my clients' company in the forfeiture application was not able in the end to enjoy the whole benefit of Mr Hin-Shing Lo's ruling.

Upon notice of appeal being filed by the Hong Kong government in the case, M.K. Lam came to my chambers again to consult me about our chances of success on appeal.

This time I told him with complete confidence that in view of the nature of the evidence called, and the manner in which the case was presented to Mr Hin-Shing Lo, there was no way, as far as I could see, that the appeal court could set aside his judgment.

M.K. Lam responded by saying that he was delighted to find me feeling so confident about winning the appeal. He added however that as no less than four to five million dollars was involved, he had decided to brief leading counsel to lead me in the appeal.

He asked how I would like to be led by Mr Leo D'Almada e Castro, QC in the case. Leo D'Almada and I had worked successfully and happily as a team in quite a number of cases. So I said I would readily welcome him as my leader.

Leo D'Almada was an outstanding member of the local Bar, and a long-standing legislative councillor. He was one of the only two silks actively practising in the courts of Hong Kong throughout the 1950s and 1960s, and until his retirement in the late 1960s was invariably involved in almost every court case of any importance in Hong Kong.

He was a brilliant lawyer, and a consummate advocate. His command of the language was superb, and his sense of humour and his choice of words never failed to entertain whether he was making a legal submission in court or an after-dinner speech. He always prepared his cases meticulously and methodically, and never took anything for granted.

Retaining him as Leading Counsel for the appeal would no doubt further enhance our chances of success, so I thought at least.

As things turned out however, the appeal brought by the Hong Kong government against the ruling of Hin-Shing Lo was never heard by the appeal court.

Leo D'Almada rang me up several days after M.K. Lam had been to see me. He said that he had been retained by M.K. Lam & Co. to team up with me in the gold case, and that he had been told to ask me what it was all about. This was hardly surprising as M.K. Lam never once turned up at the hearing before Hin-Shing Lo, but only sent a representative on every occasion.

Accordingly, I gave Leo D'Almada a summary briefing of the relevant facts, the evidence led before Mr Hin-Shing Lo, the legislation applicable, my submission, and Hin-Shing Lo's judgment in the case.

After my briefing, Leo told me that he had been specifically instructed by M.K. Lam to sound out the attorney-general on the possibility of a settlement of the case out of court, and accordingly inquired what sort of a settlement would be warranted by the prospects of the appeal.

I said I was surprised to hear that a settlement was contemplated.

M.K. Lam had not broached the subject with me when he came to my chambers. Besides, I had told him all along that we were in no danger whatever of losing the appeal. Accordingly I failed to see the need at all to approach the attorney-general for a settlement.

Our dialogue ended with Leo D'Almada saying that he would have to speak to M.K. Lam again about the matter.

I heard no more from either my learned leader or my instructing solicitors until about a week later when the former rang me up again, full of good cheer, just to let me know that he had already successfully finalized a deal with the attorney-general, whereby one half of the metal pieces would be forfeited to the Hong Kong government, while the remainder would be returned to M.K. Lam and Co. representing the local company. The appeal was in due course abandoned.

In the circumstances, I could hardly be blamed for feeling truly annoyed.

It was obvious that I had been deliberately excluded from what was happening behind the scenes. It was a fair surmise that I was not consulted because the confidence I had expressed in Mr Hin-Shing Lo's judgment might prove to be an unwitting obstacle to an overall settlement.

In any event, at no time was I a party to those negotiations with the attorney-general, and I only learned of the deal after the event.

To this day I just cannot see how Mr Hin-Shing Lo's judgment could possibly have been set aside by the appeal court. However I suppose settlements out of court are never unwelcome if only because they save a lot of time and hard work.

Despite my annoyance, I have no real regrets about the ultimate result of the case. Lay client had obviously intended to flout the law, and must be considered lucky to have been able to recover any part of the gold at all.

I cannot help wondering what really went on behind the scenes.

On the face of it, the settlement would guarantee recovery of at least one half of the gold in dispute. I can still recall M.K. Lam's meaningful advice to me earlier on, namely, that even a reasonable percentage of the gold recovered would far exceed many many times my brief fee. Leo D'Almada would of course have known nothing of such advice.

In the aftermath, the definition of 'Gold' was amended in 1972 to read:

> *'Gold' means 'gold bullion, gold coin, and articles, substances or liquids made wholly or partly of gold'.*

In 1973, the prohibition against the importation of gold into the colony was rescinded altogether, so that today gold can be freely imported into Hong Kong.

5 The Case of the Traffic Policeman and the Pak-pai Taxi Driver

Traffic cases are normally dull affairs. Wild car chases are of rare occurrence, and even if one does take place, it need not necessarily make the case any more interesting or exciting in the eyes of the law.

The case I am going to write about, however, does have a number of unusual features which are of exceptional interest, and I do hope the reader will not be disappointed after reading my account of it.

There was a time before the underground railway was constructed, when there was a distinct shortage of taxis and other forms of public transport in Hong Kong. As a result, many were those who operated a profitable business plying their private cars for hire.

These unlicensed taxis were commonly referred to as 'Pak-pai' (that is, white licence), because they did not sport the red licence plates commonly assigned to taxis. Although they helped to alleviate the transport shortage problem, these unlicensed taxis were nevertheless illegal, and those plying such illegal taxis for hire were violating the law.

It was, however, far from easy to catch them and bring them to justice. This was the background against which the relevant events of this particular case took place.

There were two separate trials involving the same traffic policeman and the same Pak-pai taxi driver.

In the first trial, the traffic policeman was the complainant, and the Pak-pai driver was the defendant. In the second, they switched roles, and the Pak-pai driver became the complainant, while the traffic policeman, the defendant. I was only involved in the second trial as defence counsel for the traffic policeman. By that time, the first case had already concluded some months before.

At the first trial, the Pak-pai driver appeared in person before a magistrate charged with (1) plying a private car for hire, (2) attempting to cause grievous bodily harm to the traffic policeman, and (3) resisting arrest.

Evidence was given at that trial that the traffic policeman had been very active in the Kowloon City area in the months leading up to the first case, and had succeeded in hunting down quite a number of people plying private cars for hire.

On the day in question, the traffic policeman said he saw the Pak-pai driver touting a fare outside the Shamrock Hotel, accordingly accosted him, and placed him under arrest.

While this was taking place, the Pak-pai driver stepped on the accelerator and tried to drive away. The traffic policeman barely escaped being knocked down by the car, but hung on to the side of the car and was dragged some two hundred yards. He was eventually knocked down when the Pak-pai driver suddenly stopped the car, pushed open the car door and ran away.

The traffic policeman gave chase, and duly caught the Pak-pai driver in the next street.

These allegations were denied by the Pak-pai driver who alleged instead that the traffic policeman had tried to solicit a bribe from him.

At the end of the hearing, the magistrate found the Pak-pai driver guilty of each of the three charges, and sentenced him to a total of nine months' imprisonment.

Surprisingly, after the conclusion of the first trial, the police launched a further investigation into the case.

Fresh evidence was allegedly discovered when a hawker and a newspaper boy each gave a statement claiming to have witnessed the whole incident. Both contradicted the account of the traffic policeman as to what happened.

According to them, the Pak-pai driver after being accosted came out of his car to speak to the traffic policeman. Together the two of them then walked a little distance away from the crowd which had gathered. The traffic policeman had his arm around the Pak-pai driver's shoulder, and the two seemed to be quietly talking to each other all the time. There was no sudden driving away, no knock-down of anyone, and no chase undertaken. This clearly corroborated the account of the Pak-pai driver especially that there was an attempt on the part of the traffic policeman to solicit a bribe from him.

As a result, a Governor's executive pardon was obtained for the Pak-pai driver in respect of his conviction and sentence, and the second trial was brought on when the traffic policeman was charged in turn in the Kowloon District Court with (1) soliciting a bribe, and (2) perverting the course of justice.

There were several features in this sequence of events which were out of the ordinary. Two of them had me somewhat puzzled, and a third positively had me alarmed.

To begin with, I wondered how and why further investigation into the case came to be undertaken after the first trial. Experience told me that it was highly unlikely that the authorities would on their own initiative and without very special reason undertake such an unusual step, unless someone, or some subsequent happening, had intervened to make them do so.

For example, the trial magistrate might have sent the court file to the Attorney-General and invited further investigation into the case. Apparently nothing of the sort happened here. Alternatively, some responsible member of the public might have actually witnessed the incident and written in to the authorities to say that the report he had read about the case did not tally with what he had seen. Again, it would seem that no such member of the public had thus voluntarily come forward. The hawker and the newspaper boy were only discovered allegedly upon further investigation being conducted by the police at the scene. In other words, the cause of this further investigation still remained altogether unexplained.

I mentioned this to the traffic policeman, but he was unable to enlighten me as to what could have happened.

From a lawyer's point of view, I found it difficult to understand why, in the light of the alleged fresh evidence uncovered, application was made, not for a retrial of the first case, or an appeal out of time from it, but for an executive pardon instead.

Normally, this prerogative of the Governor would only be resorted to in cases in which judicial process could offer no alternative remedy. This was obviously not the case here.

As defence counsel for the traffic policeman, I was especially alarmed by the granting of the executive pardon in the circumstances of this case.

As far as I could see, there was no reason whatever why the Pak-pai driver should be thus spared his conviction and sentence before the conclusion of the second trial, and before he was vindicated by an alternative finding by a court of law.

Such a premature pardon necessarily postulated the dangerous assumption that the magistrate was wrong or mistaken in his findings in the first trial, and that the truth of the matter lay with the Pak-pai driver, the hawker, and the newspaper boy, and not with the traffic policeman.

This was tantamount to prejudging the issue in the second trial which was still pending, and was no less than an attempt by the executive to interfere with and to prejudice the judicial process.

It was difficult to imagine how anyone directly or indirectly involved in the process of obtaining and granting the pardon could have overlooked the dire detrimental effect of such a step on the defence in the second trial.

Be that as it may, the trial of the traffic policeman came on for hearing in due course in the Kowloon District Court before a district judge sitting without a jury. I agreed to defend him free of charge at the request of my brother Ping Tsung, who had just joined one of the local firms of solicitors as an assistant solicitor, and was responsible for instructing me in the case.

There was one aspect of the defence about which I had never been happy. It was the traffic policeman's obvious exaggeration of the injuries he had allegedly sustained during the incident.

The traffic policeman insisted that the Pak-pai driver was trying to kill him, and that he suffered injuries to his arm, leg, and body, as a result of his having been dragged by the Pak-pai car some two hundred yards.

However, a medical examination carried out at Queen Elizabeth Hospital showed little or no sign of such injuries. I warned him that he was bound to be cross-examined on this aspect of his account, and it would have an important bearing on whether the rest of his evidence would be believed.

At the trial in the District Court, the Pak-pai driver admitted plying his car for hire outside the Shamrock Hotel.

I asked the Pak-pai driver why he had denied this in the magistrate's court. He replied that there were other subsisting charges preferred against him, and that at the time he had no idea that he could plead guilty to the first charge, and yet fight the remaining charges. For someone with his background, it was not altogether a bad answer.

He reiterated that the traffic policeman tried to solicit a bribe from him. He said he had no clue how he came to be pardoned. He did not know either the hawker or the newspaper boy, or how and where to look for witnesses in support of his own evidence in the first place.

In the end, I felt that if he was not an honest witness, he must have had a good coach to teach him exactly what to say.

I also cross-examined the hawker and the newspaper boy at some length.

I enquired in particular why they had not come forward to give evidence in the first case. They said that no one had asked them to, and they had no idea how to go about offering to give evidence.

I further enquired how their evidence came to be discovered. Their answer was simply that police officers had subsequent to the first trial suddenly turned up, asked them about the incident and, in due course, told them to attend court.

Although I succeeded in discrediting them in one or two aspects of the alleged account of the actual incident given by them, by and large they told a simple story rather well.

Once again, I was left with the unhappy impression that they might well be telling the truth, because I just could not see any obvious reason why these two strangers should choose falsely to incriminate the traffic policeman whom they did not even know.

At the close of the prosecution case, the judge as usual advised the traffic policeman on the three alternatives then open to him under our system of jurisprudence. A short adjournment was granted to enable me to advise the traffic policeman on those alternatives, and in due course, I called him to give evidence on his own behalf.

He repeated more or less the account he had given in the magistrate's court in the first trial. As expected, he was subjected by prosecution counsel to a lengthy and extremely effective cross-examination on his exaggerated injuries.

In the end he had to admit he had given a false account to his superior officers in the first place, and thus felt obliged to persist in the account. I must say that he cut a very poor figure in the witness-box.

After prosecution counsel and I had in turn addressed the court on the case, judgment was delivered almost immediately. The trial judge said that whilst the discrepancies in the Pak-pai driver's evidence in the magistrate's court and his subsequent evidence in his court had given rise to some doubt and anxiety on his part, he could not help being impressed by the straightforward accounts of the two independent witnesses, namely, the hawker and the newspaper boy, who were unknown to the parties involved, and had no reason to perjure themselves.

Furthermore, the trial judge said he was not happy at all with the established fact that the traffic policeman had lied first to his superior officers, subsequently to the magistrate, and finally in his court, about the injuries he said he had sustained. The trial judge said that this invariably led him to disbelieve the traffic policeman's account, not only as to his alleged injuries, but also as to the overall events on that day.

The trial judge accordingly convicted the traffic policeman on both charges, and sentenced him to a total of three years' imprisonment, saying he could not take a lenient view of a policeman soliciting a bribe, and perjuring himself to pervert the course of justice.

As I listened to the judgment pronounced and the reasons advanced therefor, I was not altogether surprised. Nor was I surprised by the sentence of three years. What did surprise me was that this was not by any means the end of the matter, as I soon discovered.

It had long been my practice, immediately upon any of my clients being convicted, to have an immediate conference with him in order to advise him on the prospects of an appeal, whether against conviction or sentence or both, and to enquire whether there was anything else that he would like to have done for him in the light of his conviction.

Thus shortly after the court had adjourned, I found myself face to face with the traffic policeman again in the cells of the Kowloon District Court.

I must say that he took his conviction extremely well although he kept saying that he was innocent. He thanked me repeatedly for representing him free of charge, and said it was a pity that despite my efforts, the trial judge still preferred to believe the Pak-pai driver and those two new witnesses in the case.

He asked whether there was any chance of a successful appeal against conviction and/or sentence, saying that he would not want to take advantage of my free services again, unless I thought there was a good chance of success.

I told him that in my opinion, the chances of a successful appeal were nil, because the judge had made a finding of fact on the evidence, with which I could not in all frankness disagree.

When he heard that even I disbelieved him, he appeared for the first time to be truly disheartened. If he was not innocent, he said, he would not have asked me to defend him in the first place.

I told him that the time for believing or disbelieving had passed, and all I wanted to know was whether there was anything else that I could do for him.

He responded in a sorrowful and apologetic voice, 'If you don't believe me, why don't you ask those two women in the car?' When he said that, I nearly fell out of my chair, because that was the first time anything was said by anybody, anywhere, at any time about there being two women in the car, who must therefore have witnessed the whole incident.

My brother Ping Tsung, who was the solicitor instructing me in the case, and I had been given to understand, and were under the definite impression, both before as well as throughout the trial, that the Pak-pai driver had only been seen touting a fare, so that throughout there was no question of any one having boarded the car, and there was no ready witness available to corroborate our client's account of the knock-down and chase.

I soon learnt that in fact at the time when the traffic policeman went up to confront the Pak-pai driver outside the Shamrock Hotel, two women were already in the car, and that they subsequently even went with the traffic policeman and the Pak-pai driver to the Kowloon City Police Station.

In due course, investigation followed up by my brother Ping Tsung and myself at that station revealed that those two women were Thai ladies due to fly to New York that day. Further enquiry disclosed that they were the respective spouses of two senior officials in the Thai Embassy in Washington, where they had flown that same afternoon.

Crying over spilt milk never helps anybody. Thus it serves no purpose in this account to blame either myself or my brother for the late discovery of the existence of those two Thai ladies.

This unfortunate state of affairs had been caused at least in part by the fact that when my brother and I came into this second case, the first case in the magistracy had already been concluded for some time.

The two Thai ladies were never even mentioned in the first trial, and in the magistrate's court file and record which my brother and I had duly examined and studied there was no reference whatever to their very existence, not to say, their presence in the car at any time.

Even if their presence had been known, it was of course doubtful if they could have been brought back to Hong Kong as witnesses in the second trial, although the defence could always apply to the court for their evidence to be taken abroad.

Despite the presence of those two ladies in the car, my lay client, the traffic policeman, probably thought that it would be impossible to trace them because they must have departed form Hong Kong on the same day.

Furthermore, their presence had appeared to be altogether immaterial in the first trial, as neither he nor the Pak-pai driver had made any reference to them. Consequently and understandably it did not occur to our lay client to mention them in his instructions to us, or at all in the second trial, that is to say, not until after his conviction and then only accidentally.

After tracing the identity and the whereabouts of those two ladies to the Thai Embassy in Washington, I lost no time before contacting prosecution counsel who had been and was still in charge of the case.

He was an extremely able and fair-minded prosecutor with a keen sense of justice. I told him that I accepted full responsibility for the oversight on the part of the defence, and in the interest of justice sought his support and assistance in following up on the matter.

He was as surprised as I was by the latest revelation, and readily supported the idea of sending a letter in the joint names of the Attorney-General and myself to those two Thai ladies, requesting that affidavits be supplied by them in respect of what they saw and experienced on that day.

He only laid down one condition, namely, that nothing should be said in the letter as to why these affidavits were required. Accordingly, I drafted a letter to those ladies which I signed on my own behalf, and he signed on behalf of the Attorney-General.

In passing, I should mention that prosecution counsel had told me in confidence before the second trial that he had had nothing to do with the pardon granted to the Pak-pai driver, that he endorsed my misgivings entirely regarding the likely prejudicial impact it might have on the second trial, but regretted that there was nothing he could do about it. When he first learned about it, the pardon was already a *fait accompli* referred to in the file handed to him in respect of the impending trial with instructions simply to proceed with the prosecution.

Three weeks after we sent off our letter to Washington, a polite reply was received informing us that the two ladies could not provide us with the requested affidavits, because the Thai Ambassador would not, on religious grounds, allow the swearing of such affidavits.

So, I drafted another letter, requesting the two ladies at least to provide us with an unsworn statement about what had taken place on that day outside the Shamrock Hotel.

Another six weeks passed by without anything further happening, and I was just beginning to despair, when a somewhat lengthy letter arrived from the two Thai ladies, setting out in great detail how they had waited in vain outside the Shamrock Hotel for a taxi before finally deciding to board a Pak-pai car, how a policeman came up and accosted the driver, how after a short conversation the driver suddenly started the car nearly knocking down the policeman, how the policeman hung on to the side of the car and was dragged some distance before the driver banged the car door at him, knocking him to the ground, how the driver then ran away, but was eventually chased, and caught by the policeman, who took him back with a stranglehold on one of his arms, and how everybody went to the Kowloon City Police Station, where after giving their names and intended whereabouts, the two ladies were eventually allowed to proceed to Kai Tak Airport and fly to New York.

This, of course, completely corroborated the traffic policeman's account of the knock-down and chase, and clearly refuted the alternative account given respectively by the Pak-pai driver, the hawker, and the newspaper boy, regarding the two men walking away peacefully with the traffic policeman's arm around the Pak-pai driver's shoulders, and their talking to each other all the time, just a little distance away from the crowd, without any knock-down or chase having taken place.

To say I was stunned would indeed be the biggest understatement of the year as far as I was concerned. However, one should at least be thankful for small mercies. The truth of the matter was discovered after all, albeit somewhat belatedly and by pure accident.

Almost immediately upon receiving this second letter from the Thai ladies, prosecution counsel and I jointly attended at the Attorney-General's personal office, and advised him of everything that had occurred.

Naturally as a result, my client was **duly pardoned** by the Governor, reinstated in his job, and aptly compensated for his wrongful conviction and imprisonment.

The most disturbing aspect of all these happenings was the startling audacity and cunning with which the attempt to set up the traffic policeman had been made.

Obviously an ingenious story, cleverly dovetailing into the bribe soliciting allegation at the Shamrock Hotel, had been carefully worked out in great detail for that purpose. Two total strangers, namely, the hawker and the newspaper boy, were then handpicked out of nowhere, and coached to tell that simple story to great effect in order to justify the Pak-pai driver's pardon in the first place, and bring about the traffic policeman's conviction in the subsequent trial.

The plot was utterly deadly, had in fact actually succeeded, and was only frustrated in the end.

Having gone this far, I naturally could not allow the matter to rest. As soon as the traffic policeman was discharged from prison, I sent for him to enquire whether he had any idea who could have trumped up the second case against him.

He took his time before replying. Eventually he said he could not say for certain who could have done such a wicked thing. But he wondered whether it might not have had something to do with an unpleasant confrontation he had had a short time before with a European police inspector who had driven his car out of the wrong end of a one-way street one evening.

The traffic policeman had already given the European inspector a ticket for so driving on that occasion before the inspector, who was in civilian clothes, disclosed he was a fellow police officer. It was too late for the ticket to be withdrawn, whereupon the inspector warned him in no uncertain terms that he was very foolish to be so stubborn, and would live to regret it.

I must say I could not quite believe that a police inspector would go so far to vent his vengeance on a traffic policeman all because of a traffic ticket justifiably issued against him. At any rate, I asked him for the name of the European inspector with whom he had had the unpleasant encounter.

I then wrote to the Attorney-General requesting the name of the party who had spearheaded the purported discovery of the so-called new evidence of the hawker and the newspaper boy after the first trial, and initiated the subsequent pardoning of the convicted Pak-pai driver as a result.

In due course the Attorney-General supplied me in writing with the name of the party sought. It was indeed the same European police inspector who had been involved in the traffic ticket incident.

Once again I felt obliged to approach the Attorney-General to reopen the subject of the two trials. More particularly, I singled out the following chain of events for his special attention, namely, the traffic ticket incident, the threat made by the European inspector, and the significant coincidence of his role in the material events leading up to the second trial.

I also laid special emphasis on the fact that the Pak-pai driver, the hawker and the newspaper boy had obviously all been extremely well coached in the evidence they gave in the district court trial. The letter of the two Thai ladies had now proven that evidence to be a complete fabrication. This could hardly be just another coincidence.

Without actually saying it in so many words, I made it quite clear by discrete implication that while as defence counsel for the traffic policeman, I was not entirely free from blame myself, nonetheless, in my humble and impartial opinion with the benefit of hindsight, the Governor, and the Attorney-General or his legal representative, had obviously been duped into serving as tools of a plot to set up the traffic policeman by granting the premature executive pardon of the Pak-pai driver and staging the second trial against the sinister background of the so-called fresh evidence of the hawker and the newspaper boy.

There was no attempt on the part of the Attorney-General to play down the force and logic of my argument, as he responded simply by promising that an investigation would be made.

Another eight weeks went by before I was finally advised, after yet another letter from me to the Attorney-General, that the European inspector had left the Colony on early retirement, and that the matter was treated by the authorities as closed. No further explanation whatever was given.

In the circumstances, there was nothing more that I could do in the matter, even though I was very disappointed. I could, I suppose, reveal everything to the press, and leave it to public opinion to decide what should have been done.

To be absolutely fair, I could visualize difficulties in bringing home any criminal charge against the inspector in question. The hawker and the newspaper boy would no doubt all have conveniently vanished into oblivion, long before my client had even secured his pardon.

Even if available, it must be extremely doubtful whether they would be willing to reveal the details of the whole ugly truth of the matter. In the absence of such revelation, the traffic ticket incident and the overall suspicious circumstances leading up to the second trial would surely be wholly inadequate by themselves to sustain a conviction in yet another criminal trial.

As a practising member of the Bar, I was particularly perturbed and alarmed to find that in Hong Kong which, we would like to believe, is governed by the rule of law, a police inspector could succeed so far in his devilish efforts to frame a fellow officer and be allowed after due enquiry by the Attorney-General, to get away without having to pay a higher price than an early retirement.

Epilogue

For some time after the case, the traffic policeman continued to turn up regularly at my chambers on festive occasions with baskets of food, fruit, and the odd bottle of wine, to show that he still remembered what I had done for him.

On one occasion, he took me into his confidence and told me that he was leaving the police force, because after his reinstatement, he discovered quite accidentally that some of those flourishing Pak-pai taxi drivers in Kowloon City were in fact close friends of his colleagues in the traffic division of the Hong Kong police, at least some of whom, he suspected, had obviously been compromised already one way or another.

Consequently he felt that the only safety for him was in quitting because he could not afford to be set up again. Fortunately he no longer had to rely on his police pay for a living because with the money paid him by government as compensation, he planned to open a small department store with a relative and friend of his to sell tinned food and other edible items in the New Territories.

I naturally hastened to wish him every success in his new life.

6 The Case of the Ruptured Kidney

1967 was a truly traumatic year for Hong Kong.

In the month of April, the Cultural Revolution in China, which had swept like wild fire through most parts of the mainland, reared its ugly head in this mainly Chinese populated colonial outpost of the British Commonwealth.

Overnight, thousands of political agitators took to the streets. Wearing head and arm-bands, shaking their arms and fists, shouting anti-British slogans, and carrying pro-communist banners, they marched daily in thunderous but well-organized formation through the heart of town, taunting the authorities, and blatantly brushing law and order aside.

At one stage those agitators even tried in vain to storm Government House, only just failing to break through the police lines, but leaving not a few battered policemen behind.

On both sides of the harbour, countless packages of varying description and sizes containing bombs some real and some otherwise were found each day in the streets as well as in other public places. Despite repeated warnings from the authorities to stay away from them, quite a number of people including children were injured when curiosity led them to examine some of those packages.

The few explosive-disposal specialists available in Hong Kong were kept fully occupied racing against time to detonate these lethal packages before more people were hurt, and in the course of carrying out his duty one of them tragically lost an arm.

This bomb scare was a real nightmare, which, together with the intimidating marches of the militant demonstrators, had the people of Hong Kong living daily in awesome fear and misgivings.

For a while a curfew was imposed every evening by the government, rendering it an offence for anyone without special permission to be found in the streets after dark. This state of affairs lasted some eight weeks, during which the police were specifically instructed to exercise utmost self-restraint in dealing with demonstrators, and to avoid, if at all possible, any head-on confrontation with them. As a result the police, more often than not, found themselves on the receiving end of insults and physical injury without redress.

On numerous occasions, the police were compelled to intervene when harmless bystanders and other law-abiding citizens were harassed, intimidated, or molested by those demonstrators. Yet in the ensuing fracas, the police had to back down every time from making any arrests despite breaches of the peace having obviously been committed, despite dire abuse being regularly hurled at them, and despite physical injury having frequently been sustained by them.

In one particular instance, a police station was literally besieged by a splinter group of demonstrators for almost two hours. Windows were broken as a result of stones and other objects being thrown, and officers and men of that station were jostled and insulted as they departed from or returned to the station.

The situation at times looked so ugly that not a few of the local newspapers ventured to ask whether our much vaunted police force was still capable of maintaining law and order.

Came the month of June. The demonstrators disappeared as suddenly as they first appeared, and sanity returned to Hong Kong to the relief of its four million inhabitants. But the ugly taste of the happenings of the preceding weeks and months lingered, especially with the rank and file of the Hong Kong police who had watched their comrades battered and humiliated without being able to do much, if anything, about it.

This was the background against which three policemen were tried for murder in Hong Kong in the latter part of 1967. In those days the police were responsible for looking after and guarding the prisoners in the court cells. The first accused Cheung Kam Yin was a police corporal, while the second accused Chan Man Chin, and the third accused Cheung Ying Ki, were both police constables. At the relevant time, these three policemen were solely responsible for the custody of the prisoners in the North Kowloon Magistracy. The victim of the alleged murder was one of their prisoners.

In this account, there will be innumerable references to the exact hour of the day when various happenings took place and from which vital inferences would have to be drawn. I must invite the reader to pay particular attention to these specific references to the time in relation to each significant happening.

Events began at about 5 p.m. on Saturday 24 June 1967, when two men, Lee and Wong, were accosted and searched by the police at the Shaw Film's Studio in Kowloon, and an inflammatory poster was found in their possession.

Although by this time there were no more political agitators roaming the streets of Hong Kong, inflammatory posters were continually put up to incite people to rise against British colonial rule, and the police had their hands full trying to clamp down on these offenders.

Accordingly, Lee and Wong were arrested and taken to Wong Tai Sin Police Station. There they remained in custody for some forty-four hours until shortly before 2 p.m. in the afternoon of Monday 26 June, when they were taken to the North Kowloon Magistracy to answer a charge for possession of an inflammatory poster.

They arrived at the magistracy between 2.10 p.m. and 2.20 p.m., and were duly delivered into the custody of the three above mentioned policemen who were solely responsible for the prisoners in the cells at the said magistracy.

Between 2.30 p.m. and 3 p.m. Lee and Wong duly appeared before the magistrate Mr F. Stratton, who immediately noticed their extremely poor physical condition, and ordered them to be taken to hospital forthwith. This was accordingly done. Lee died subsequently in hospital at 5.45 p.m. the same afternoon.

A hand-picked team of senior police officers was appointed to investigate the circumstances of Lee's death. Statements were taken from three sources, the first source comprising the police pathologist and some government doctors who had examined Lee at different times, the second source, a large number of police officers from Wong Tai Sin Police Station regarding the condition of Lee before he was delivered into the custody of the three accused policemen at the North Kowloon Magistracy, and the third source, a number of other prisoners occupying cells in the North Kowloon Magistracy at the relevant time regarding alleged assaults on Lee and Wong by the three said policemen. In due course these three policemen were charged with the murder of Lee.

The news that the three policemen had been charged with murder was received by the public with mixed feelings. It must have been difficult for people in Hong Kong to forget the recent faultless discipline and conduct of the police in dealing with the defiant political activists in the preceding weeks and months. On the other hand, it was no less difficult for law-abiding citizens to condone police brutality culminating in death occurring in a courthouse right below where the magistrates were sitting.

Committal Proceedings

In due course, I was instructed to represent the first accused police corporal Cheung Kam Yin at the Committal Proceedings. The second and third accused policemen were represented by leading counsel.

Committal proceedings are a preliminary hearing by a magistrate of the available evidence against an accused person, at the end of which the magistrate will decide whether or not a prima facie case has been made out by the prosecution. If so, the accused will be committed for trial, and the case will be transferred to the High Court to be heard before a judge and jury. If not, the accused will of course be discharged. As of today, witnesses for the prosecution at committal proceedings will only be called if required by the defence for cross-examination, otherwise their statements will be made available to, and accepted by the magistrate automatically as prima facie evidence. However in 1967, the procedure was less expeditious, and each witness for the prosecution had to be called, and their evidence recorded by the magistrate.

The prosecution case in this instance was built upon the following grounds. First, Dr Pang Teng Cheung, a police pathologist, had performed a post mortem on Lee on Tuesday 27 June, and concluded that the cause of death was an injury rupturing the kidney inflicted not more than four hours prior to death, that is, not before 1.45 p.m. on Monday 26 June. Secondly, according to a number of police officers from Wong Tai Sin Police Station, Lee had been delivered in apparent good health into the custody of the three policemen between 2.10 p.m. and 2.20 p.m. on Monday 26 June. Thirdly, one of the prisoners detained in the cells of the North Kowloon Magistracy by the name of Yam Cheong claimed to be an eyewitness of physical assaults by the three accused policemen on Lee and Wong shortly before their appearance before the magistrate Mr Stratton between 2.30 and 3.00 p.m.

This chronological sequence of events appeared at first sight to wrap up the murder charge somewhat tidily against the three accused policemen.

I noticed, however, that with regard to the fatal injury, Dr Pang had hesitated quite a while before expressing the view that it could not have been inflicted more than four hours prior to death. Dr Pang must have been aware that his expert evidence could well determine the time when the fatal injury had been inflicted, and thus, in the particular circumstances of this case, where, and by whom, it must have been so inflicted.

In Hong Kong, it was unusual for the opinion of a police pathologist not to be automatically accepted in court. However, in this instance, because of Dr Pang's noticeable hesitation, I decided to seek separate medical advice on the four-hour limit. As things turned out, it was just as well that I made this decision.

In passing, I should mention that initially there was a second charge against the three accused policemen for causing grievous bodily harm to Wong. Like Lee, Wong was incarcerated in the cells at Wong Tai Sin Police Station after his arrest, taken for a medical examination at 10 a.m. on Sunday 25 June, and found to have sustained a couple of minor bruises. In the afternoon of Monday 26 June, after Wong had been taken with Lee to the North Kowloon Magistracy, all that he could remember was fainting there after feeling pain and giddiness, and being subsequently taken to Queen Elizabeth Hospital. His inability or unwillingness to tell the court anything else led inevitably to the dismissal of the charge of causing grievous bodily harm against all three accused policemen.

At the conclusion of the committal proceedings, the magistrate held there was a case to answer on the murder charge in respect of each of the three accused policemen, and committed all three for trial before a judge and jury in the Supreme Court.

In those days, it was not easy in Hong Kong to find a medical expert willing to challenge the opinion of another, especially when murder was involved. However, in the present case, I was fortunate to secure the assistance of Professor G.B. Ong, who at the time headed the Surgery Department at the Hong Kong University Medical Faculty, and was an internationally renowned surgeon of long standing.

Professor Ong did not take long to arrive at his own conclusions on the timing of the fatal injury causing death. According to him, it would be impossible for medical skill to determine from the discoloration of a bruise, or from the healing process in an organ in a dead body, that it had been inflicted within as short a period as four hours. Furthermore, he thought that Lee could easily have been carrying a ruptured kidney before he arrived at the North Kowloon Magistracy.

Trial

The trial took place in September 1967 before the late Mr Justice Rigby sitting with a jury. The Solicitor-General appeared for the prosecution.

In the course of the post mortem conducted on Lee, Dr Pang had found two sets of injuries. The first set of injuries comprised **thirteen bruises**, which had already become discoloured. The second set of injuries comprised **nine bruises**, together with cracks in certain ribs and the breast bone, and a laceration on the anterior wall of the stomach. He concluded that the ruptured kidney must have been caused by one of the bruises in the second set of nine bruises not more than four hours prior to death.

At the Committal Proceedings, Dr Pang had advanced four reasons for his conclusion, namely, the absence of any blood in the urine in the bladder; the presence of a recent lacerated wound on the anterior wall of the stomach; the discoloration in a bruise immediately adjoining the ruptured kidney; and the stage reached in the healing process in the kidney itself.

However at the trial he made a number of concessions which were more than favourable to the defence. Thus in respect of the first of his four reasons, Dr Pang conceded at the trial that without a microscopic examination, it was not in fact possible to say there was no appearance of blood in the urine, and furthermore that this non-appearance of blood in the urine in fact proved little or nothing as to time because it could have been due to paralysis of the kidney resulting from the severity of the injury, or to a blockage between the kidney and the bladder. In other words, the first of his four reasons had to be discarded.

In respect of the second of his four reasons, Dr Pang had assumed that both the laceration in the stomach and the fatal injury had taken place at the same time, and as the laceration looked fresh, he had accordingly concluded that the rupture of the kidney was equally recent. At the trial however, he conceded that there was in fact no solid or apparent justification for that assumption and consequent conclusion. As no other reason was advanced for the suggestion that the laceration in the stomach helped to fix the time of the injury to the kidney, Dr Pang's second reason likewise would not hold up.

As to his reliance on the discoloration and healing process for his third and fourth reasons respectively, Dr Pang surprisingly and readily agreed with Professor Ong's opinion put to him by me in cross-examination that the rate of discoloration varied in different parts of the body and from individual to individual. Similarly with the healing process. As a result, Dr Pang was not in a position to relate either the discoloration or the healing process observed in Lee's body to any established norm, and thus could not rely on his third and fourth reasons respectively.

The sum total of all these concessions was that there was little or nothing left of the four reasons given by Dr Pang for his estimate that the fatal injury to Lee's kidney could not have been inflicted more than four hours before death.

Of no less importance to the defence was the fact that although Dr Pang declined to accept the opinion of Professor Ong extending the timing of Lee's fatal injury to eight to twelve hours prior to death, he did agree to extend his own estimate of four hours, first to four and a half hours, and finally, albeit reluctantly, to five hours prior to death. The estimate of four hours would put the clock back to 1.45 p.m., four and a half hours to 1.15 p.m., and five hours to 12.45 p.m.; that is, respectively ten minutes, or forty minutes, or one hour ten minutes, prior to Lee being taken to the North Kowloon Magistracy from Wong Tai Sin Police Station at 1.55 p.m. on Monday 26 June.

Even the four hour limit would of course already be logically sufficient to open up the possibility that the fatal injury had been inflicted before his delivery into the custody of the three accused. Thus it could well have been inflicted between 1.45 p.m. and 1.55 p.m. while Lee was still at Wong Tai Sin Police Station, or between 1.55 p.m. and 2.10/2.20 p.m. when he was on his way to the North Kowloon Magistracy.

Extending that limit to four and a half hours, or even five hours, must necessarily render that possibility more likely.

Professor Ong's estimate of eight to twelve hours prior to death would, of course, put the clock further back to 9.45 a.m. or 5.45 a.m. on Monday 26 June. This would surely provide still more time for the likelihood that, prior to the delivery of Lee into the custody of the three accused policemen at the North Kowloon Magistracy, the fatal injury had already been inflicted.

However, none of the foregoing reasoning, important though it obviously was to the issue of identification of the parties responsible for the fatal injury to Lee's kidney, and where it could have taken place, appeared to have made any impression on the trial judge, as was apparent in his summing-up to the jury in due course.

The first set of Thirteen Discoloured Bruises, according to Dr Pang, had been inflicted twenty-four to forty-eight hours prior to death, that is, between 5.45 p.m. on Saturday 24 June and 5.45 p.m. Sunday 25 June. This set of bruises played an unexpectedly big part in undermining the prosecution case against the three accused policemen. Dr Tsui Leung Chiu of Queen Elizabeth Hospital testified that he had examined Lee at 3 a.m. on Sunday 25 June, and found him to have at that time only two fresh bruises. The incontrovertible inference from this was that at least eleven of these discoloured bruises must have been sustained subsequently between 3.00 a.m. and 5.45 p.m. on Sunday 25 June. As Lee was known to have spent the whole of this period at Wong Tai Sin Police Station, it followed that those eleven bruises could have been inflicted by none other than the police officers of that station, unless the prosecution could call evidence to the contrary, and there was no such evidence.

No evidence was called at any time as to when exactly the second set of **nine bruises** found on Lee had been inflicted, other than that they were more recent, and that one of them was the cause of the ruptured kidney. This left it altogether open to speculation whether this second set of nine bruises had been sustained before or after 1.55 p.m. on Monday 26 June when Lee was finally taken to the North Kowloon Magistracy from Wong Tai Sin Police Station.

Again, what was undisputed was that throughout the period between 5.45 p.m. on Sunday 25 June and 1.55 p.m. on Monday 26 June, Lee had remained at Wong Tai Sin Police Station. No evidence was adduced and nothing was known as to what happened at the police station during this period.

The only evidence on the condition of Lee on Monday 26 June at the time when he was delivered into the North Kowloon Magistracy, came from three police officers of Wong Tai Sin Police Station who had escorted him there. One of them said that Lee appeared to be in good condition; another said that he could see nothing wrong with Lee; and the third said that Lee was walking properly. Not one of the three mentioned the presence of any of the thirteen discoloured bruises, far less explained how, when, where, by whom, and in what circumstances these bruises came to be inflicted. As these bruises were incontrovertibly shown to have been inflicted when the deceased was detained at Wong Tai Sin Police Station, the election of those witnesses to turn a blind eye to them necessarily rendered it difficult to accept without reservation their claim that Lee had been delivered to the North Kowloon Magistracy in apparent good health.

Several other police officers from the Wong Tai Sin Station were called to give evidence on Lee's condition during the whole of the forty-four odd hours when he was in custody there. Each and every one of these officers was thoroughly discredited in cross-examination.

One of these police officers, for example, said Lee had left the station on Monday 26 June in good health. He subsequently admitted under cross-examination, after checking certain entries in an official book supposedly made by him, that he had been mistaken in having asserted earlier on that he had been on duty throughout that weekend. In fact, he was not on duty at all, and thus would not have known anything about the physical condition of Lee. Another officer who was on duty at the cells in the Wong Tai Sin Station on Monday 26 June was so evasive and unsatisfactory under cross-examination that his evidence was interrupted by the Solicitor-General, who, with the permission of the Court, ordered him to be 'taken away, searched, and checked'. Yet another officer present at the cells in Wong Tai Sin Station said that both Lee and Wong were then in good health, but, under cross-examination, admitted that he did not really remember what they looked like, and even if they had been ill or in pain, he would not have noticed.

The clear impression left was that the police officers in Wong Tai Sin Police Station had gone out of their way deliberately to hide the truth. For, if the fatal injury to Lee had not in fact been inflicted during the half hour or so when he was in the cells of the North Kowloon Magistracy, it could only have been inflicted by the officers of Wong Tai Sin Station at that station.

Yam Cheong's 'eye-witness' account of the alleged assault on Lee by the three accused policemen varied somewhat at the trial from the account he had earlier given at the committal proceedings. For example, he said at the trial that he saw the first accused kicking Lee and Wong. At the committal proceedings, he had only said that the first accused policemen hit Wong once with his hand before walking away, and that this was followed by the second and third accused policemen kicking Lee and Wong until they fell to the ground.

Under cross-examination, Yam Cheong admitted to feeling extremely unwell and drowsy on the afternoon of Monday 26 June. He conceded that apart from his health, his eyesight had also been very poor. Partly because of this, and partly because of the awkward position he occupied in the cell, he could not really see very clearly what was happening outside the cells where Lee and Wong were. Furthermore, he agreed that there were numerous other prisoners occupying his cell, as a result of which, more often than not, his view was completely blocked. However, he denied having been motivated by his resentment of the police, as a result of his many previous convictions, to formulate false accusations against the three accused.

There was an amusing episode during the cross-examination of this particular witness. A large clock was hanging on the back wall of the court some fifteen to twenty yards from where he was standing in the witness box. He agreed that this was roughly the same distance between him and Lee and Wong when the latter were allegedly assaulted in the cells of the North Kowloon Magistracy. He was asked whether from where he stood, he could read the time of the day indicated on that clock. He looked at it for some time before telling the court that the time indicated on the clock was shortly after 3.30 p.m. This was of course the correct time of the day. But unfortunately for him, that clock in court had in fact been out of order for some considerable time, and the hands stood at ten minutes past one o'clock!

Furthermore, Yam Cheong's evidence of the alleged assaults on Lee and Wong was refuted by another witness, a police officer who at the relevant time, was occupying the duty room which commanded a full view of the scene. This police officer said that he did not see any assault committed.

In the face of these vital gaps and weaknesses in the prosecution case, it was difficult to see how any properly directed jury could return a guilty verdict against any of the three accused policemen. Accordingly, at the close of the prosecution case, I advised my client, the first accused, that apart from Professor Ong, there was no necessity to call any other evidence in his defence. I explained to him the three alternative courses which under the law applicable at that time were open to an accused person. I pointed out to him that if he elected to give evidence, he would of course be liable to be cross-examined.

The first accused took some time to decide on the various alternatives open to him, and eventually elected to remain silent. The second and third accused likewise elected to remain silent.

Accordingly, I proceeded to call Professor G.B. Ong to give evidence on behalf of the defence. He turned out to be an impressive witness. He was clear, precise, and confident. Professor Ong was not cross-examined by the Solicitor-General at all, so that his evidence remained altogether unchallenged.

Briefly, Professor Ong disagreed with Dr Pang's opinion that the fatal injury had been inflicted within four, or four and a half, or even a maximum of five hours, prior to death. He expressed the view that no up-to-date medical expertise could fix with any degree of certainty the time of such injury to anything less than eight to twelve or even twenty-four hours. In this connection, Dr Leung Ling Kai had testified that at Queen Elizabeth Hospital he had examined Lee in the afternoon of Monday 26 June shortly before Lee's death. Dr Leung Ling Kai had also estimated that the fatal injury had been inflicted within twenty-four hours prior to death. Professor Ong was of the opinion that it was more than possible that Lee had been carrying a ruptured kidney for some time prior to his arrival at the North Kowloon Magistracy on 26 June.

At the conclusion of Professor Ong's evidence, the Solicitor-Attorney duly made his final address to the jury on behalf of the prosecution, while counsel for the several accused policemen likewise made their respective final addresses for the defence. This was followed by Mr Justice Rigby's summing up of the case to the jury.

In his final address, the Solicitor-General reiterated the three grounds relied on by the prosecution, but said very fairly that the jury should not return a guilty verdict against the three accused policemen or any one of them unless they were satisfied beyond reasonable doubt that the three accused were responsible whether individually or jointly for the fatal kidney injury sustained by Lee.

In my final address to the jury, I emphasized on behalf of the first accused that the many vital gaps and shortcomings in the prosecution evidence must leave more than a reasonable doubt as to where, when, and by whom, the fatal injury to Lee's kidney had been inflicted. I maintained, as I did at all relevant times throughout the trial, and, indeed, subsequently on appeal, that in the face of the two sets of injuries found by Dr Pang on Lee's body of which at least the first set of thirteen discoloured bruises had obviously been sustained by Lee at the Wong Tai Sin Police Station, the prosecution must fail unless it could be shown that his kidney had suffered no injury prior to his arrival at the North Kowloon Magistracy between 2.10 and 2.20 p.m. on Monday 26 June, or that the fatal injury could only have been inflicted after his arrival at the North Kowloon Magistracy. (This assessment of the evidence was subsequently endorsed by the judgment of the Court of Appeal.) Since at no time did the prosecution call evidence to prove the first, and the medical evidence failed altogether to substantiate the second of the two said vital grounds, I submitted that as a result it was no longer relevant whether or not the three accused or any one of them had assaulted the deceased as alleged.

Leading Counsel on behalf of the second and third accused addressed the jury more or less along the same lines as I did.

Unfortunately Mr Justice Rigby very surprisingly failed altogether to read the evidence in that light, or even to appreciate what the crux of the defence really was. Accordingly, his summing-up was inadequate and misconceived, and misdirected the jury.

It became apparent, as Mr Justice Rigby summed up the case to the jury, that he preferred Dr Pang's evidence to Professor Ong's because the former was a police pathologist, and had carried out the post mortem on Lee's body. Yet where Dr Pang and Professor Ong had differed was in respect of the limits of present day medical knowledge in enabling particular deductions to be made from known data, in which area, Dr Pang whether as a pathologist or the person who had conducted the post mortem could claim no advantage over Professor Ong.

Mr Justice Rigby attached little or no importance to the effect of the various estimates of time made respectively by Dr Pang and Professor Ong in relation to the fatal injury. He did not realize that even taking Dr Pang's original estimate of four hours prior to death, there would be that impossible half hour gap in the prosecution case, not to say the four and a half hours, or even five hours, subsequently conceded by Dr Pang. Mr Justice Rigby did not seem to appreciate that the estimated timing of the fatal injury had a direct bearing on the identification of the venue where it had been inflicted, and thus the party or parties likely to be responsible.

Mr Justice Rigby's summing-up was, in short, almost a complete endorsement of the prosecution case. After reminding the jury very briefly of the evidence of the various witnesses, he laid singular emphasis on:

(1) the medical evidence of Dr Pang that the fatal injury had been inflicted not more than four hours before death, while dismissing Professor Ong's alternative opinion as mere fanciful possibilities;

(2) the evidence of the eyewitness Yam Cheong of assaults by the three accused on Lee, and the failure of the three accused policemen or any one of them to give evidence and deny on oath those allegations of Yam Cheong; and

(3) the evidence of the Wong Tai Sin police officers that Lee had been delivered in apparent good health to the North Kowloon Magistracy notwithstanding devastation of this evidence under cross-examination.

Mr Justice Rigby said that the jury should have little or no difficulty in being satisfied beyond reasonable doubt that the three accused were responsible for the death of Lee and thus guilty of the murder charge laid against them. He failed altogether to direct the jury as to what the defence was. He made no reference whatever to the crucial assessment of the evidence I made in my address to the jury. This subsequently formed an essential part of the Court of Appeal decision in allowing the appeal by the three accused policemen against conviction.

As a result, the jury after due deliberation, found the three accused policemen guilty, although not of murder, but only of manslaughter. While I was not unhappy with the dismissal of the murder charge, I was nonetheless dissatisfied with the manslaughter verdict. The first accused almost immediately acceded to my advice that an appeal be lodged.

Appeal

The appeal brought by the three accused policemen against conviction was duly heard in the early part of January 1968 by a full court of three judges, presided over by the Chief Justice Sir Michael Hogan. The appeal judges, unlike Mr Justice Rigby, had no difficulty in appreciating the exact nature of the defence and the material issues involved in the case.

The first ground of appeal which was argued was based on Mr Justice Rigby's misdirections to the jury on the medical evidence.

The other ground of appeal argued was based on Mr Justice Rigby's failure to appreciate the importance of the different possibilities of when the fatal injury could have been inflicted, and consequently his failure altogether to direct the jury as to what the defence was.

The Judgment of the Court of Appeal on those two grounds was so succinctly and felicitously phrased, and so accurately reflected the arguments addressed to the jury at the trial that I feel I can do no better than set out the relevant parts of it herein.

Ground One

In respect of this ground, the Court of Appeal had the following to say:

'It was quite correct to say that Dr Pang, a very experienced pathologist, had had the advantage of seeing the dead body, an advantage not open to Professor Ong, but it was important to ascertain and determine how far that advantage assisted him on those matters in which he and Professor Ong were in conflict.

Professor Ong was not seeking to contradict or contest what Dr Pang had seen on the dead body. The matter which he questioned or the conclusions which he queried were those based on medical science and the practice and application of medicine. In respect of matters such as these, Dr Pang had no proved advantage over Professor Ong through having seen the particular body. This was a conflict between two eminent medical men as to the limits of present day medical expertise and, if the jury were to be asked to decide which was the more accurate in this field, it was important to remember that whereas Dr Pang, in cross-examination, and, indeed, to some extent in examination-in-chief, had accepted the existence of factors which appeared to throw doubt on his conclusion, such as differing rates of discoloration and healing in different people and different rates in different parts of the body, there had been no cross-examination of Professor Ong and his testimony appeared to be unscathed by any admissions or qualifications volunteered or extracted from him.'

Ground Two

In respect of this ground, the Court of Appeal had the following to say:

'. . . Indeed it seems doubtful whether the judge fully appreciated the importance of these timings. Their significance does not emerge clearly from the summing-up. There was an error which minimized the impact of the time factor in Dr Pang's evidence when he told the jury that the defence relied on the contention that the evidence did not show, with any reasonable degree of certainty, that the kidney was ruptured by a blow struck within 4 hours of death. In fact, the defence was that the prosecution had failed to prove the injury was sustained within three and a half hours of death, the limit which would bring it to the time when the deceased reached North Kowloon. The half hour was significant because it meant that Dr Pang's evidence, even in its original form, failed to establish this important element in the prosecution case.

. . .

To sum up, it is apparent that if the prosecution were to succeed in this case in bringing the charge of murder or manslaughter home to one or more of the accused, it was necessary for them to show by the evidence of Yam that such accused had participated in assaulting the deceased in a manner capable of producing the fatal injury and to show, by means of the medical evidence and the testimony of the Wong Tai Sin witnesses, either that the deceased was demonstrably free from this injury when he reached North Kowloon or that it had not been inflicted upon him during the period, prior to delivery, medically established as the limit within which it could have been sustained.

. . .

In our view a jury, properly directed and acting reasonably, could not have convicted the accused upon it. The medical evidence was incapable of showing that the injury to the kidney could only have been inflicted within a period later than the deceased's arrival at North Kowloon whilst this evidence and that from the Wong Tai Sin witnesses did not show that the deceased was free from the fatal injury to his kidney when he arrived at North Kowloon or that it could not have been inflicted at Wong Tai Sin.'

The Court of Appeal accordingly allowed the appeal against conviction of each of the three accused policemen.

This brought an end to a sensational trial in the Hong Kong Courts, which had for many weeks and months captured the imagination of both the public and the press, particularly in view of the political events outlined in the introduction to this case and the part played by the police in those events.

The grand finale to the Case of the Ruptured Kidney was a happy one. Chinese New Year arrived shortly after the Court of Appeal quashed the conviction of the three accused policemen, who were instantly released and reinstated. My client, Cheung Kam Yin, the police corporal, was overjoyed to be reunited with his wife and four children, a free man to welcome the arrival of the Chinese New Year. I found their filial joy more than infectious, when they all turned up surprisingly on Chinese New Year's Day at my residence to wish me 'Kung Hei Fat Choi!' (a common Cantonese greeting at Chinese New Year). To demonstrate their far from transitory appreciation of my services rendered in the court case recorded above, they continued to visit me every year on Chinese New Year's Day for the next fifteen years.

7 *The Case of the American Who Was in Two Places at the Same Time*

No one, not even David Copperfield, the world famous illusionist, can be in two places at the same time. Thus, if an accused person who is charged with having committed an offence on a particular day, or at a particular time, can establish that he was on that particular day, or at that particular time, elsewhere than at the venue of the offence, he will be entitled, to say the least, to the benefit of the doubt, and be acquitted.

The defence of alibi, however, is not free from drawbacks. For example, if the charge is murder, the defence of alibi would necessarily exclude such alternative defences as provocation, self-defence or insanity.

Furthermore, in order to establish the defence of alibi, corroborative evidence would be required to substantiate the accused's claim. Any witness or witnesses called to corroborate the defence would have to satisfy the court how and why the meeting with the defendant on the relevant occasion came to be remembered. Because of the difficulties involved, it does not happen too often that the defence of alibi is relied on in a criminal trial. It happens even less often in fraud cases.

The case of *The Queen* v. *Charles Tashjian* took place in the Victoria District Court in 1973 before the then District Judge T.L. Yang (who later became the first Chinese Chief Justice of Hong Kong). The accused was a businessman from the east coast of the United States of America. He stood charged with attempt to defraud Messrs Jardine Matheson & Co. Ltd. of Hong Kong.

The events in the case began in 1972, when the accused Charles Tashjian, while touring South America, purchased a consignment of precious gems in Venezuela worth some US$500 000, and ordered them to be dispatched to Hong Kong for delivery to be taken at the offices of Jardine Matheson & Co. Ltd. After returning to his home town of Watertown outside Boston, he subsequently visited several other places outside the United States of America before arriving in Hong Kong at the beginning of October 1972.

After checking into a hotel in Kowloon, he called at the offices of Jardine Matheson & Co. Ltd. to take delivery of the precious gems. He was attended to by a junior member of the staff. But instead of the precious gems being delivered, the police were sent for, and he was arrested and charged with attempted fraud. Apparently someone with the name Charles Tashjian had already some weeks previously taken delivery of the gems from Jardine Matheson & Co. Ltd. Furthermore, the same junior member of the Jardine Matheson staff claimed that the man who had done so was none other than the accused. In other words, the accused was seeking to take delivery of the same gems a second time. That was why the police were called in.

The case was first brought up for hearing in the Victoria District Court on 10 November 1972 when the defence asked for a summary of the prosecution case, which was duly supplied. Application was then made for a longer than usual adjournment of the hearing, in order to enable the defence to be prepared, and witnesses to be called. The court was naturally somewhat reluctant to grant the application, as there was no guarantee that the accused, who was an American tourist, would return to Hong Kong to stand trial. Be that as it may, the application was eventually granted, and the trial was set down for hearing from 26 February 1973 to 2 March 1973 inclusive.

In due course, Peter Hon, the solicitor instructing me, brought the accused to my chambers, and apprised me of the relevant facts of the case. I must confess that the prosecution case immediately struck me as being extremely odd. It was difficult to understand why, if the accused had already earlier on collected the gems from the offices of Jardine Matheson & Co. Ltd., he should reappear and try to collect them a second time. He must know that this could only lead to trouble.

On the other hand, there was the young man at Jardine Matheson & Co. Ltd. who claimed to be able to identify my client. Furthermore, a handwriting expert had been called in to examine and compare a specimen of the signature and handwriting of the man who had actually collected the gems, with those of the accused appearing in chits and bills recovered from the hotel where he was staying. According to the handwriting expert, the two sets of signatures and handwriting were written by the same man. If so, the accused must have been the man who had signed for and taken delivery of the gems at the offices of Jardine Matheson & Co. Ltd.

Another piece of evidence relied on by the prosecution as throwing suspicion on the accused was the fact that his passport was brand new. The old one had apparently only recently been surrendered to the American Consulate in Hong Kong in exchange for the new one. When the American authorities at the request of the police produced the accused's old passport, several pages were found to be missing. The American Consulate maintained that this was the condition in which the old passport had been surrendered. The contention of the prosecution was that if those pages had not been missing, they could well show a stamp imposed therein by the Hong Kong Immigration Department on a date prior to the taking of delivery of the gems at the offices of Jardine Matheson & Co. Ltd. If so, it would confirm that the accused had been to Hong Kong on the date of the Immigration Department stamp, and would thus have had ample opportunity to collect the gems.

The date on which the gems had been collected from the offices of Jardine Matheson & Co. Ltd. was of course clearly stated in the synopsis supplied by the prosecution. The first thing that the accused told me in conference was that he had checked his own itinerary, and found that on that day he was still in the United States, and therefore could not possibly have been in Hong Kong. I responded by telling him that if he could prove that, he would have nothing to worry about. I pointed out to him that, of course, his word alone would not be good enough for the court, and that he would need corroboration of his alibi.

I also stressed the importance of the handwriting expert's evidence. I suggested that if we could produce an expert witness of our own to challenge the evidence of the prosecution, our case would be much stronger. But handwriting experts were scarce in Hong Kong at the time, because hitherto such experts would normally be called only by the prosecution and were rarely, if ever, challenged in our courts. I thus advised the accused that since he was returning to the United States to look for witnesses to substantiate his alibi, it would be advisable for him to try also to secure, if possible, the assistance of a competent handwriting expert, preferably someone who had been accepted in American Law Courts, to give him advice on the opinion of the Hong Kong handwriting expert. The three-month adjournment of the case should give him ample time to secure his witnesses and fly them to Hong Kong to attend trial.

I naturally also asked the accused what had happened to the pages missing from his old passport. His explanation was that they had accidentally been soiled and damaged to an extent which necessitated the surrender of the old passport in exchange for a new one. Although this sounded a little odd and not altogether convincing, I decided not to speculate whether or not it was the truth of the matter. Much of course would depend on what other supporting evidence, if any, the prosecution could produce. If the prosecution's contention as to the missing pages were to stand alone, it could rank only as mere speculation and suspicion. On this last note, the accused departed from my chambers to return to his home country.

Nothing further happened until the latter part of February 1973 when my instructing solicitor telephoned to say that our client had returned to Hong Kong from the United States of America and would like to bring me up to date regarding the latest developments in his search for witnesses. I could not help feeling somewhat relieved, because it would be embarrassing to appear in court just to tender my apologies to the trial judge in the event of my client having jumped bail. Furthermore, my instructing solicitor hinted at improved prospects in the case. So, another conference was arranged.

Obviously the three months' adjournment fulfilled the purpose for which it was applied, because the accused Charles Tashjian had brought back with him two vital material witnesses for his defence.

At our second conference, I was introduced first to an assistant manager of a bank in the accused's home town who had had an appointment with him on the very day the precious gems were stated in the prosecution synopsis to have been collected from the offices of Jardine Matheson & Co. Ltd.

The assistant bank manager brought with him two expired calendars for 1972 from his bank. The first was a desk calendar with two holes punched into the left upper half wherein two curled pins would normally be put, so that the pages could be turned over from day to day, or forward and backward as desired. The second calendar was in fact his bank's appointments book which had the day of the week, the month, as well as the year, together with the name of the bank printed on each page.

According to the assistant bank manager, social appointments with his bank by telephone would initially be entered into the desk calendar. Business appointments would however invariably be entered into the appointment book.

When I examined the two calendars, I found there was indeed the name Charles Tashjian written into each of them on the day the delivery of the precious gems was actually taken in Hong Kong. There were of course many other entries, and many other names recorded in the said two calendars throughout 1972.

I thought it expedient to point out immediately to the accused and the assistant bank manager that delighted as I was to see those two calendars, in law certain documents such as cheque stubs and entries in calendars are not admissible in evidence because they are self-serving.

The reason is simple. A witness can easily manufacture such self-serving documents to suit his own purpose. However, whilst a party may not rely on self-serving documents as evidence, he may with the Court's permission look at them in order to refresh his memory. For example, the assistant bank manager in this case could ask the Court for permission to consult his calendars to confirm whether he did or did not have an appointment with a particular customer on the particular day.

Whilst the accused appeared somewhat upset and disappointed when I gave my advice on self-serving documents, the assistant bank manager took it all in very calmly. In the end he disclosed he had been similarly advised in the past, because this was not the first time he was required to give evidence in Court involving banking appointments with clients, which had been entered in calendars. He said that the law in the United States of America and Hong Kong must have been more or less the same in this connection.

The assistant bank manager was a calm, soft-spoken, well-educated man of about forty-five years old; he promised to be an excellent witness who could easily clinch the verdict for the defence. For, if his evidence was accepted, the court could not possibly find that the accused and the party who had actually collected the precious gems from the offices of Jardine Matheson & Co. Ltd. were one and the same person, bearing in mind that the east coast of the USA was normally twelve hours behind Hong Kong in time, and furthermore that it would take more than twenty hours to fly from Boston across the North American continent and the Pacific Ocean in order to get to Hong Kong.

The second witness brought by the accused to Hong Kong was an eighty-year-old American lady who could only walk with the assistance of a huge stick and laboured breath. I must say that when I first saw her limping into my chambers, I was not a little worried lest she might not last the trial! But I soon found out why she had been flown to Hong Kong despite her age and her far from perfect health. She had given expert evidence in innumerable civil and criminal cases in the American courts involving handwriting and forgery, and for some forty years had been looked upon as the leading handwriting expert in a large number of States in America. I very much regret I can no longer remember the name of this elderly lady.

At the conference in my chambers, however, she could not

immediately make any material contribution to the case, because she had as yet no opportunity to find out what the case was all about, and what contribution, if any, she could make to the defence.

So, I asked my client to provide her with a copy of the written opinion of the prosecution expert regarding the two sets of signatures and handwriting, and requested her to let me have her views thereon in writing if possible, so that I could familiarize myself with them before the trial, and thus be enabled to cross-examine the prosecution expert witness in due course where her opinion should differ from his. On this note, our second conference ended.

The trial commenced on 26 February 1973 as scheduled and lasted four days.

The young employee of Jardine Matheson & Co. Ltd. was the first witness called for the prosecution. He was a proud young man who was obviously pleased with his prompt action leading to the arrest of the accused. Surprisingly, though, he was totally unable to tell the court anything about the circumstances under which the management of Jardine Matheson & Co. Ltd. had decided to allow delivery of the precious gems to be taken on the earlier occasion. He said that the investigation into a claimant's identity, and his entitlement or otherwise to the gems, was no part of his duties at all, and that his superior officers were solely responsible for those aspects of the matter.

It was certainly more than curious that none of those superior officers was called to give evidence, and at no stage of the trial, did the prosecution seek to enlighten the Court as to the exact circumstances under which Jardine Matheson & Co. Ltd. came to be satisfied that the first man claiming these gems was the person legally entitled to them. By what documentary or other proof or other means that man had succeeded in satisfying Jardine Matheson & Co. Ltd. of his identity and entitlement to the gems remains a mystery to me to this day.

For example, was that man's passport examined and were particulars of it entered into the company's records? Did the claimant produce any banking and/or other commercial documents to show that he had purchased and was the legal owner of the gems? And so on. Positive evidence on these aspects of the matter would not only vindicate Jardine Matheson & Co. Ltd.'s decision to part with the gems, but also strengthen the prosecution case against the accused. In the absence of such evidence one could hardly accept the very limited, and, indeed, one might say, at best second-hand account of a junior clerk to justify his company's parting with the gems to the party who actually took delivery of them.

As far as the young employee called to give evidence was concerned, he remembered only physically handing over the parcel said to contain the gems to the man claiming it. He said, however, he was able to recognize the accused as the man who had thus taken delivery of the parcel on the earlier occasion.

I asked him how long the handing over of the gems lasted altogether. 'Half a minute or so,' he said. Had he seen that man before or after the event? I asked. 'No,' he said. In other words his claim of recognition was based on his having seen that man for no more than half a minute whilst a parcel was handed over by him quite some months ago, and he had never seen the man before or again until the accused turned up to seek delivery of the same gems. However he added after a short pause that he remembered also that the man who took the delivery had the same name as the accused.

I asked him whether that man had any peculiar features. He said yes. I asked him to particularize. He looked at the accused in the dock for a little while before answering, 'Just like those of that man.' I pressed him again to particularize and he was totally silent.

I asked him whether he was a big man or small man. He said average size.

I asked him if he had noticed the colour of that man's hair. After some hesitation he again pointed at the accused in the dock, and said it was of the same colour without saying what colour that was.

I asked him whether the earlier man spoke with an English or American accent. He said he did not know the difference. When I pressed him once more as to whether he had noticed if that man spoke with any peculiar accent, he said in the end, he had noticed nothing unusual about his accent.

I requested the Judge to note this answer in particular. The accused, of course, to my knowledge, spoke English with a distinct and very noticeable foreign accent which could probably be traced to his eastern European heritage. I was sure the Judge would notice this when the accused went into the witness box.

Finally I asked the young employee whether it was common practice for parcels to be dispatched to his company for delivery to be taken at its offices. He said this happened regularly. 'How often?' I asked. 'It varies,' he said. 'Sometimes as many as twenty to thirty parcels within the week would be collected from his company. Sometimes not quite as many, but seldom less than ten per week,' he added.

In other words, the occasion of the gems was only one of a substantial number when parcels were delivered at the offices of Jardine Matheson

& Co. Ltd. Notwithstanding this and despite the lapse of several months, the young employee claimed to be able to recognize this one man on this one occasion.

So much then for the young employee of Jardine Matheson & Co. Ltd. and his claim to recognize the accused.

The next witness for the prosecution was an Immigration Officer whose evidence turned out to be a complete fiasco. Apparently it has been intended that he would produce certain cards, documents, or other records which purported to relate to the accused's date of arrival in Hong Kong. But what he sought to produce, turned out to have nothing whatsoever to do with the accused or the case in question. Furthermore, in the witness box he kept referring the court to one of the cards in his custody which had for some mysterious reason been categorized under the letter 'O'. But when the letter 'O' was examined by the Court under a magnifying glass, it became obvious that the 'O' was in fact a 'C'. In short, his evidence was such an utter mess that the Judge, who was a very patient man, turned to prosecution counsel and enquired whether any useful purpose could possibly be served by pursuing this witness' evidence further. Prosecution counsel readily agreed, and the witness' evidence was discontinued. Curiously, no alternative evidence was led from the Immigration Department.

Dr E. Edgely was called next as a witness. A doctor of chemistry primarily, he had undertaken a special course on forgery and handwriting in the UK, and had given evidence as an expert witness in quite a number of forgery cases in the Hong Kong Courts. As far as I was aware, his expert evidence had invariably been accepted as it was virtually impossible in Hong Kong at the time to secure an alternative opinion.

But one of the fascinating facets of litigation is that the unpredictable frequently occurs. And so it did in this case.

When Dr Edgely went into the witness box, he had no idea that the defence would be calling its own expert witness who was already sitting with the Judge's permission in Court to listen to his evidence.

Dr Edgely expressed the familiar view that if a certain number of similarities were found in two sets of handwriting, one would be entitled to conclude that both sets must have been written by the same person. He then proceeded to illustrate with enlarged photographic specimens the similarities he found in the specimen signature and handwriting of the man who had collected the gems, (which specimen had been retained by Jardine Matheson & Co. Ltd. and subsequently produced to the police), and the specimen signature and handwriting appearing in the chits and bills signed by the accused in his hotel. Finally he concluded that in the light of those similarities, the two specimens must have been written by one and the same man.

I should mention that, on the previous day, my instructing solicitor had supplied me with a brief note of the opinion of our lady expert where she differed from Dr Edgely. So, in cross-examination I put her opinion point by point to Dr Edgely questioning several of the alleged similarities which he had relied on for his conclusions. I further questioned him as to the exact number of similarities required to be found which he had specified as adequate to entitle him to arrive at that conclusion. Dr Edgely, I must say, stood his ground quite well where his opinion differed from what I had put to him as the opinion of the handwriting expert I intended to call.

After I had completed my cross-examination of Dr Edgely, prosecution counsel got up, and very smugly, asked Dr Edgely in re-examination (which the prosecution was perfectly entitled to do) on what authority, if any, Dr Edgely had based his opinion regarding the nature and number of the similarities which led him to his conclusion that one and the same man had written both specimens. 'Harrison' was the answer. Of course, Harrison's name as author could be found in leading textbooks on forgery and handwriting. Prosecution counsel then quietly announced he would be calling his last witness.

This witness turned out to be a police inspector who had obtained from the American Consulate in Hong Kong the accused's old passport from which a number of pages were missing. I had nothing to ask him about this expired passport which was the accused's responsibility alone to explain.

That closed the prosecution case.

Thereupon I submitted to the Judge that the prosecution had failed to make out a case against the accused. I pointed out that essentially the prosecution case was that the accused had taken delivery of the precious gems previously, and was nevertheless seeking to collect the same gems a second time. He must therefore have realized that there would be no gems for him to collect on the second occasion. So, if anything, it could only mean that on the second occasion he was merely going through the motion of requesting and not obtaining delivery of the gems, so that he could subsequently bring a fraudulent claim against Jardine Matheson & Co. Ltd. or the insurance company for non-delivery of the gems. In other words, he was merely preparing the way for such a claim to be brought. Otherwise, the attempted fraud charge would be totally meaningless.

At law, there is a clear distinction between mere preparation and attempt to defraud. While the latter is an offence, the former is not, and my submission to the Judge was that the evidence led by the prosecution in this case at best showed mere Preparation but fell far short of an Attempt.

I cited a case in the United Kingdom in which a man had put away his wife's jewellery, then tied himself up, and called the police, falsely claiming that burglars had broken into his house, bound and gagged him, rifled his safe, and made away with his wife's collection of jewellery kept inside it. When eventually the husband admitted to the authorities that it was all a sham in order to enable him later to make a false claim against the insurance company which had insured his wife's jewellery, he was charged with and convicted of Attempted Fraud. But the Court of Appeal in England held that as the intended claim against the insurance company had not in fact as yet been brought, the sham could only be said to be in its embryo. He had indeed made preparation to put forward a fraudulent claim, but had not yet made any actual attempt to defraud, even though he had told falsehoods to mislead the police. He was accordingly acquitted.

As a consequence, I urged the Judge forthwith to discharge the accused.

The Judge ruled, however, that in his opinion the case before him was distinguishable from the UK case, and accordingly held that the accused had a case to answer.

In the face of this ruling, I had to decide whether to call the accused and his witnesses to give evidence, and let the defence run its normal course, or alternatively, rest on my submission without calling evidence, and rely on a successful appeal against the Judge's ruling in the event of a conviction.

There were advantages and disadvantages in either course. Calling evidence would of course score if such evidence was accepted by the Court. On the other hand the evidence might be rejected, and furthermore, it might have the untoward effect and the undesirable result of filling up gaps otherwise existing in the prosecution case. There was no way to tell how the accused and his witnesses would perform in the witness box, especially under cross-examination. Relying solely on a successful appeal against the Judge's ruling would mean a void on the defence slate as far as evidence was concerned and could lead to disaster in the event that the Court of Appeal disagreed with my view on the law on Attempt and Preparation, and the Judge's ruling was upheld.

Although I remained undaunted by the Judge's adverse ruling, I nevertheless decided in the end that it was much too risky not to call the accused and his witnesses to give evidence, as I was especially impressed by the quality of the corroborative evidence proffered by the banker from America.

I explained the situation in great detail to the accused who indicated he would abide by my advice in the matter.

Thus, after a short adjournment, I put the accused in the witness box. As he took the oath and told the court his name, the Judge watched and listened to him with obvious interest. He then turned to ask me whether it was the peculiar accent of this witness's which I had in mind when I cross-examined the young employee from Jardine Matheson & Co. Ltd. Indeed, Your Honour, I said, happily content that I had scored a point for the defence.

The accused's evidence-in-chief was quite short and simple. He told the Court how he had purchased the precious gems in Venezuela because they were cheap, why he had consigned them to Hong Kong for delivery to be taken there because he believed that in Hong Kong the gems would fetch a good price, how he had returned to the United States of America for a short time before setting off again for other parts of the world, how he had regular appointments with the assistant manager of one of the banks in his home town, especially before and after he went on business trips whether local or abroad, which were frequent.

What happened after his arrival in Hong Kong was, of course, already known to the Court.

I deliberately refrained from asking him about his old and his new passport, because I knew the prosecution would no doubt try to make as much capital out of it as possible. In the light of the explanation given to me about the matter at the first conference in my chambers, I decided that it would be best for it to come out in the Prosecution Counsel's cross-examination rather than in my examination-in-chief.

The accused naturally denied the charge. He further denied that he was the man who had collected the precious gems previously.

Prosecution Counsel went straight into the attack as soon as I sat down. Did the accused know whether the young employee of Jardine Matheson & Co. Ltd. had any grudge against him? None was the answer. If that was the case why should he falsely accuse him of trying to collect the precious gems a second time? The accused could not think of any reason why the witness should do so, but suggested that he could have been mistaken.

Prosecution Counsel then put to him that there was no mistake, and that the accused was indeed the same man who had previously collected the gems, and was trying to collect the same gems a second time. The accused disagreed with him, and, after a short pause, added that he could not have been very smart to try something as ill-advised and stupid as Prosecution Counsel had suggested.

Prosecution Counsel remained unperturbed, and turned instead to the handwriting evidence, asking whether the accused agreed he had signed the chits and bills recovered from his hotel. The accused readily agreed. The accused was then asked what he thought of Dr Edgely's opinion, namely, that both sets of signature and handwriting must have been written by the accused. To which the accused replied with confidence that Dr Edgely must have been mistaken, because another handwriting expert would be called to tell the Court otherwise. Prosecution Counsel's response thereto was to observe, somewhat smugly, that he could hardly wait to hear the evidence of the accused's expert.

He then turned to the two passports.

I have already observed that the accused's account of the accidental soiling of his old passport did not sound entirely free from suspicion. But I had decided not to speculate whether that was or was not the truth of the matter, because accidents and coincidences sometimes do sound even stranger than fiction although they are in fact nothing but the truth.

The accused, it must be said, gave his explanation extremely well, however suspect it might have sounded. Despite being cross-examined at great length in this connection, he stood his ground, and Prosecution Counsel could do no more in the end than put to him that his whole account was a bundle of lies, and that he had had to destroy those missing pages in the old passport because they would otherwise have revealed a stamp of the Hong Kong Immigration Department proving his prior arrival in Hong Kong to collect the gems. To which the accused simply said, how could you possibly assert that as a fact?

At this juncture, Judge Yang surprisingly intervened to enquire whether Prosecution Counsel had other evidence to back up his statement. When the latter said that he had none, the Judge indicated that as far as the Court was concerned, there was hardly any point in persisting in such sinister but unproven insinuations.

That ended Prosecution Counsel's cross-examination of the accused, and I could see no necessity whatever to re-examine him on any of the matters raised.

I proceeded to call the lady handwriting expert next, so that she could be released as soon as possible because of her age and her poor health.

I could see that Prosecution Counsel could hardly wait to cross-examine her in order to recover some of the ground already lost. So, after taking her through her long recognized experience in the American Courts, I was as short with her in my examination-in-chief as propriety permitted. In fact, she merely repeated the views I had already put to Dr Edgely on her behalf. Her conclusion, very briefly, was that she disagreed with some of the alleged similarities relied on by Dr Edgely, and that while she agreed with him to the extent that there were indeed some similarities in the two sets of specimen signature and handwriting, they were not sufficient to justify Dr Edgely's conclusion that they had been written by the same man.

As soon as I sat down, Prosecution Counsel jumped to his feet. 'So you differ from Dr Edgely on the following points, do you?' he asked, and then proceeded to enumerate those points.

'Indeed,' she said.
'You heard Dr Edgely tell this court that he based his opinion on the authority of Harrison?' he asked.
'I sure did,' she said.
'Have you heard of Harrison?'
'Indeed I have,' she said.
'Yet, you still disagree with and disapprove of Dr Edgely's opinion?'
'Indeed,' she repeated.
'On what authority?' he uttered those words, one by one, as slowly and deliberately as if he was teaching a child what to do.
'On my own authority, and many years of experience in the courts of law in the United States of America,' she replied.
'So, on your own authority you disagree with Harrison?'
'I do, and I have frequently so disagreed,' was her answer.
'In what circumstances?' he pressed.
'When I taught him!' she replied. This time she was the one who was slow and deliberate in her answer.

You could almost hear a pin drop in the court for at least the ensuing seconds, at the end of which Prosecution Counsel sat down as abruptly as he had got up, no more than a shadow of his former confident self. He was obviously so stunned and surprised by the old lady's dramatic disclosure that she had taught Harrison, that he failed altogether to follow up by pursuing an inquiry into the rationale behind her non-acceptance of and her disagreement with Dr Edgely's conclusion. I must say that that last answer of the old lady took even myself by surprise!

The last witness for the defence was the assistant manager of the accused's bank. His evidence was short but no less effective and convincing.

He told the court how the accused had for some time banked with the witness' employer bank, how, as assistant manager, he had always kept two calendars in his office, into which entries would be made from day to day of appointments with clients whether social or business, and how the accused had frequent appointments with him at his bank.

I then singled out the day on which the precious gems had been collected from Jardine Matheson & Co. Ltd., and asked him whether he had any appointment with any of his clients on that day, and if so, with whom. To which his reply took the form of a query whether he could consult the two calendars he had with him.

I immediately applied to the Judge for permission for the witness to refresh his memory from his two calendars, which application was granted without objection from Prosecution Counsel.

Accordingly, the witness checked his two calendars regarding the date signified by me before saying that he remembered interviewing the accused in his office in the bank in the late morning of the day in question.

At that point, I sat down, wondering whether Prosecution Counsel would launch into another lengthy but futile cross-examination of this particular witness in whom I had the greatest confidence.

But all that Prosecution Counsel did was to ask for permission to inspect the witness' two calendars which was duly granted. At the end of the inspection, he merely asked meekly whether the witness could possibly have been mistaken about the exact date of that particular meeting with the accused. The answer, as expected, was naturally in the negative.

To this day, I cannot help wondering whether prosecution counsel's failure or unwillingness to ask this particular witness any more questions was because he was still trying to find his feet again after having been floored by the last answer of the old lady.

That concluded all the evidence adduced in the case. This was followed by the respective final addresses of Prosecution Counsel and myself to the Court.

Prosecution Counsel was obviously still so deflated that he was content to leave the matter entirely to the Judge.

I, too, said that I would not labour the evidence again, although I would be failing in my duty if I did not make a few observations, namely, that there was simply little or no logic in the contention of the prosecution that the accused was trying to collect the same gems twice, because if that were the case, he must know that he would only have got trouble but no gems the second time. On the other hand, if some other party had in fact collected the gems, that would automatically exonerate the accused on the charge before the Court. Although one might be inclined to ask how the other party came to know of the gems and their dispatch to Jardine Matheson & Co. Ltd., and how he had succeeded in persuading the company to allow him to take delivery of the gems, those were neither questions within the ambit of the Attempted Fraud Charge before the Court, nor the concern of the defence, and might best be directed at the management of Jardine Matheson Co. Ltd. I also repeated my earlier submission on the difference between mere Preparation and Attempt to defraud. In conclusion, I submitted that there could only be one logical verdict on the evidence.

Judge Yang reserved judgment.

On the following morning, Judge Yang delivered a verbal but prepared judgment saying very briefly that he found this a very interesting case in which there were quite a number of curious features. In the end, he said, the case boiled down to the question whether the evidence adduced by the prosecution left him, in the face of the alibi evidence, with any reasonable doubt as to whether the accused was in fact the man who had collected the gems from Jardine Matheson & Co. Ltd. in the first place and was trying to do so again a second time, which was in itself a peculiar suggestion by the prosecution. He said that it was not the function of the Court to investigate what had actually happened at the offices of Jardine Matheson & Co. Ltd. or behind the scenes. His function was simply to decide whether the prosecution had proved the offence alleged against the accused. He said he had little difficulty even on the banker's evidence alone, which he accepted without reservation, in coming to the conclusion that he had more than a reasonable doubt whether the accused could be in Hong Kong on the day the gems were collected. This would of course suffice for him to acquit the accused, and any ruling on the differing opinions of the two handwriting experts would be purely academic. But in view of the trouble undertaken by both the prosecution and the defence in this connection, Judge Yang said he would like to make it known that if he must choose between the two experts, he would prefer the old lady's opinion to Dr Edgely's. He accordingly acquitted the accused.

After the court adjourned, the accused immediately consulted me as to what to do about the gems. I said there were several options open to him. He could sue Jardine Matheson & Co. Ltd., or the vendors in Venezuela, or the insurance company involved. But as I had not been fully apprised of the exact terms of sale, or of the provisions of the insurance policy, or the instructions given to Jardine Matheson & Co. Ltd., I was in no position to give sound advice off-the-cuff on any of the said options.

However neither my instructing solicitor nor I heard anything more from the accused.

8 The Case of the Hunter Who Became the Hunted

If I were asked which was the most extraordinary case I had ever handled, I would have no hesitation in naming the case of *the Queen v. Augustine Chung*. This was the summary trial of a solicitor in the Victoria District Court in Hong Kong in October 1975 for blackmailing for monetary gain, or, alternatively, attempting to obtain property by deception. At the time, I thought it deserved the epithet of being the case of the year. I see no reason to think otherwise today.

Augustine Chung read Sociology at the University of Hong Kong in the 1960s with the aid of a monetary grant from the Hong Kong government. Upon his graduation he worked as a social welfare officer for two years in order to fulfil the terms of his grant. After leaving the Social Welfare Department, he joined a local solicitors' firm as an articled clerk, qualified as a solicitor in 1970, was employed initially as an assistant solicitor, but soon became a partner of a prominent local firm. In no time, he built up a substantial practice in the magistrates' courts representing drivers and owners of public cars and light buses in traffic summons. He was appointed legal adviser and official spokesman for their trade union, and represented them in a miscellany of other matters including suing government for the cancellation of the New Territories taxi licences and public light bus licences.

By 1975, Augustine Chung was a solicitor of five years' standing who had not only done well professionally and financially, but had also won considerable publicity for himself. He owned a deluxe flat, a Rolls-Royce, a Maseratti sports car, a Volvo and an expensive motor launch. He and his wife also had substantial holdings in a number of publicly listed companies.

With that background, it might be difficult to understand why a person in Augustine Chung's position would want to blackmail anyone for monetary gain or attempt to obtain property by deception.

No less remarkable was the fact that the victim of the alleged blackmail or deception should be none other than Donald Cheung, another prominent solicitor, who was at the time the senior partner of a leading local firm of solicitors, and a former President of the Law Society of Hong Kong. If for some unknown reason, Augustine Chung had indeed sought financial gain, he might have picked easier prey.

At the relevant time, Donald Cheung, apart from being a solicitor, was also a director of a well-known firm of building contractors namely, Paul Lee & Co. Ltd., whose affairs were under investigation by the authorities. Paul Lee was a local builder and contractor whose company became publicly listed.

Between 1969 and 1971, the share market enjoyed a boom unheard of before. Local businesses suddenly became aware of the immediate fiscal advantages of becoming publicly listed, and consequently queued up to offer their shares to the public. To add respectability to their management, prominent citizens and eminent professional men were regularly invited to join their respective boards of directors. The value of shareholdings in these newly listed companies frequently jumped several times in the space of a few months as a result of wild rumours and hushed tips.

For a while the people of Hong Kong seemed to be interested only in making a quick return from the stock market. Those with ready cash hastened to invest it all in one or other of the new companies. Others secured overdrafts from the only-too-willing banks to do the same. The newly purchased shares would, more often than not, be pledged as fresh security for more purchases on credit.

As a result, prices kept spiralling upwards until eventually the inevitable occurred. In 1973 the bubble finally burst after the local Hang Seng Index hit an up-to-then record dizzy height of 1780, and in due course crashed to a record low of 158.

Paul Lee & Co. Ltd. had appeared to be carrying on a flourishing business until it suddenly failed in 1973 almost immediately following upon the Stock Market crash. Upon investigation of its affairs by order of the Financial Secretary, vast sums of money were found to be missing. Fraud, larceny, misappropriation of the company's funds to speculate in the stock market, as well as other offences were suspected.

In the months which followed, rumours were rife as to what action the authorities would take upon completion of the investigation, for example, who, if anybody, would be held responsible for the failure of the company's business and for the disappearance of the company's money, and further whether anybody would be charged criminally, and if so, who, how, and when.

It was not surprising that Donald Cheung, a director of Paul Lee & Co. Ltd., should protect himself by taking legal advice from leading counsel in London as well as from his brother Oswald Cheung, a leading counsel and Councillor in Hong Kong.

Against this background a number of meetings took place between Augustine Chung and Donald Cheung in the month of July 1975. The first of these meetings occurred on Monday 7 July 1975 when the former contacted the latter by telephone, and met him for coffee in town. Hitherto the two men had only known each other professionally.

Augustine Chung said he had information from 'up-top' that certain directors of Paul Lee & Co. Ltd. would imminently be charged with criminal offences, and that because Donald Cheung had made a bad statement to the authorities, he had been put on the Immigration Stop-List and would not be permitted to leave Hong Kong. Nothing much else was said at that meeting, so that Donald Cheung must have been left pondering over what he was told, why he was told, and what, if anything, was to follow.

Two days later, i.e. on Wednesday 9 July, Donald Cheung was stopped at Immigration Control when he tried to take his wife to Macau. It may be interesting to note that subsequently Augustine Chung divulged in the witness box that this Stop-List information about Donald Cheung, which turned out to be 100% accurate, had in fact been supplied to him not by anyone 'up-top' but only by the brother of another director of Paul Lee & Co. Ltd. The precise source of that information was not known.

On Friday 11 July 1975, a second meeting by appointment took place between the two solicitors. This time Augustine Chung told Donald Cheung that he was acting on behalf of friends involved in deciding whether or not to institute criminal proceedings in the Paul Lee investigation. He said those friends had in their possession a document damaging to Donald Cheung, which they were prepared to destroy for half a million US dollars. He added very ominously that even if Donald Cheung was acquitted, he would be finished professionally.

If Augustine Chung had expected Donald Cheung to be overawed by the Stop-List information or the disclosure that he, Augustine Chung, had friends who had in mind instituting criminal proceedings in the Paul Lee investigation, he could not have been more mistaken.

Donald Cheung's reaction was, instead, to suspect corruption, and, immediately after that second meeting with Augustine Chung, to contact Oswald Cheung QC, who in turn brought the matter to the attention of the Attorney-General.

As a result, officers of the ICAC, the Independent Commission Against Corruption, went to Donald Cheung's home on Saturday 12 July. There they connected a tape-recorder to his house telephone, and another to his body, so that any future conversations with Augustine Chung could be recorded.

That same evening i.e. on Saturday 12 July, Augustine Chung took Donald Cheung out for a drive in his car, unaware of the trap laid waiting for him. Augustine Chung told Donald Cheung that the incriminating statement mentioned on 7 July had not in fact been made by Donald Cheung but by a third party, and that the price for destroying it had been reduced to HK$1 million payable by five cashier orders of $200,000 each.

Augustine Chung further offered himself as a stakeholder of the cashier orders, so that even if there was a double cross and the charges were not eventually dropped, or it turned out to be all a false pretence, Donald Cheung would still be able to recover his money and not be out of pocket.

On the following day, i.e. Sunday 13 July, Augustine Chung, still not suspecting that the trap was closing in on him, took Donald Cheung out again in his car, and told him that as soon as the cashier orders were handed over, his name would be taken off the Stop-List. However, the matter must be finalized within forty-eight hours. A discussion then followed between the two men as to how best to raise the money.

At each of the three previous meetings, Donald Cheung had apparently tried unsuccessfully to find out who the 'up-top' connections of Augustine Chung were. He tried again on Sunday 13 July. As soon as it became obvious that the information he sought was not forthcoming, he gave a pre-arranged sign to a number of ICAC officers who had been waiting for the two men to return from their drive. As a result, Augustine Chung was placed under arrest on suspicion of conspiracy to solicit bribes.

Immediately upon his arrest, Augustine Chung said that he could explain everything, that no corruption was involved, and that he had only been conducting an experiment on Donald Cheung to whom he wished genuinely to apologize. This was of course to no avail, and he was taken back to the offices of the ICAC.

On Monday 14 July, I returned from Court to my chambers shortly after 5 p.m. There I found waiting for me my old friend, a senior solicitor W.I. Cheung, who said he would be instructing me as defence counsel for his partner Augustine Chung. He asked if I could request bail for Augustine Chung. Accordingly I got in touch with the ICAC, and bail was agreed.

After the conclusion of the arrangements for bail, I had my first conference with Augustine Chung in my chambers. I soon learnt that no fewer than 6 ICAC officers had taken turns the previous evening to record a lengthy voluntary statement from him. This began a little after 11 p.m., continued throughout the night and the following morning and day, and only ended in the late afternoon of Monday 14 July.

My first conference with Augustine Chung commenced shortly after 6 p.m. on Monday 14 July. It continued until 2 a.m. on the following Tuesday morning 15 July when I terminated the meeting arbitrarily until another date could be fixed.

While my instructing solicitor and I were both completely exhausted, Augustine Chung remained fresh and enthusiastic, and could and no doubt would have gone on for many more hours if I had not put an end to the conference. This was the more amazing bearing in mind that he had just previously been involved night and day in giving the long statement to the ICAC.

From the very outset of this account, I have indicated that this was an extraordinary case. Augustine Chung, who was the principal character in the case, was undoubtedly an extraordinary man.

This must be borne in mind when one tries to ascertain whether or not his unusual and surprising defence was bona fide. In his judgment, Judge Hopkinson said of Augustine Chung's defence that 'such an idea is crazy and half-baked. In the case of an ordinary normal individual one would dismiss it out-of-hand as utterly absurd. But here we were dealing not with an ordinary normal individual, but with a crank.'

To say that Augustine Chung's defence was simply that it was all an experiment in psychology and he had no intention of depriving Donald Cheung of anything would be to over-simplify the issue. Otherwise it would be difficult to understand why it had taken him so very long to explain it initially to the ICAC officers, subsequently to his legal representatives, and finally to the Court. His statement to the ICAC took many working hours, his instructions to his lawyers on separate occasions took several times as long, and eventually his evidence in Court lasted two and a half painful hearing days.

As far as the case went, and particularly where Augustine Chung himself was concerned, his defence was necessarily tied up completely with his whole life, about which he took great pride in talking. Thus he was invariably at pains to tell the world at every opportunity that he was born of humble parents, survived a poverty-stricken and unhappy childhood, had to overcome many hurdles before he could complete his education and finally qualify as a lawyer. He said that he had chosen the legal profession because the law offered not only monetary and other material attractions, but also ample opportunities to fight against social, legal, as well as other forms of injustice.

At the ICAC, Augustine Chung first mentioned a number of existing articles written by him in both English and Chinese on psychology and social problems, some while he was still an undergraduate at the University of Hong Kong, others when he was working as a social welfare officer. When, on a later occasion, I asked him in my chambers whether any of those articles was still available, he surprised me by immediately producing from his briefcase quite a collection of somewhat tattered privately printed literature, some in English and others in Chinese, all bearing his name as author. These specimens of his personal literature were all produced in Court subsequently.

Although in due course the trial Judge described these specimens of his printed literature as unoriginal and tedious, he concluded nevertheless that only someone with a social conscience could have written them. Since there was no way they could have been trumped up just for the defence, their existence necessarily made Augustine Chung's explanation that he was only carrying out an 'experiment' on Donald Cheung more readily believable.

In one of those printed pamphlets, in particular, Augustine Chung propounded the view that because the underprivileged classes of society were constantly suffering from poverty and hunger, it was only to be expected that they would stoop to crime from time to time. The privileged classes on the other hand were spared such suffering and thus were far less susceptible to committing crimes. He believed however that if the privileged members of our society should be subjected to the appropriate kind and amount of pressure, they too would crack at some stage and be involved in crime. Unfortunately, he said, opportunities to prove his theory were necessarily scarce, if they occurred at all. He felt destined to be a champion of the underprivileged, and would dearly love to be able to put his pet theory to the test.

This latter pamphlet in particular introduced a ring of truth into his defence. For, if he had hitherto entertained a constant desire to prove the vulnerability of the privileged classes under pressure, the Paul Lee investigation rumours and the Stop-List information would certainly appear to offer a golden opportunity for the psychological experiment to be carried out on somebody such as Donald Cheung. For Augustine Chung, to be able to describe the result of such an experiment subsequently in print would truly satisfy a life-long ambition.

Beside his writings, another unrelated piece of evidence would also appear to lend support to Augustine Chung's claim to having a social conscience. In November 1974, he had taken out a life insurance policy for US$700 000 for the joint benefit of his wife and the Community Chest. It was to take effect only if he was injured or died within a period of five years. Presumably he must have genuinely believed in his own worth to the community if he should survive the prescribed period. In case he died, the sum insured would presumably replace the loss of his service to the community.

At one of our many conferences, it was suggested that in the face of the unusual nature of the defence it might be of assistance if our client was psychiatrically examined. Augustine Chung himself did not initially accede to the suggestion but was eventually persuaded to agree to be examined.

Dr David Chen was the best qualified and best known psychiatrist in Hong Kong. He had then just left government service to set up private practice. In due course, he examined Augustine Chung on a number of occasions.

Augustine Chung was tried before Judge Hopkinson in the Victoria District Court at the beginning of October 1975. The hearing lasted seven days. On each day the Court was packed to overflowing. This was not surprising because both Augustine Chung and Donald Cheung were well-known in Hong Kong and not only in the legal profession. Besides, it was unique for a lawyer to be charged with blackmailing another lawyer for monetary gain.

As the trial progressed, and Donald Cheung and the ICAC officers had all given evidence in turn, those who had packed the court expecting to see fireworks must have been somewhat disappointed, because none of the prosecution witnesses were cross-examined by me at all. In addition to the evidence of those witnesses, three tape-recordings were admitted as evidence and played back in Court. Two of these were taken from the tape-recorder carried on the person of Donald Cheung and merely confirmed the conversations which took place between him and Augustine Chung on 12 and 13 July respectively. Light entertainment was provided when the play-back of one of those two tapes reflected a miscellany of other sounds recorded when Donald Cheung apparently went into the wash-room and forgot to switch off the machine he was carrying! The third tape was a long recording of the statement made by Augustine Chung at the ICAC, the play-back of which in Court took the greater part of a day.

This third tape set out in great detail not only Augustine Chung's explanation in answer to the charge, but also his whole life story. Accordingly the defence became an open book even before Augustine Chung went into the witness box. The sole issue of the trial in fact hinged on Augustine Chung's state of mind when he met and spoke to Donald Cheung on the four occasions respectively on 7, 11, 12 and 13 July. That those several meetings and conversations took place was never disputed. The only dispute was whether Augustine Chung had intended thereby to secure monetary gain or obtain property from Donald Cheung, or, whether, as Augustine Chung claimed, it was all part of an 'experiment' which he had dearly wanted to put to the test all his life.

At the conclusion of the prosecution case, Augustine Chung duly took the witness stand, and in no time was once more performing his long solo act, talking and rambling for two and a half days about his past life, his unhappy childhood, his success story, and his social conscience. There could be little doubt in the mind of anyone watching and listening to him that at times he was thoroughly enjoying himself. He looked every inch the proud author when he produced and read out his several papers on psychology and social problems in Hong Kong, and explained to the Court, how as champion of the underprivileged he had consistently longed for an opportunity to test the reaction of the privileged classes to psychological and other forms of pressure. He said that if he were to miss this opportunity to test Donald Cheung's resistance to psychological pressure, he would never get another chance. He told the Court unashamedly of his achievements in the magistrates' courts, his relative financial affluence, his numerous rich possessions, and the many expensive gifts showered on him by his grateful clients. He could hardly contain his pride when he referred to and produced the insurance policy he had taken out for the benefit of the Community Chest and explained why he had done it. Once again he was profuse in his apologies for picking Donald Cheung as the guinea pig for his experiment. He explained that the case of Donald Cheung offered him an opportunity he simply could not resist for putting his life-long theory to the test.

His repeated professed apologies to Donald Cheung, tendered first upon his arrest, then at the ICAC, time and again when instructing his defence lawyers, yet again when interviewed by Dr David Chen, and finally in the witness box, were not entirely insignificant, because they not only reflected consistency on his part, but perhaps would not normally be expected from a genuine blackmailer.

Augustine Chung was cross-examined somewhat sparingly by Prosecution Counsel. He was pressed only to explain his intent behind each of the several meetings he had had with Donald Cheung. Eventually it was put to him very simply and succinctly that the whole exercise was by no means just an experiment as claimed, but, instead, a real attempt to secure monetary gain from Donald Cheung, and that he would have kept the five cashier orders of $200,000 each for himself if and when Donald Cheung handed them over to him.

Augustine Chung replied that he had never intended to secure anything for himself because he was so well-off that another million dollars would not make any difference to his way of life, and that if and when the cashier orders were produced, they would prove that Donald Cheung had succumbed to pressure, and the experiment would have been completed. He would there and then have told Donald Cheung the truth, apologized to him for everything, and happily asked him to keep his money.

After Augustine Chung had concluded his evidence, I called Dr David Chen to give evidence. He told the court that in the month of August he had interviewed and examined Augustine Chung on a number of occasions in his clinic. As a result he was of the opinion that his patient was suffering from a mental disorder called hypomania, which could get progressively worse as time goes on, and which invariably left the invalid totally disjointed, and completely preoccupied with his own importance and image. It was a disturbance of mood, he said, and necessarily affected the invalid's way of thinking as well as his behaviour from day to day. He was not cross-examined.

At the conclusion of the evidence, Prosecution Counsel submitted that on the undisputed evidence before the Court, Augustine Chung had clearly attempted to blackmail Donald Cheung for monetary gain or alternatively to obtain property from him by deception. The explanation of 'experiment', even if believed, was no defence because the admitted request for the cashier orders showed adequate intent either to secure monetary gain or obtain property by deception. He further suggested that the so-called explanation reflected no more than a prepared defence carefully planned before the commission of the crime.

I maintained and submitted that each of the two charges required a criminal intent to be proven, so that if the Court should be left in reasonable doubt whether or not the accused was only carrying out an experiment on Donald Cheung, it must follow that the requisite guilty intent to secure monetary gain for himself or permanently to obtain property by deception would not have been proven, and the accused must be acquitted. I said the offences with which Augustine Chung stood charged were clearly distinguishable from the simple offence of intimidation in respect of which no criminal intent was required to be proven. I further submitted that the suggestion of a prepared defence could hardly be squared with the existence of the personal literature of the accused and the insurance policy taken out for the benefit of the Community Chest.

On 18 October, Judge Hopkinson read out a carefully prepared written judgment upholding my submission on the law and giving the benefit of the doubt to Augustine Chung who was accordingly acquitted. In brief, Judge Hopkinson said he had been led by the following factors to find in his favour, namely, relative financial sufficiency and affluence, and his personality and characteristics. He had watched Augustine Chung very carefully not only during the two and a half days when he was in the witness box but also when Dr David Chen was giving evidence. Furthermore, he took into consideration the overall consistency of Augustine Chung's account from the very moment of arrest; his repeated wish to apologize to Donald Cheung; the purport and significance of his numerous writings and the support they lent to his defence, the fact that he was suffering from the mental disorder hypomania, which must have affected his mind and behaviour according to the evidence of Dr Chen, which was not challenged by the prosecution at all, and finally the insurance policy he had taken out in favour of his wife and the Community Chest in the event of his dying within five years which indicated not only the fact that he had a social conscience but also the extent to which he genuinely believed in himself being a net asset to society as champion of the underprivileged. The Judge said that in the face of all those factors, he was not convinced that the 'experiment' was merely a prepared defence. Augustine Chung was accordingly discharged.

However, I represented him when he was brought before the disciplinary committee of the Law Society of Hong Kong for intimidating Donald Cheung after his acquittal in the Victoria District Court. This resulted in his being struck off the Roll of Solicitors.

Index

15–17 Upper Shelley Street 7–9, 72

Alexandra House 129
American Flying Tigers 41
Amoy 49
ancestor worship 32, 33
Anderson, Mrs 93, 94, 101
Androcles and the Lion 30, 31
Ann, T.K. 131
Atlee, Clement 85

Bamboo Curtain 182
Bank of Communications 44, 53
Bernacchi, Brook 144
Bishop Yu Bin scholarship 70
Blair-Kerr, Alastair 156
Bradman, Don 76
Briggs, Sir Geoffrey 146
British Army Aid Group 58
Burnett-Hall 109–111

Caine Road 7
Cairo 84
Canton 35, 61
Chan Chi-tang 62
Chan, Patrick 132, 133
Chang, Denis 132
Chang Fa-kwei 61
Chen, Dr David 241, 242, 243, 244

Cheng, Kitty 132
Cheung, Donald 236–239, 241–244
Cheung Kam Yin 204, 206, 217
Cheung, Sir Oswald 25, 129, 238
Cheung Wing In 239
Cheung Yam San 176
Chiang Kai-shek 47, 56, 57
China Building 163
Chinese Customs and Excise
    Department 43, 44, 53
Chinese Students' Union 103
Chinese Third War Zone 46
Chinese University of Hong Kong,
    The 26, 131
Choa, George 31, 32
Chui, Marjorie 132
Chung, Augustine 235–244
Chung Chi College 131
Chungking 43, 59
Churchill, Winston 84
College May Ball 75
Colonial Legal Service 125
Columbus, Christopher 94
Conveyancer of the Court 111
Corpus Delicti 175, 177
Cronin, F. 12, 13

D'Almada, Christopher 124
D'Almada, Frank 163

D'Almada e'Castro, Leo 163, 189
Davies, John (Lt. Commander) 45, 46, 47, 48, 49, 51
Davies, Michael 130
Deng Xiaoping 145
Dignam, Mrs 99
Diocesan Boys' School 25
Director of Education 69
Donnelly, Rev Fr D. 12, 27
Downey, Bernard 131
Downing College, Cambridge 69, 114
Dussek, Mr 93

Earls Court 26, 99
Edgely, E. 185, 226, 227, 230, 231, 233
Evans, Dafydd 131
Faculty of Social Sciences and Law 131
Faid, Mrs 24
first Chinese Crown Counsel 124
French 17, 18, 31
Fujian 45, 46, 47, 49
Fung, Lucia 121
Fuzhou 46, 47, 49, 50

Gallagher, Fr 12, 33
Ganzhou 47
Gibbs, Norman 73, 75, 108
Gibson and Weldon 101
Glasgow 26
Gough Street 103
Gould, Mr Justice 147
Graham, G. 130
Gray's Inn 135
Greene, Alan 186
Gregg, Mr Justice 170, 172, 173, 182
Griffin, John Bowes 124
Guangxi Province 38
Guangzhou Wan 38, 39, 40
Guilin 40, 41, 43, 56

He Shi 59
Helena May Institute 169

Hiroshima 60
Hogan, Chief Justice Sir Michael 215
Hollywood Road 11
Hon, Peter 220
Hong Kong Bar Association 26, 132, 144
Honorary Senior Counsel 140
Hopkinson, Judge 241, 244
Howe, Sir Gerald 126
Hsiang Hon-ping (General) 50
Hsiung, S.I. 30
Huang, Rayson 25
Huggins, Mr Justice 147
Huizhou 61–66

Inner Bar 132, 133, 139
Inner Temple 135
institution of Silk 139

Japan 35
Japanese Occupation Army 37
Jardine Matheson & Co. Ltd. 131
Jiangxi 47
Jiao Ling 50
Jimmy's Kitchen 163
Junior Bar 139

Kam Yee Fai 165
Kam Ying Hei 26
Kao, Mary 132
Kong Ching Tong 176
Kowloon 8
Kuala Lumpur 113
Kutrakal, Ratna 31, 32
Kwan, Susan 132
Kwok, Kenneth 131

La Bohème 26
Lam Pak Chung 36
Lam Yung Tai 27
Lam, M.K. 184, 188, 189, 190
Lancashire 13
Landau, Leo 163, 164, 169, 170
Landlord and Tenant Ordinance 123

Lau Din Cheuk 25
Law Tripos 135
Lawson, Professor 86, 90, 93, 101, 102
Lee Yen-wor (Lt. General) 47, 54, 55, 56, 57, 65, 66, 67
Legal Aid Department 154
Legal Department 124, 125, 129, 156
Li, Chief Justice Andrew 132, 133, 148
Li, Lillian 77
Li, Simon   77, 98
Lian Ping 51
Lien Cheng 50
Life Member 144
Lim Hoy Lan 13
Lim, Joseph 13, 30, 31
Lincoln's Inn 6, 98, 103
Lingnan University 40
Liverpool 5
Lo, Helen 165, 167, 168, 169, 172, 174
Lo, Hin-Shing   165, 184, 187, 188, 189, 190
Long Chuan 51, 58, 59
Long Nan 59
Lord Chancellor 141
Low, CM 80
Low, Mary 80, 81
Low, Mrs 80
Low, Peter 80
Low, Suzanne 80, 81

Ma, Kam (Professor) 24
Macau 38
MacDonnell Road 165
malaria 41
Malaya 113
Mao Zedong 57, 62, 84, 85, 114
Martie, Madame 31
Marxist doctrine 85
Matthews, Mr 81, 97
Matthews, Clifford 26
McDougall 81, 85
McMullin, Mr Justice 147

McNeil, John QC 164
Mei Lu 40
Mei Xian 50
Merton College, Oxford 5, 71, 72, 73, 76, 77
Miles, Sir John 73
Mills-Owen, Mr Justice 147
Mok Yeuk Chi 132
Morley-John, Michael 185
Mosque Street 7
murder 175

Nagasaki 60
Nan Ping 47, 48, 50
New Asia College 131
No. 1 Wyndham Street 163
No. 2 Robinson Road 9
No. 211, Circular Road 118
No. 9 Ice House Street 130
No. 9 Queen's Road Central 130

Ong, G.B. (Professor) 207, 209, 212, 213, 215

Pang Teng Cheung 206, 207, 208, 209, 213, 215, 216
Pauper Cases 154
Peak tram railway 166
Pembroke College, Cambridge 5
Personnel Department, Seventh War Zone 56
Pingshi 40
Political Institutions 74, 108
Poon, Herman 132
Portia 13
Prince's Terrace 7
Public Services Commission 125, 126
Public Works Department 167
punting 76

Queen's Counsel 137, 139, 140, 141, 142
Qujiang 40, 43, 44, 47, 51, 53, 54, 56, 58, 61, 65, 67
Quzhou 66

Rea, Dermot 170, 180
Rear, John 131
Remedios, Denis 177
Ricci Hall 13
Ridehalgh, Arthur 126
Rigby, Mr Justice 146, 208, 213,
　214, 215
Roberts, Sir Denys 146
Roberts, James 81
Roman Catholic faith 85
Room 711B 130
Roosevelt, Franklin 84
Russell Square 103
Ryan, Rev Fr T. 16

Sagamoto, Mr 39, 40
San Francisco 71
Sanguinetti, Albert 144
School of Oriental and African
　Studies in London 26
Scott, Sir Walter 27
secondary evidence 175
Sedgwick, Mr 41
Selangor 118
Senior Bar 139
Senior Citizen 140
Senior Counsel (資深大律師) 140
Senior Non-Expatriate Officers'
　Association 127
Seventh War Zone 40
Shang Rao 47
Shanghai 38
Shantao 49, 50, 51
Shaw, George Bernard 30, 31
Shenzhen 38
Sheridan, T. 12
Shook Lin and Bok, Messrs 114
Shylock 13
'silks' 139
Sneath, Graham 155, 160, 161
Society of Jesus 11
Somerville College 80
South China Building 163
Southeast Asia 113
SS Britannic 5
SS Menelaus 5

St Albans Quad 73
St Frances College, Illinois 70
St John's Apartments 169
St John's Hall 26
St Louis University 70
Stonyhurst College 13
Strickland, George 124
Stubbans 3 73

Tan Teow Bok 114
Tang, Magdalene 121
Tang, Ignatius 121
Tashjian, Charles 219
The Merchant of Venice 13
The Professor from Peking 30
Theatre Lane 163
Thompson McLintock & Co.
　136
Tong, SY 69
Tort 102
Trench, Sir David 130
Tsui, Peter 11

United College 131
University College 25
University Grants Committee 130
University of Illinois in Chicago 27
Urquhart, Major 58

Vatican 33
Victory Scholarships 5
voir dire 177

Wadham College 85
Wah Yan College 9
Walton, Arthur 69, 79, 80, 83, 84,
　95, 110, 111
War Auxiliary Services 36
War-time Rice Control Department
　36
West Cromwell Road 99
Wicks, Mr Justice 154, 159, 160,
　161
Williams, Bill 117
Wilson, Charles 82
Wilson, James 81, 82

Wilson, Julia 81
Wong Chun Kau (General) 43
Wong Wai Wa 59
Wright, Leslie 144, 163

Xing Ning 50

Yam, David 132
Yang, Judge T.L. 219, 233
Yau Yiu Tim 165
Yeo, Dr 124
Yong Shook-lin 113
Yong Pung-how 113, 114, 120
Yong Siew Chin 114
You Never Can Tell 30
Yu Hon-mou (General) 47, 57
Yu, Mrs Norma 38, 59

Yu Wan 38, 73, 110
Yu Wan, Mrs 36, 37, 38, 40, 41
Yu, Brian 8
Yu, Josephine 8, 30, 38, 40
Yu, Margaret 8, 30, 38, 40, 69, 70
Yu, Pak Chuen 8, 15, 43, 54, 59
Yu, Ping Tsung 8, 12, 15, 16, 17,
   18, 31, 47, 54, 55, 59, 194, 196,
   197
Yu, Quok Chung, Denis (余國充)
   57, 132, 133, 140
Yu, Rosalind 8, 33, 38, 41
Yu, Sheung Woon 8, 15, 69
Yu, Winnie 8, 33, 38, 41

Zhejiang Province 66
Zhongshan University 40